SOCIALISM AND THE CITIES

Kennikat Press

National University Publications

Interdisciplinary Urban Series

General Editor
Raymond A. Mohl
Florida Atlantic University

SOCIALISM
and the
CITIES

Edited by BRUCE M. STAVE

With an Appendix "ON MUNICIPAL SOCIALISM, 1903"
From the Correspondence of the late
WALTER LIPPMANN

National University Publications
KENNIKAT PRESS • 1975
Port Washington, N.Y. • London

Manufactured in the United States of America

Published by
Kennikat Press Corp.
Port Washington, N.Y./London

Library of Congress Cataloging in Publication Data
Main entry under title:

Socialism and the cities.

(Interdisciplinary urban series) (Kennikat Press national university publications)
    Bibliography: p.
    Includes index.
    1. Socialism in the United States—History—
Addresses, essays, lectures. 2. Municipal government
—United States—History—Addresses, essays, lectures.
I. Stave, Bruce M.
HX89.S58   335'.00973   75-34435
ISBN 0-8046-9133-9

CONTENTS

ACKNOWLEDGMENTS

A collective effort such as this volume incurs many debts. First and fore-most, the editor wishes to thank the contributors for their patience and cooperation. This is especially so for those who joined this project from the beginning several years ago and who survived the changes in personnel and subject matter so common to symposium volumes.

An earlier version of James R. Green's essay was presented at the 87th meeting of the American Historical Association on December 29, 1972, in New Orleans at a session on American Socialism in the Twentieth Century. He wishes to thank his comrades James Weinstein, Mari Jo and Paul Buhle, who participated in the panel discussion, and also Staughton Lynd and H.L. Mitchell, two experienced Socialist agitators, who raised important questions from the floor. Paul Cullinane helped with the tabu-lating and coding for the biographical information that appears in Green's essay and Cliff Romash assisted with computer programming.

An abbreviated, modified version of Sally Miller's chapter was read to a conference at the University of Wisconsin-Milwaukee in April 1974. Kenneth E. Hendrickson's contribution is an expanded and altered version of an article he published in the January 1966 issue of *New York History* and he appreciates the agreement of that journal's editor, Wendell Tripp, to its publication in revised form. Garin Burbank wishes to thank Donald Graham and Douglas McCashin, who were graduate history students at the University of Saskatchewan, Regina Campus, for assisting with the statisti-cal work that appears in his essay. Michael Ebner presented an earlier ver-sion of his contribution to a faculty seminar of the history department at the City College of New York. His former colleague there, Ari Joel Perlman, provided him with an insightful critique. James P. Shenton of Columbia University, and sometime public official in Passaic, also read a preliminary draft, making illuminating comments as to how the final product could be improved. Professor Ebner also benefited from the comments of Eugene M. Tobin of Kutztown State College, Peter Romanofsky of Jersey City State College and Joel Schwartz of Montclair State College. Arthur McMahon, retired Executive Editor of the Passaic-Clifton *Herald-News*, was instrumental in locating *The Issue*, a monthly Socialist party tabloid. An earlier version of William Pratt's article was read at the Southwest Social Science Association Meeting in San Antonio, March 30, 1972. Professor Pratt is indebted to the Woodrow Wilson Foundation and the University of Nebraska at Omaha for financial assistance in support of his research.

I wish to thank contributor James R. Green for suggesting that Walter Lippmann's 1913 letter be published in its entirety as an appendix to this book and the Duke University Library for granting permission to do so; before his death, Mr. Lippmann, through his attorney, Louis S. Auchincloss, graciously agreed to publication. The University of Connecticut Research Foundation supported this volume and my own research with a grant for which I am most appreciative. My contribution dealing with Bridgeport is a much revised version of a paper originally delivered before the Association for the Study of Connecticut History's fall meeting in 1970 at Yale University. It has benefited from readings by my colleagues in the University of Connecticut's history department: Robert Ascher, who enthusiastically commented upon several of the essays in this volume; Richard D. Brown, Richard O. Curry, and R. Kent Newmyer; also helpful in their comments were Everett Carll Ladd, Director of the University of Connecticut's Social Science Data Center, and Fred W. Grupp, Jr., Executive Director of the University's Peoples of Connecticut Ethnic Heritage Project, as were William Henry Harbaugh of the University of Virginia, Thomas A. Krueger of the University of Illinois, and my good friend and critic, John M. Allswang of California State University at Los Angeles. Two University of Connecticut doctoral students, Bruce Clouette of the history department and Edmond J. True of the department of political science, helped make my voting data understandable to a computer and its reply comprehensible to me. Joan Serwanski and Kay Macht graciously typed part of the manuscript. While they are not individually named, the assistance of the large number of archivists and librarians who helped the contributors with their research does not go unappreciated. From the outset, Cornell Jaray's enthusiasm for this project made working with Kennikat Press a most pleasant experience, which was increased by Ray Mohl's encouragement and criticism offered in his capacity as general editor of the Press's Interdisciplinary Urban Studies series.

viii

ACKNOWLEDGMENTS

Final thanks is extended to my wife, Sondra Astor Stave, who took time from her own career in local politics to assist me in my more academic study of the activity which she practices. Her partnership in scholarship is exceeded only by her partnership in life. As for our son and junior partner, Channing, he has come to understand what historical writing and editing is about. Perhaps that's why at the tender age of five, he chooses to be an architect—at least that is his choice for today—rather than an historian. Since he refuses to accept responsibility for any errors of fact and interpretation in this volume, as editor, I do.

B.M.S.

Coventry, Connecticut

SOCIALISM AND THE CITIES

BRUCE M. STAVE

SOCIALISM AND THE CITIES:
An Introduction

In a recent discussion of the deficiency of studies dealing with American socialism, one scholar has written, "There are, for example, few detailed examinations . . . of their [the Socialists'] success in building local organizations, their campaigning, and how socialists performed in office as in Milwaukee, Reading, Pennsylvania and Bridgeport, Connecticut. . . ."[1] This volume is offered to assist in filling this historical gap and to help provide the detailed studies necessary for scholars to formulate a coherent critical theory for the investigation of American socialism. Moreover, it is intended to afford some insight into the politics and society of urban America in the twentieth century. It is hoped that the goals for the volume are achieved; however, one cannot quarrel with Walter Lippmann's remark that "A man standing on a soapbox has to be cocksure. But about the tactics of a revolutionary movement only a fool is convinced that his is the last word."

The contributors to this volume come to their subjects without soapbox certainty and recognize that further words on socialism in the United States will undoubtedly follow their own. In writing these essays for *Socialism and the Cities* no single point of view has been assigned for repetition throughout each essay. No one methodology, except for the

---

This Introduction is based primarily, but not totally, on the essays included in this volume. The interpretive synthesis that has evolved, however, is entirely the responsibility of the editor. While external sources are cited below, references to, and quotes from, essays in this book are not footnoted.

3

historian's analysis of things past, has been followed. Where appropriate, the tools of the social sciences, such as collective biography, the formulation of an index of dissimilarity, and correlation voting analysis have been combined with the more traditional historical discipline to produce essays which attempt to provide a social analysis of political history. The subject matter, American municipal socialism, provides the one common bond for the essays in this volume.

In an attempt to offer a national overview of rank and file Socialists during the Progressive era, the first essay, James R. Green's study of the "salesmen-soldiers" of the "*Appeal* Army," breaks this bond of total emphasis on municipal socialism in order to highlight another concern of this volume. This is the desire to study not simply the party's leadership and rhetoric, but also its rank and file "Jimmie Higginses" and its mass base in the electorate. Special emphasis also is given to these topics in William C. Pratt's study of the grass-roots workings of the Reading Socialist party (SP) and my own study of Bridgeport's electoral behavior during the twenty-four-year administration of Mayor Jasper McLevy.

Reading and Bridgeport are post-Progressive era socialist cities; the first to elect a mayor, the largest, and probably the most influential of the socialist municipalities studied in this volume is Milwaukee. Sally M. Miller's work provides a detailed analysis of the effects of ethnicity, primarily German, and labor in that city from the period prior to the election of Socialist Mayor Emil Seidel in 1910 through World War I, with all of the problems and opportunities it created for the municipal socialists, and finally to the defeat of Mayor Dan Hoan in 1940. Milwaukee's influence led George R. Lunn, newly converted to socialism, to visit that city in June 1911 in order to study its administration. The visit helped Lunn establish his socialist credentials prior to winning the party's mayoralty nomination in Schenectady during the fall of 1911. Once in office, he bowed again to midwestern socialism by importing his commissioner of public works from Milwaukee. Kenneth E. Hendrickson's essay chronicles how reformism and factionalism marked the Schenectady experience as Christian Socialist Lunn, in the words of his newspaper, *The Citizen,* attempted "to stand for the great silent majority."

At the same time, in Oklahoma City, Socialists led by Oscar Ameringer made a conscious attempt to "Milwaukeeize" their municipality. In 1910, 5,842 Sooners had contributed to the Party, making the state's SP dues-paying membership the largest in the nation. Solidly based in the discontent of impoverished farmers, Oklahoma's Socialist party could not make effective headway in the new state's namesake city.[2] In his contribution to this volume, Garin Burbank explores the reasons for this failure. He emphasizes the differences between the long established, industrialized,

4

ethnic Milwaukee and the newly settled southwestern boomtown, with its largely WASP population, whose work was organized primarily in small-scale trade and service enterprises and whose craft union leaders were generally more favorable to Gompersism than socialism. With the collapse of the Sooner city's building boom in 1911, the chances of urban socialism diminished with each construction worker who left the area in search of a new job.

In the four cities under study where socialism came to power, a common pattern emerges as to the type of government they provided. Sally Miller's conclusion that socialism in Milwaukee "epitomized progressive municipal reform more boldly than those who bore the name" applies equally to Schenectady, Reading, and Bridgeport. Similarly, a dozen years before the Socialists won in Milwaukee's City Hall, John C. Chase, the Socialist mayor of Haverhill, Massachusetts, summarized his first term's achievements as "confined mainly to minor reforms in municipal government."[3] If this was true of that New England shoe manufacturing town of 37,000, it also held for the nation's largest metropolis. New York City's municipal Socialists, whose most ardent support rested with the city's Jewish needle trade workers, pursued a distinctly reformist, non-revolutionary program. While no Socialist mayor was ever elected in New York City, in 1917, the Party's candidate for that office, Morris Hillquit, won almost 22 percent of the vote; moreover, ten Socialists were elected to the state assembly, five to the board of aldermen, and the first socialist judge in the United States, Jacob Panken, won election to the municipal court. Many voters apparently agreed with one New York reformer, who wrote Hillquit several years before his strong showing in the mayoralty election, "What I feel about Socialism is that it is a very important element in the whole Progressive movement."[4]

Often coming to power as a consequence of voter reaction to corruption within major party administrations, fearing programs that would raise taxes and alienate business and the public, limited by city charters and at loggerheads with hostile state legislatures, believing that a socialist municipality in a capitalist nation had little chance of success, the city Socialists determined to be both "in the world and of it."[5] They sought to win elections, stay in power, and work for reform within the existing framework of government and economy. As a result, they advocated "clean," streamlined government, and were often as interested in cost accounting, central purchasing, and maintaining a sound city credit rating as in extending municipal services, establishing public ownership of utilities and transportation, and curbing the hostility of the police toward strikers. It appears that American socialism was most successful in winning power when it was most progressive; as "gas and water socialism," it espoused democ-

5

racy rather than revolution, and as John Laslett has pointed out, often "left much of its potential constituency on the Left disillusioned and dissatisfied—among western farmers and miners, exploited immigrants, or blacks working in northern industry, and . . . by doing so it failed to establish itself as a viable alternative to existing movements for reform."[6] Preoccupation with immediate demands left the ultimate demands of socialism unsatisfied; nationalization of the means of production and distribution, democratic planning, and production for use rather than profit have not been accepted in this nation.[7] Municipal socialism in the United States did little to further these goals.

In this context of urban socialism, it is not difficult to understand why the president of General Electric in Schenectady remarked that "Dr. Lunn was the best man that had ever been Mayor" of his city,[8] why Dan Hoan was praised for being "one-tenth Socialist and nine-tenths businessman," and why a Bridgeport manufacturer remarked, "To McLevy this city is *his* business, just as much as my factory is my business." Nor is it hard to comprehend the disillusionment of Walter Lippmann after serving in Schenectady as Mayor Lunn's secretary. In a letter reprinted in the Appendix of this book, Lippmann, in the fall of 1913, wrote to the Party's national office noting what he thought the true business of socialism should be—"it is quite clearly the business of a Socialist administration to cut into the returns of property, take as much of them as possible to be spent for social purposes." He went on to remark that "if Socialists are to make anything of political action they have got to keep themselves clearly distinguished from the progressives."

James Green, after studying the *Who's Who in Socialist America* for 1914, reminds those of us who see urban socialism as the left wing of progressivism, that the SP's main source of strength, its working-class membership, did distinguish it from the Progressives. Only one quarter of the *Appeal* salesmen lived in large cities, but they were overwhelmingly working class; moreover, Green finds that with most Socialist workers concentrated in the "Middletowns"[9] of America, the Party's agitational work and effectiveness improved. The proximity and social structure of the small town and city, according to this interpretation not unlike Herbert Gutman's earlier work,[10] permitted the SP's working-class base to join closely with discontented professionals and petty bourgeoisie. Moreover, it is often forgotten that in Schenectady with a population of almost 75,000 in 1910, twenty-three other Socialists elected with Lunn were workers, half of them being machinists. Green believes that the strength and style of Socialism in Schenectady was not determined by Lunn as much as by the lesser-known workers, who served the Party as well as the city, and who remained loyal to socialism after Reverend Lunn became a Democrat.

6

While this volume maintains that the rank and file of the Party cannot and must not be disregarded, one must question whether "socialism as progressivism" was really antithetical to Jimmie Higgins's desires. More than two decades after Lunn, a minister, was first elected in Schenectady, Jasper McLevy, a roofer, became mayor·in Bridgeport; the large majority of the Socialist aldermen who served with him in his first term were skilled workmen. The essential story of socialism in Depression-ridden Bridgeport under the leadership of McLevy and his fellow workers differs little from that under socialism in Progressive-era Schenectady under a clergyman and his non-fellow workers. Progressive reform did not appeal solely to the middle classes. As J. Joseph Huthmacher and John Buenker have demonstrated, the new stock urban working class frequently lent support to both social and, less expectedly and with several noted exceptions, to structural reform. In New York City, "most Socialist voters wanted reforms not revolution."[11] The workers may very well have desired just what municipal socialism offered to them.

On the other hand, one package of urban structural reforms that Socialists generally opposed, with good reason, included the often successful attempts to institute city manager or commission forms of government. Along with substituting nonpartisan city-wide elections for ward-based elections to city councils and school boards, such reform diluted areas of socialist strength and grass-roots neighborhood control over municipal politics. Conversely, it enhanced the power of urban elites, who had the resources and expertise to take advantage of the new rationalized structures.[12] Michael Ebner's analysis of the successful effort to change the form of government in Passaic, N.J., provides a useful case study of the effect of commission government on the Socialists and why they proved ineffective in combating such changes. As the Passaic socialist newspaper editorialized after the municipal election, "The great mass of the working class of this city have been neatly eliminated from politics." The Passaic Socialists offered no concrete alternative to the commission except to advocate the status quo at a time when the public sought—or, at least, was willing to accept—reform. In this instance, the difference between socialism and progressivism appears manifest.

Aside from advocating no positive program during the change-of-government contest, Passaic's Socialists made little effort in the municipal elections to attract the "new" ethnics of the city's First Ward, especially its large Slavic Catholic community. In Milwaukee, on the other hand, the ability to win the city's Polish vote aided the German-based SP immeasurably. Nationally, an absence of "new" immigrants marked the *Appeal Army*."[13] According to James Green, this reflected "the lack of an organic connection between the Party's new immigrant members and the old

7

rank and file in the towns and small cities of the heartland." This finding raises several questions worthy of consideration. If we accept socialism as reformist, despite its opposition to the urban structural reforms mentioned earlier, did "socialism as progressivism" have a greater appeal to "new" immigrants than to native white males or older assimilated immigrants who formed the *"Appeal* Army"? If so, what of the experience of prevalently "old" immigrant German Milwaukee and Pennsylvania Dutch Reading? Should we look to the small industrial cities, railroad towns, and coal camps, where corporate capitalism victimized the salesmen soldiers, rather than to the larger cities for the true American radical experience? Finally, rather than asking whether rank and filers more than leaders like Lunn and Victor Berger in Milwaukee shaped municipal socialism and provided it with its strength and style, one might ponder what the Party offered to these individuals.

William C. Pratt submits that for many dedicated workers, the SP offered nothing less than a "complete way of life." Just as alleged Democratic and Republican "political hacks" found a structure for their lives in the everyday wheeling and dealing of urban machine politics, the Jimmie Higginses often centered their existence around party activity. "Smoking a Socialist-made cigar, listening to the Socialist orchestra and chorus, working the concession at Socialist Park—all of these things tended to hold the party together between elections and after defeats." As an index to the continuity of urban politics in the United States as well as to the similarities between the social structure of party activity among city Socialists and organization Democrats, one might consider the following. A 1972 description of Brooklyn Boss Meade Esposito's Thomas Jefferson Democratic Club paints a portrait of at least one hundred people meeting in the Club's main hall, "which looks like the rec room of a very large suburban home." Committees not only planned campaign strategy, but also a fundraising fashion show. Coffee and cake were served and checkered cloths covered little round tables on which rested Chianti bottles topped by candles.[14] The clubhouse was, in short, the social center of a political institution and, for today's party activists, enhanced the vibrancy of what to them was the only game in town.

This seemed no less the case for the Jimmie Higginses who enjoyed the camaraderie associated with attending Socialist meetings and picnics and generally immersing themselves in the social side of politics. While the similarity in social structure between the Socialists and the major parties is apparent, one might conjecture that for an active member of the Socialist party the esprit de corps provided by party structure may have been more important than that needed by members of the two major parties. As sociologist Betty Yorburg has pointed out in her collective portrait of

8

American Socialists, individuals whose beliefs do not conform to those of the majority in their society and who wish to act upon these beliefs are particularly in need of group reinforcement and support. Upton Sinclair captured this feeling when he wrote in his autobiography, "It was like the falling down of prison walls about my mind; the amazing discovery after all those years, that I did not have to carry the whole burden of humanity's future upon my two frail shoulders! There were actually others who understood. . . . The principal fact the socialists had to teach me was that they themselves existed."[15]

The Party, then, supplied many dedicated Socialists with a sense of community. In Reading, where factionalism demoralized the SP and the New Deal siphoned off electoral support, a more ominous signal of the Socialist loss of vitality appeared. The youth movement of the Party had disappeared by the late 1930s and despite several efforts, the "Yipsels" were never reorganized, moreover, by 1944, the average age of Reading's SP membership climbed to over fifty. While this increase in the age of Party members suggests the diminished effectiveness and vitality of municipal socialism, a study of Democratic precinct committeemen in Pittsburgh has shown that the collective aging of the rank and file reflected the party's success in that city. As the Democrats consolidated their power in the two decades between the 1930s and 1950s, it grew increasingly difficult for younger people to enter the party structure; in an effort to maintain control over the tangible rewards of politics, precinct workers remained in office blocking easy access to the young.[16] Thus, the variable of age appeared to have played a different role for the Socialists in decline than it did for the Democrats in ascendancy.

In both of these instances, information regarding age is based on party activists. The evidence from studying Bridgeport indicates that age is also a most important variable when considering Socialist electoral support. Voting analysis of the support for Jasper McLevy when he first came to the mayor's office in 1933 and when he was finally defeated in 1957 suggests that at the time of his initial victory in the throes of the Depression, McLevy received his strongest vote from those areas having the largest proportion of young voters; by the time of his defeat after twenty-four years in Bridgeport's City Hall, the youngest areas offered him little support, while he did best in voting districts with a high proportion of older voters. Conversely, the situation for Bridgeport's Democrats was exactly opposite. The data suggests that McLevy attracted the same voting constituency throughout his hold on the mayoralty. It grew old and middle class with him. Many of the voters might have known no mayor other than the one who had led them out of the Great Depression. However, as new generations moved into the electorate and new minority groups into

9

the city, Bridgeport's brand of socialism attracted few of them. Ironically, it simultaneously grew too fiscally conservative for the city's businessmen, who had once ardently supported McLevy, but who came to desire urban redevelopment that he refused to endorse.

Chronologically, this volume's analysis of socialism and the cities ends with the defeat of McLevy's administration and the conclusion, three years later, of Socialist Frank P. Zeidler's third term in Milwaukee's City Hall, which Sally Miller views as "a ghostly reminder of a dynamic past." Thus, *Socialism and the Cities* covers a broad span of twentieth-century urban history in the United States, roughly from the turn of the century through 1960, but makes no claim to exploring every instance of municipal socialism in America.

In 1912, alone, as James Weinstein has pointed out, Socialists held "some 1,200 public offices in 340 municipalities from coast to coast, among them 79 mayors in 24 states." He continues that Socialist strength ranged over a wide variety of places; in 1911, it was strongest in semirural towns and small cities, whereas by 1917 the Socialist vote "increased principally in the larger cities of the industrialized East and Midwest."[17] The cities studied herein are all large—none under 50,000 population during the time for which they are analyzed—but are not atypical metropolises like New York City. They were chosen in the expectation that the essays concerning the two cities in which the Socialists never gained power provide significant case studies of the Party's municipal failures, while those relating to Milwaukee, Schenectady, Reading, and Bridgeport analyze the most important examples of *urban*[18] socialism in the United States. And, it is hoped that if, in the future, the Cooperative Commonwealth has not yet arrived, and someone poses the question raised by the title of Werner Sombart's 1906 work, *Why is There No Socialism in the United States?*, this volume will serve as a reference for analyzing what happened when there *was* socialism in the United States.

NOTES

1. D.H. Leon, "Whatever Happened to an American Socialist Party? A Critical Survey of the Spectrum of Interpretations," *American Quarterly* 23 (May 1971), 242; in their dialogue, "Social Scientists View the Problem," Chapter 2 of John H.M. Laslett and Seymour Martin Lipset, *Failure of a Dream? Essays in the History of American Socialism* (Garden City, New York, 1974), the editors call for local case studies which compare the socialist experience within the United States and internationally.

2. For membership figures, see: David A. Shannon, *The Socialist Party of America* (Chicago, 1967), p. 34; for the view that Oklahoma socialism was not mainly the result of a Populist resurgence as historians like Shannon suggest, see: Chapter 1 of James R. Green, "Socialism and the Southwestern Class Struggle, 1898–1918:

A Study of Radical Movements in Oklahoma, Texas, Louisiana, and Arkansas" (Ph.D. dissertation,Yale University, 1972).

3. Henry F. Bedford, *Socialism and the Workers in Massachusetts, 1886–1912* (Amherst, Mass. 1966), p. 103.

4. For socialism in New York City, see: Melvyn Dubofsky, "Success and Failure of Socialism in New York City, 1900–1918: A Case Study," *Labor History* 9 (Fall 1968), 361–75, quote from p. 374; for Hillquit's proportion of the vote, see: James Weinstein, *The Decline of Socialism in America, 1912–1925* (New York, 1969), p. 175. Weinstein indicates that seven aldermen were elected.

5. Daniel Bell has contended that the great problem of United States socialism was that "it was trapped by the unhappy problem of living 'in but not of the world,' so that it could only act, and then inadequately, as the moral, but not political, man in immoral society." See: Daniel Bell, *Marxian Socialism in the United States* (Princeton, N.J., 1967), p. 5; see: Weinstein, *Decline of Socialism,* p. 108, for the limits on municipal socialism.

6. Laslett and Lipset, eds., *Failure of a Dream?* pp. 41–42.

7. Leon, "Whatever Happened to an American Socialist Party?" p. 258.

8. Weinstein, *Decline of Socialism,* p. 109.

9. This refers to the study of Muncie, Indiana, by Robert and Helen Lynd, *Middletown* (New York, 1956).

10. Herbert G. Gutman, "The Workers Search for Power" in H. Wayne Morgan, ed., *The Gilded Age: A Reappraisal* (Syracuse, N.Y., 1963), pp. 36–69.

11. For "urban liberalism" see: J. Joseph Huthmacher, "Urban Liberalism and the Age of Reform," *Mississippi Valley Historical Review* 44 (September 1962), 231–41; and John D. Buenker, *Urban Liberalism and Progressive Reform* (New York, 1973); the quote concerning New York City socialism is from Dubofsky, "Success and Failure of Socialism in New York City," p. 374.

12. For discussion of the city manager and commission forms of government, see: Samuel P. Hays, "The Politics of Reform in Municipal Government in the Progressive Era," *Pacific Northwest Quarterly* 55 (October 1964), 157–69, and Chapter 4 of James Weinstein, *The Corporate Ideal in the Liberal State: 1900–1918* (Boston, 1968). See: Melvin G. Holli, *Reform in Detroit: Hazen S. Pingree and Urban Politics* (New York, 1969), especially Chapter 8; and Bruce M. Stave, "Urban Bosses and Reforms" in Raymond A. Mohl and James F. Richardson, eds., *The Urban Experience: Themes in American History* (Belmont, California, 1973), pp. 182–95 for the differences between social and structural reformers. For a first-hand account of socialist attitudes toward urban structural reform, see: "Report of Committee on the Commission Form of Government for Cities," *Proceedings of the National Congress of the Socialist Party* for 1910 (Chicago, 1910), pp. 290–95 and the ensuing debate on pp. 295–301 and the committee's report published in the 1912 *Proceedings,* pp. 179–91.

13. For the relationship of the Socialists to the "new" immigrants, see: Charles Leinenweber, "The American Socialist Party and 'New' Immigrants," *Science and Society* 32 (Winter 1968), 1–25; and Paul Buhle, "Debsian Socialism and the 'New Immigrant' Worker," in William O'Neill, ed., *Insights and Parallels: Problems and Issues of American Social History* (Minneapolis, 1973), pp. 249–77.

14. Hendrik Hertzberg, " 'Hi boss,' said the judge to Meade Esposito," *The New York Times Magazine* (December 10, 1972), pp. 80, 82.

15. Betty Yorburg cites Sinclair and others in her *Utopia and Reality: A Collective Portrait of American Socialists* (New York, 1969), pp. 87–95.

16. See: Bruce M. Stave, *The New Deal and the Last Hurrah: Pittsburgh Machine Politics* (Pittsburgh, 1970), pp. 175–76.

17. Weinstein, *Decline of Socialism,* pp. 93–103, 115.

18. While "urban" is a difficult concept to define, I have chosen the 50,000 population to distinguish between semirural and small towns and cities and the industrial cities emphasized in this volume. While the division might appear arbitrary to some, I believe that political scientist Daniel Elazar's statement about city size and political orientation can be projected back through the twentieth century. He has noted, "There is considerable evidence to the effect that even today virtually all cities below 50,000 in population excepting only a few older suburban cities which face 'central city'- type problems, really do not develop a 'city' outlook in the political arena. As a rule, they align themselves with the so-called 'rural' areas (really a misnomer in the demographic sense today) against the 'big city' in urban-rural conflict situations." I am somewhat more skeptical of his suggestion that this also applies to cities of less than 150,000 population. See: Daniel J. Elazar, "Urban Problems and the Federal Government: A Historical Inquiry," *Political Science Quarterly* 82 (December 1967), 505–25.

JAMES R. GREEN

1. THE "SALESMEN-SOLDIERS" OF THE *APPEAL* ARMY":
A Profile of Rank-and-File Socialist Agitators

Who were the "Jimmie Higginses" of the Socialist party, the rank and file agitators in the movement who spoke from soapboxes on street corners, collected dues, and sold radical literature? Historians have shown that in the years before World War I, the Socialist Party of America (SP) included a diverse membership from many classes, sections, and nationalities, but they have not examined the lives of these regular dues-paying members. Jimmie Higgins remains the fictional character portrayed in Upton Sinclair's novel.

This profile of nearly 500 rank and file Socialist agitators is intended to provide some insights into the lives of the regular party members who did most of the political and organizational work in the years when the SP was on the rise. The analysis may also provide some answers to questions raised by previous historical studies of the old Socialist party.

What was the class composition of the party's membership? Was it largely middle class, as David Shannon and Daniel Bell suggest, based on their examination of the Socialist party national leadership? If so, how does the party's membership compare with that of the Progressive party which, according to Alfred Chandler, had a leadership composed largely of urban businessmen and professionals? Did the Socialists recruit members of the "old" middle class, a *petite bourgeoisie* of struggling shopkeepers and farmers, small-town doctors and lawyers, rather than members of the "new" corporate, professional middle class who, according to Robert Wiebe, led the Progressive crusade?[1] Or, has the middle-class presence in the Socialist party been exaggerated? Recent studies by Melvyn Dubofsky, James Weinstein, and John Laslett have stressed the support Socialists

13

received in several important labor unions.[2] Does this suggest that the Party's rank and file agitators were also recruited largely from the working class? If so, what kind of workers were involved in socialist activity? Were they largely skilled workers continuing in a nineteenth-century tradition of artisan radicalism that initially emerged as a political response to the destruction of the old crafts by industrialization? Were factory workers and other industrial proletarians also among the "Jimmie Higginses" who did the Socialist party's agitational work? If so, were they largely native born or were they "old immigrants" from northern and western Europe? Did the "new immigrants" who came to the United States after 1880 play a significant role before they swelled the Party's foreign language federations during World War I?

These questions have been difficult to answer because historians have lacked sufficient information about rank and file Socialists. A few years ago, while I was doing research on the Socialist movement in the Southwest, I found a source that helps to fill this gap in the social history of the Party. In 1914 a booklet was printed by a Socialist publisher in Girard, Kansas, entitled *Who's Who in Socialist America;* it contained excellent biographical information about 495 activists who sold record numbers of subscriptions to the *Appeal to Reason,* the largest Socialist weekly published in the United States.[3] The sketches include information on age, occupation, birthplace, and residence as well as interesting evidence concerning party activity and earlier partisan affiliations. Most significantly, the biographical sketches contain accounts of why these leading activists converted to socialism. After coding and cross-tabulating the information contained in this *Who's Who,*[4] I was able to study the class and cultural characteristics of a large sample of rank and file Socialists. I was also able to investigate the political ideas and strategies these activists brought to their crusade for the Cooperative Commonwealth. And finally, I was able to make a few generalizations about why people became Socialists during the early years of the twentieth century.

The 495 Socialist agitators listed in the *Who's Who* of 1914 were the leading "salesmen-soldiers" of a remarkable subscription "army" organized around 1900 by Julius A. Wayland, publisher and editor of the *Appeal to Reason.* By the turn of the century this colorful "one-hoss editor" had already attracted 140,000 subscribers to his newspaper by cleverly mixing sensational reporting, folksy commentary, and excerpts from the classical socialist texts.In the next few years Wayland's *Appeal* "Army" attracted thousands of new subscribers to the Girard, Kansas weekly. By 1913 the *Appeal* editors boasted a national circulation of over 750,000, larger than any other weekly periodical, including popular magazines like the *Saturday Evening Post* which took a somewhat different line on the "social

14

question." At this time the *Appeal* Army contained about 80,000 "salesmen-soldiers" who traveled around the country hawking papers, hustling subscriptions, organizing study groups, and founding Party locals.[5] In some states, like Kansas and Oklahoma, the Army's organizational work was almost as important as its educational work.[6]

The *Appeal* Army's *Who's Who* indicates that most of the leading salesmen came from the sections in which Wayland's weekly had the largest readership. (See Table I.) Just over one-fifth of the best soldiers came from the Southwest (Kansas, Missouri, Arkansas, Oklahoma, Texas, and Louisiana), where the *Appeal* had its headquarters and its strongest political influence. Oklahoma and Texas had the largest "armies" in the nation and the third and fourth largest *Appeal* circulation rates. The Midwestern and Western states followed with 35 percent of the total *Who's Who* Army. The states of Ohio and California were particularly important in supplying *Appeal* salesmen and subscribers. Despite its Populist origins and its popularity with hard pressed farmers in rural sections, the *Appeal* Army included a significant number of star salesmen from the Mid-Atlantic states, especially New York and Pennsylvania (which led the nation in *Appeal* subscriptions and *Who's Who* listings). The states of the Great Plains and the Old South also contributed significant numbers of people to the *Who's Who*. By comparison, New England's contribution was relatively insignificant.

TABLE 2-1

Residence of Rank and File Socialist
Agitators by Section, 1914

Section	%	(N)
Southwest	20.8	(103)
Midwest	18.2	(90)
Far West	17.2	(85)
Mid-Atlantic	15.8	(78)
Great Plains	11.5	(57)
Old South	10.9	(54)
New England	4.6	(23)
No Information	1.0	(5)
Totals	100	(495)

This correlation between the size of the *Appeal's* circulation and the success of the Army around 1914 holds even in states where Wayland's weekly had significant competitors in the socialist press. For example, in Texas, one of the leading states in both categories, "Red Tom" Hickey edited a militant socialist paper called *The Rebel* which enjoyed a circulation of 25,000, largely within the Lone Star State.[7] By 1913 workers in New York City supported a thriving radical press led by the daily *Call* (circulation: 22,000) and Abe Cahan's giant *Jewish Daily Forward* (circulation: 142,000). As a result, the *Appeal* had relatively few readers in the city, but it enjoyed a large circulation in New York State at large, especially in industrial cities like Schenectady where most of the workers read English. The influence of the *Appeal* was also limited in some states like Massachusetts which had Finnish and Lettish papers with large circulations and in cities like Milwaukee, St. Louis, and Chicago which supported older German socialist papers.[8] But for the most part the strength of Wayland's journalistic competitors in the cities did not seriously limit the popularity of the *Appeal* and the strength of its Army in the rural sections and smaller industrial cities.

Women were quite active in the Socialist party before World War I.[9] They also read the *Appeal to Reason,* especially when the articles were written by agitators like Caroline Lowe, Kate Richards O'Hare, May Wood Simons, and Grace Brewer. But women were not active in the *Appeal* Army. Only ten females appeared in the *Who's Who* of 1914. This may reflect the fact that selling things was mainly a male role in the 1910s. The leading soldiers listed in this directory were being rewarded for their aggressiveness. The male leaders of the party, who held very traditional attitudes toward women, certainly did not encourage female comrades in this kind of assertive behavior.[10] A few famous women like Lena Morrow Lewis and Kate Richards O'Hare, were widely praised for their aggressive speaking sytle, but they were the exception. The rank and file women in the Party were certainly not encouraged by the men to be forward soldiers in the *Appeal* Army.

The backgrounds of the exceptional women in the *Who's Who* are rather interesting. Five of the ten were housewives or "housekeepers" (three from the Midwest and two from Oregon). Three were converted to socialism by reading the *Appeal* and one, an ex-teacher named Jesse Hawthorne from Illinois, became a Socialist after reading a pamphlet called "Servant in the House."[11] Socialist publications like the *Appeal* focused mainly on the crusade for female suffrage and the exploitation of women wage earners. The men who controlled these publications were as reluctant to advocate complete sexual equality as they were to agitate for "social equality" of the races. As Mari Jo Buhle points out, the Party never stressed the domestic problems of working-class wives and mothers.[12] Nor did the rural radicals in the Party emphasize the special oppression of farm women[13] Nevertheless, pamphlets like "Servant in the House" and occasional feminist articles in socialist papers raised important questions in the minds of female party members. For example, one Socialist farm woman from Kansas, who undoubtedly read the *Appeal,* gave this response to government investigators who inquired about the "Economic Needs of Farm Women":

It is not the lack of cosmetics that ages us women of the farm before our time. It is the treadmill, the life of hard incessant labor without reward. The wife has no definite share of her husband's income. She is the stewardess of riches, the actual possessor of none. Moneyless, she can project nothing. She gives up, loses her individuality, grows dull. Could every farmer's wife receive the wages of an ordinary hired girl for her very own, it would open her eyes to new vistas of accomplishment.[14]

The other five women in the *Who's Who* worked outside the home. One, Annie Hart, was a rubber worker in Williamsport, Pennsylvania; another, Mrs. Nels Johnson, was a tailor in a small Texas town; and a third, Mary Sanborn, was a librarian in New Haven, Connecticut. Two were professionals. Flora Foreman, who was converted to socialism in Kansas by "observing the ardor of her father in the cause he loved," taught school in Oregon where she was dismissed from one teaching position and threatened with dismissal from another "because of her revolutionary teachings." Frances Dickinson, of Orange City, Florida, was a physician who converted to socialism "through observation and experience of the effect of capitalist environment on human nature." Before this she was president of Harvey's Medical College for twelve years, an unusual distinction for the time.[15] Unfortunately, there were not a sufficient number of women in the *Who's Who* to allow a general analysis of their role as agitators within the Socialist movement.[16]

One-third of the 485 men who appeared in the directory of leading "soldiers" were born in the Midwest, one-quarter were natives of the Mid-Atlantic states, and one-fifth came from foreign countries. Surprisingly, 17 percent of these top salesmen were natives of the Old South (i.e., southern states east of the Mississippi); this was partly the result of the *Appeal* Army's great strength among Southern-born "poor whites" in Oklahoma and Texas.[17] Only 5 percent of these agitators were born in New England, that great breeding-ground of nineteenth-century radicals and reformers.

Table 2 indicates that most of these "salesmen-soldiers" were middle-aged. The largest number were in their forties. There were equal numbers in their fifties and in their thirties.

Over half of these successful Socialist agitators lived in towns and small cities (under 10,000) while only one-quarter lived in large cities; this suggests that socialism attracted fewer big city promoters than progressivism, which, as Alfred Chandler shows, was led largely by the urban bourgeoisie.[18] The contrast is reinforced by the fact that one-fifth of these leading Socialist supporters were residents of rural America (see Table 3); they were mainly tenants and indebted yeomen from the West and Southwest (55 of 98 rural dwellers or 60 percent) and not from the Southern and Plains states (29 of 98 rural dwellers or 30 percent) that produced the strongest Populist movements in the 1890s.[19]

This sample of Socialist agitators is undoubtedly skewed away from the big cities by the *Appeal's* populistic origins, its concern for the farmer's problems, and its folksy American idiom. The large socialist dailies and ethnic papers in the cities made it difficult for Wayland's salesmen to make inroads into the established immigrant readership of the urban radical press. In fact, Table 3 shows that, even in urbanized sections of the country, big city representation in the *Who's Who* was exceeded by that of the smaller cities and country towns. Only New York and Ohio provided enough

TABLE 2-2

Ages of Socialist Agitators, 1914

Age	%	(N)
70s	5	(23)
60s	18	(84)
50s	20	(96)
40s	29	(137)
30s	20	(96)
20s	8	(32)
Totals	100	(468)*

*No information on ages of 27 persons

salesmen from big cities to comprise a majority. However, this limited representation from the big cities does not mean that the *Appeal* Army was solely a country phenomenon, because there were more salesmen in the *Who's Who* from urban areas over 10,000 in population than there were from rural areas. Furthermore, the large representation from the towns included many soldiers from crowded factory cities and mining camps as well as salesmen from country villages. For example, in the Western states 57 percent of the best *Appeal* hustlers came from towns (the same percentage as the national average). About half of them came from mining centers which, according to Melvyn Dubofsky, recreated urban conditions on the frontier even though they rarely exceeded a population of 10,000.[20] In any case, despite the small percentage of agitators from big cities, the *Who's Who* came close to representing the residential distribution of the Socialist party's rank and file membership in the years before 1914. It did not reflect, however, the urban-rural differences in the party's membership as accurately as it represented the regional distribution of socialist strength.

TABLE 2-3

Residence of Socialist Agitators by Section and Location, 1914

Regions	Location*							
	City		Town		Rural		Total	
	%	(N)	%	(N)	%	(N)	%	(N)
Southwest	12	(12)	59	(61)	29	(30)	100	(103)
Midwest	38	(34)	56	(50)	6	(6)	100	(90)
Far West	14	(12)	57	(48)	29	(25)	100	(85)
Mid-Atlantic	41	(32)	53	(41)	6	(5)	100	(78)
Great Plains	11	(6)	61	(35)	28	(16)	100	(57)
Old South	24	(13)	52	(28)	24	(13)	100	(54)
New England	26	(6)	61	(14)	13	(3)	100	(23)
Avg. Percent & Total (N's)	23	(115)	57	(277)	20	(98)	100	(490)**

* City = over 10,000 population; town = incorporated area less than 10,000; rural = unincorporated area.
** No residence listed for five agitators.

The size of the *Appeal* Army in the Southwest clearly reflects the Party's disproportionate strength in states like Kansas, Missouri, Arkansas, Louisiana, Texas, and, especially, Oklahoma. As David Shannon pointed out, "it was Oklahoma, with a predominantly rural population and less than one fifth the total population of New York, that led all states in paid up membership" in 1911. "In the congressional elections of 1914 Oklahoma polled 15,000 more Socialist votes than New York," he added. "This rural strength of the party, particularly in Oklahoma, is a subject that merits further consideration," Shannon observed more than twenty years ago.[21]

I have shown elsewhere that the strength of socialism in the Sooner State was not mainly the result of a Populist resurgence as some historians suggest.[22] The Socialist party achieved remarkable gains in Oklahoma because railroad corporations, extractive industries, land speculators, and agricultural capitalists rapidly transformed the state from a promising frontier in the 1890s to a sink-hole of rural poverty in the 1910s. With the fastest growing white tenant population in the South and the most militant trade unions in any agricultural state, Oklahoma presented a wonderful opportunity for Socialist agitators. As a result of union militancy among miners and construction workers in the towns and cities (like Oklahoma City) and agrarian unrest among the rural poor, the Socialists won thousands of supporters away from the progressive Democrats (or "Bryanites") after 1908. Excellent leadership from outside agitators like Oscar Ameringer and Otto Branstetter and indigenous radicals like Pat Nagle and Kate Richards O'Hare helped the Party grow in Oklahoma. From the start, the *Appeal* Army in the Sooner State (the nation's largest) helped to plant the seeds of grass-roots socialism. In fact, during the early years, the *Appeal* editors claimed that the Party's vote correlated directly with the circulation of Wayland's weekly; when Eugene Debs polled almost 17 percent of the Oklahoma vote in 1912, the total Socialist tally roughly equalled the *Appeal's* statewide circulation, 42,000.[23]

The *Appeal* Army could also claim credit for the growth of socialism in Kansas (its home base), Texas, and other Southwestern states. However, the size of the Army in the Southwest may exaggerate the relative strength of socialism in the region to some extent, because Wayland's weekly was unusually influential in these states. The Party probably polled a larger total vote in the more populous Midwestern states, but the Socialists were stronger proportionately in the Southwest than they were in any other section. And the activity of the *Appeal* Army, and especially of the "soldiers" listed in the *Who's Who,* helped to create this surprising strength.

The importance of the Midwest is of course reflected in Table 3. This region (the Old Northwest, plus Iowa and Minnesota) contributed more salesmen to the *Who's Who* than the more urbanized Mid-Atlantic states. This is reflected in the overall membership of the Party as well. "In 1910," Shannon noted, "the combined membership of Ohio, Illinois, and Wisconsin was greater than that of the total of New York and Pennsylvania."[24] Finally, the weakness of the Army in New England (the first stronghold of Debsian socialism around the turn of the century) and the Old South (where the Party never organized effectively) accurately reflects the size of SP membership and voting strength in 1914. In short, the regional distribution of the *Appeal* Army's elite summarized in Table 3 represents with some accuracy the sectional strength of the Socialist party which, in the years before World War I, drew most of its support from the industrial cities of the Midwest, the tenant farms of the Southwest, and the mining camps of the Far West.

The residential distribution of the Army's members shown in Table 3 is more interesting, even if it is somewhat less accurate, because the nature of the urban-rural breakdown raises important questions about the nature of the movement's class composition. Does the strength of the

Appeal's Socialist agitational force in the towns and on the farms mean
that the Party's rank and file was largely middle class, as historians like
Bell and Shannon suggest?[25] Table 4 shows that a majority (281 of the
495, or 57 percent of the "salesmen-soldiers" listed in the *Appeal Who's
Who)* were working class. A minority (214 of 495, or 43 percent) were middle
class. This is particularly interesting since achievement as a literature sales-
man or newspaper hustler depended to some extent on having free time, mobility, literacy, and verbal skills. In other words, if the Socialist rank and file
was largely middle class, we would expect far more traveling salesmen and
insurance agents to be listed in the *Who's Who* than factory workers and
miners. This was not the case. The latter outnumbered the former three to
one.

TABLE 2-4

Class Composition of Appeal "Army" Elite by Occupation and Residence

Class and Occupation	City %	City (N)	Residence Town %	Residence Town (N)	Rural %	Rural (N)	Total %	Total (N)
MIDDLE CLASS	13	(28)	38	(82)	49	(104)	100	(214)
Professionals	26	(11)	67	(29)	7	(3)	100	(43)
Businessmen	4	(5)	23	(31)	73	(99)*	100	(135)
Clerks and Salesmen	33	(12)	61	(22)	6	(2)	100	(36)
WORKING CLASS	33	(93)	64	(180)	3	(8)	100	(281)
Skilled Workers	32	(46)	66	(95)	2	(3)	100	(144)
Semi- and Unskilled Workers	34	(47)	62	(85)	4	(5)	100	(137)
Totals	24	(121)	53	(262)	23	(112)	100	(495)

*All but two were farmers.

Table 4 indicates that the city dwellers in the *Who's Who* were overwhelmingly working class (93 of 121 or 77 percent of the total), again
pointing up the contrast to the leaders of the Progressive party who were almost entirely upper middle-class city dwellers.[26] It is even more important
to note that a clear majority of the top salesmen who resided in small cities
and towns were workers (180 of 262 or 69 percent). Only rural residents
(about one-fifth of the total) were predominantly middle class. Nearly all
of these people were farmers (97 out of 112). A majority of these agricul-
turalists probably owned their own farms, but many in this group were
heavily mortgaged. Furthermore, a significant minority of these farmers
were undoubtedly tenants who owned no property; they rented a small farm
from a landlord and bought goods on time from a credit merchant. These
landless farmers, who constituted a majority of the Socialist party's sizeable
membership in Oklahoma and Texas, identified more with the working class

21

than the middle class of the country towns who served as their creditors, bankers, and landlords.[27] In other words, the class composition of the *Appeal* Army's elite corps reflected in Table 4 indicates that the SP's rank and file leaders were not predominantly middle class as some historians suggested after examining the social origins of a small group of national leaders.

Table 4 also reveals that only 9 percent (43 of 495) of the salesmen in this group were professionals; 7 percent (36 of 495) were largely clerks and traveling salesmen; and, with the exception of farmers, only 7 percent (38 of 495) were businessmen, mainly real estate agents, grocers, barbers, druggists, and the like, who served farmers in country towns and workers in smaller industrial cities.

The class composition of this leading group of Socialists contrasts sharply with a national sample of 260 Progressive leaders collected by Alfred Chandler. A large percentage of these reformers were businessmen (36 percent) who in many cases owned or managed corporations and in few cases ran shops or stores like the radicals. The rest of Chandler's Progressive leadership sample consisted entirely of professionals. Unlike the Socialist professionals, most of the Progressives were lawyers or editors. In the entire sample of 260 reform leaders, Chandler wrote, "there were no farmers, no laboring men and only one labor union leader."[28]

There are some problems involved in comparing this elite sample of Progressive leaders (including many national committeemen and state chairmen) with a sample of rank and file Socialist agitators. We should note, however, that Chandler's rather inclusive sample contains names of those reformers who simply gave time and money to the Progressive party as well as the names of those who served in official positions. Furthermore, the people listed in the *Appeal* Army's *Who's Who* included many who were Socialist officials and candidates, usually on a local or state level. They ranged from George H. Geobel, a New Jersey carpenter (and one of the few agitators listed who enjoyed a national reputation), who "helped organize locals in practically every state" and "filled practically every office in the Party except national secretary," to J.W. Head, a Kansas farmer who served as deputy sheriff of Cloud County.[29] Nevertheless, the fact remains that this unique sample of Socialist agitators cannot be compared strictly to Chandler's sample of Progressive leaders. The Bull Moosers never enjoyed the support of a group of rank and file activists like the *Appeal* Army, because, unlike the Socialist party, the Progressive party was organized from the top down.

In order to find a group of Socialist leaders who are more comparable to Chandler's Progressives, I have turned to a list of delegates who attended the Socialist party's "emergency" convention in the spring of 1917.[30] These people, who were called together in order to make a radical response to the United States entry into World War I, included most of the party's national and state leaders. Professor Shannon writes that "only about one-half of the delegates were farmers or workers, although many of them worked with their hands in their younger days," but he does not give a detailed occupational breakdown.[31] My examination of the list reveals that of the 119 delegates listing occupations there were 47 blue-collar workers, 22 white-collar workers, 17 businessmen (including 9 farmers, mainly Oklahoma tenants), and 33 professionals.

In short, the class background of the Socialist party's national leadership differed dramatically from that of the Progressive party. Only 1 percent of the radicals were businessmen as compared to 36 percent of the reformers while only 10 percent of the former were lawyers as compared to 29 percent of the latter. Furthermore, it is unlikely that as many middle-class Progressive leaders worked at manual labor in their younger days as was the case with the middle-class Socialist leaders. Most significantly, none of the Progressive party's national leaders were workers or farmers, as compared to 48 percent of the Socialist party's national leaders.

The delegation represented at the SP's 1917 emergency convention did contain fewer workers (39 percent) than the *Appeal*'s cadre of activists (57 percent of the rank and file agitators listed in the *Who's Who* of 1914 were workers); it also contained fewer workers than the party's national membership (66 percent of the 6,300 members responding to a 1908 questionnaire were wage earners).[32] And so it seems that the "salesmen-soldiers" who led Wayland's propaganda movement contained about 10 percent fewer workers than the SP's membership at large; their Army also contained 4 percent more professionals, 3 percent more farmers, and 3 percent more businessmen. Nevertheless, the *Who's Who* of 1914 comes fairly close to representing the class composition of the party membership at large, closer certainly than the national leadership attending at the 1917 convention.

What kind of workers comprised the Socialist party's rank and file in the years before World War I? Responses to the 1908 questionnaire revealed that about 44 percent of the Party's members were skilled workers while about 22 percent were unskilled workers. Interestingly enough, the *Appeal* Army's elite contained a smaller proportion of skilled workers (29 percent) and a larger proportion of unskilled workers (28 percent) than the national survey of all party members. Fortunately, the detailed occupational information listed in the *Who's Who* allows us to look more carefully at the workers in the Socialist party who were most active as "Jimmie Higginses."

Table 5 provides a more detailed breakdown of the various jobs held by Socialist party workers. The skilled workers were largely employed in construction (twenty-two carpenters led all other crafts) and in transportation, mainly railroads and, to a lesser extent, urban transit.[33] Another important group of skilled workers, the machinists (sixteen), included men like Walter Kruesi of Schenectady, New York, who was appointed commissioner of charities by a Socialist administration that included eleven other machinists among its elected officials.[34] The SP's strength among machinists was reflected on a national level by the election of Socialist workers to leadership positions in the International Association of Machinists.[35]

TABLE 2-5
Occupations of Working-Class
Socialist Agitators

Occupation	%	(N)
Skilled Workers in Construction and Transport	17	(83)
Other Skilled Workers	12	(55)
Factory Operatives	15	(76)
Laborers	13	(67)*
Total Workers	57	(281)
Total Others	43	(214)
Totals	100	(495)

*Includes one worker who listed his occupation as "wage slave."

Two other trades represented in the *Who's Who* by twelve shoemakers and nine blacksmiths reflected the continuation of an older tradition of artisan radicalism. The cordwainers or shoemakers led in articulating protests against the factory system throughout the nineteenth century.[36] In the late 1890s many of these leather workers, especially in Massachusetts, turned to socialism as a more radical response to the destruction of their trade and as a logical political extension of their cooperative traditions.[37] In 1895 the shoe workers elected Socialists to run the affairs of their new union and in 1899 they elected fellow Socialist workers to run the affairs of two Massachusetts cities, Haverhill and Brockton, in which they predominated. However, by 1914 the strength of socialism in these large shoemaking centers had declined drastically.[38] One shoemaker from Brockton, R. A. Nutting, was honored in the *Appeal Who's Who* of that year, but the other members of that trade came largely from small cities and towns in the Midwest;[39] this was also true of the nine blacksmiths listed. These craftsmen resembled the village artisans of the early nineteenth century who spread radicalism to other townspeople and to farmers.[40]

Skilled workers continued to play an important role in labor and radical movements, including the *Appeal* Army, during the early twentieth century. These workingmen were especially important in the Midwestern Socialist parties; the *Who's Who* entries from these states contained the

24

largest proportion of skilled workers in the nation (exactly one-quarter). The artisans and craftsmen who helped lead the *Appeal* Army in scores of small cities and country towns throughout Mid-America represented the articulate, self-confident form of working-class culture the Lynds described in Middletown just after the turn of the century.[41] Men like Finley Bickford, a stonemason from Eddyville, Iowa, S.O. Cable, a carpenter of Newton, Kansas, and John Dimond, a shoemaker with a shop in Keokuk, Iowa, represented the importance of Anglo-American craftsmen in the *Appeal's* Midwestern Army.

Other men, like the following, reflected the significance of German and Scandinavian artisans: A.O. Rosen, a blacksmith residing in Silvis, Illinois; Gustave Aumann, a bricklayer working in Manitowoc, Wisconsin; Martin Halberg, a pianomaker who practiced his art in LaPorte, Indiana; Morris Fox, a carpenter who also farmed a place near Londonville, Ohio; and E.Z. Ernest, a printer and town mechanic from Olathe, Kansas, who worked a farm outside of town.[42] The last two soldiers personified the town-country connection that was so important to the spread of Midwestern socialism in the early 1900s. Village artisans were in a good position to bring radical ideas to their farmer clients, especially when they were part-time farmers themselves.

Henry J. Schulthis, the son of German parents from St. Louis, symbolized another important characteristic of the Socialist skilled workers in the small cities and towns of the Midwest. After joining the Socialist party in Missouri, Schulthis moved to Culver, Indiana, where he worked as a baker and pastry cook while distributing "many pieces of Socialist literature" and "securing many subscriptions to the *Appeal* and other Socialist papers."[43] The patient work tradesmen like Schulthis devoted to the *Appeal* and its cause resulted in part from the proud attitude they adopted toward practicing their own skill. And, unlike laborers in factories or the extractive industries, village craftsmen often had contact with a wide range of people who enjoyed the time and the inclination to engage in serious political dialogue. Henry Schulthis expressed his seriousness about studying socialism by enrolling in a correspondence school sponsored by the *Appeal;* this kind of activity was part of a long tradition of self-education prevalent among radical craftsmen throughout the nineteenth century. In order to convert people to socialism, the agitator had to have a good grasp of economic facts, radical theories, and debating skills.

These artisans and craftsmen who helped to lead J.A. Wayland's propaganda army in scores of Midwestern towns were usually removed from contact with trade unions and industrial workers, and so their agitational efforts were directed largely towards farmers, shopkeepers, and other members of the *petite bourgeoisie* who were threatened by monopoly capitalism.

25

But in larger towns and small cities with manufacturing, mining, or railroading connections, these older artisans joined with industrial workers in building the Socialist party on a local level. The glass blowers of Muncie, Indiana, represented this older group of workers in one Midwestern manufacturing center during the early 1900s. As described by the Lynds in *Middletown*, these craftsmen of the glass-making industry were at the center of a strong, class-conscious labor movement composed largely, but not entirely, of skilled workers in craft unions affiliated with the American Federation of Labor. The glass blowers, along with other skilled workers in the building trades, the railroad yards, and several light industries, were led by self-educated, well-read trade unionists who exercised considerable control over their jobs.[44] They also had a strong influence in union and civic affairs. Some of them were undoubtedly Socialists. Interestingly enough, several glass blowers from Debs's home state of Indiana appeared in the Socialist *Who's Who* of 1914.

Unlike the village artisans of Mid-America, the salesmen-soldiers from small industrial cities like Muncie came to socialism through class struggles in which they fought on the side of embattled labor unions. This is corroborated in Frederick Barkey's important dissertation on the West Virginia Socialists whose leaders joined the cause largely as a result of their trade union experience as skilled iron moulders, glass blowers, cigarmakers, painters, carpenters, and other building tradesmen. The Socialist leaders Barkey interviewed from West Virginia mining camps and industrial cities were largely native-born Protestants.[45]

However, immigrant workers in similar industrial settings also came to the Socialist crusade through trade union experiences. For example, an Austrian named Blaise Novak who worked as an iron moulder in East Pittsburgh, Pennsylvania, said that he was converted to socialism "through the trade union." After his conversion, Novak sold 150 subscriptions to various socialist newspapers in 1913 and acted as secretary of his steelworker Party local.[46] Other salesmen-soldiers who decided to propagandize for the Socialist party as a result of labor union struggles included miners like Paul J. Paulsen who was locked in a West Virginia "bull-pen" for three weeks during the national coal strike of 1902. Unlike most West Virginia coal miners, Paulsen was born abroad—in Denmark. After being blacklisted, Paulsen moved to Wyoming where he organized for the Socialist party and the United Mine Workers. While serving as SP state secretary and as a representative to the UMW national executive board, Paulsen still found time to sell socialist literature. In 1913 he sold enough subscriptions to the *Appeal* to win a place among the champion salesmen listed in the *Who's Who*.[47]

However, like most of the Socialist miners interviewed in Appalachia by Frederick Barkey, those appearing in the 1914 *Who's Who* were largely Anglo-American workers who considered themselves skilled crafts-men. By 1914 these older miners dominated the leadership of the UMW on a district and national level, even though a majority of the work force in many areas consisted of immigrants from Southern and Eastern Europe. And, as John Laslett shows in *Labor and the Left*, a significant number of these English-speaking union leaders were Socialists.[48] They came not on-ly from large coal-mining centers like Southern Illinois (which produced well-known national leaders like J.H. Walker, Adolph Germer, Duncan Mc-Donald, and Frank Hayes), but from less important mining towns in West Virginia, Oklahoma, Kansas, and Arkansas where the district leaders of the union were all Socialists in 1914. Some of these important UMW leaders were active in many phases of Socialist propaganda work; they included men like Paulsen of Rock Springs, Wyoming; Alex Howat of Pittsburg, Kan-sas (president of District 14 and a close friend of the *Appeal* published in nearby Girard); and Fred Holt of McAlester, Oklahoma (secretary-treasurer of District 21 and the Socialist party's most successful gubernatorial candi-date in 1914).[49] They were an inspiration to rank and file miners like Ben T. Holes of Russellville, Arkansas, who organized locals, "distributed sev-eral thousand pieces of Socialist literature," and sold many subscriptions to Party papers, even though he was "persecuted and blacklisted" because of his agitational work.[50]

Because the miners listed in the *Who's Who* were all native Americans or "old" immigrants from the British Isles, Scandinavia, France, or Belgium who gained their experience in the pits before large-scale mechanization, they have been included among the skilled workers in the sample. In fact, within their communities, these older miners acted very much like the arti-culate skilled workers the Lynds described in Middletown. Like European miners whose experiences were grounded in the nineteenth century; they loved to study and discuss politics. And unlike the European peasants who later emigrated to do work in the American mines, they participated in poli-tics in various spheres (union and civic), on different levels (local, district, and national), and in several parties (Democratic, Republican, Populist, and Socialist).[51] As a result, the *Appeal to Reason* and its remarkable army en-joyed strong support in coal camps and mining centers (especially in the Midwest and Southwest) among English-speaking miners who took pride in their work and in their politics.[52]

On the average, the 144 skilled workers in the *Who's Who* were the same age (forty-one years) as the 137 semiskilled workers in the sample, but they were far more experienced in previous radical movements. Sur-prisingly, 40 percent of the skilled workers in the *Appeal* Army elite had been affiliated with the People's party before converting to socialism. This is particularly interesting given the fact that only 12 percent of the farmers

27

in the sample had been Populists. How can this apparent paradox be explained?

The small proportion of Populist farmers in the leading ranks of the *Appeal* Army can be explained in part by the fact that in 1913 most rural Socialist activists were tenant farmers, especially in important states like Oklahoma and Texas; these landless farmers were often too young or too transient to vote in the 1890s. In an unpublished study of the Southwestern Socialist movement, I have maintained that these "forgotten" farmers were often ignored by the independent yeomen and landlords who led the People's party in the South. My analysis of voting patterns in rural communities and mining towns throughout the Southwest suggested that there was less continuity between the Populist and Socialist movements than some historians hypothesized;[5][3] this discontinuity is reflected on a national level among the farmers in the *Who's Who*. The lack of Populist experience among these leading rural agitators is less surprising when we note that the vast majority of the farmers in the sample (88 percent) were converted to socialism after the founding of the Party in 1901. In other words, most of them were quite young during the heyday of the Alliance and Populist movements; they came of age politically during the early 1900s when rising tenancy rates became an issue for the first time, partly as a result of socialist agitation. The Populists never tried to make tenancy an issue, and so they attracted proportionally less support than the Socialists did from renters in the rural South and West.

As compared to the farmers in the *Who's Who*, the skilled workers in the sample were somewhat older men, including a larger percentage who converted to socialism before 1901. In fact, a surprisingly large percentage (40) went directly from populism to socialism in the decade following the takeover of the People's party by Bryan and the Democrats. Like Eugene Debs, Victor Berger, and Julius Wayland, many of these skilled workers hoped that the Populist movement would produce an independent labor party with a socialist program. After the debacle of 1896, many of them gave up hope and some joined Daniel DeLeon's Socialist Labor party which maintained a principled Marxist critique of the Populists throughout the decade. Others continued to work within radical Populist movements in states like Kansas and Texas where leftist labor leaders played a role in the formation of the People's party. Of course, many of these skilled workers were actually Socialist sympathizers while they were in the Populist crusade. Many of those who worked in towns and cities west of the Mississippi were initially interested in socialism by J.A. Wayland's first newspaper, *The Coming Nation*, which published a sort of proletarian populism in a weekly that reached over 100,000 readers in the early 1890s. When Wayland started published the *Appeal to Reason* in 1895 "he had all but given up" on his hope that the People's party would adopt a "socialist program."[54] Over the next few years most of the radical craftsmen who read *The Coming Nation* came to agree with its editor, they were among the first to subscribe to Wayland's new socialistic paper, and, when the "one hoss editor" launced the *Appeal* Army in 1900, these skilled workers were among the first to volunteer.

It is also interesting to note that a larger percentage of skilled workers (18) participated in the Prohibition party before converting to socialism than was the case with middle-class soldiers (only 1 percent of the businessmen, professionals, and farmers in the *Who's Who* had been affiliated with the antiliquor party). This suggests that a hidden tradition of working-class self-reform that Paul Faler has discovered among antebellum artisans persisted into the twentieth century. In his important study of cordwainers in Lynn, Massachusetts, Faler found that artisans adopted their own approach to the problem of drunkenness in the community. Working-class temperance workers rejected the repressive, moralistic approach of middle-class crusaders and adopted a more humane form of temperance agitation through which they could advance their own class interest.[55] The Socialists adopted the same approach to alcholism, although they blamed it much more directly on the capitalist class. The skilled workers in the *Appeal* Army probably retained some of the fear of liquor that troubled artisan agitators in the early nineteenth century. In fact, Wayland and his editors frequently appealed to this sense of native working-class morality by printing articles on the "liquor trust" and exposés of "white slavery" with headlines like "Working Girls Seduced by Commercial Buccaneers."

It is not surprising to find the traditions of early American artisans surviving within this group of dissenting workers (a majority of whom were skilled craftsmen) when we note that only about one-fifth of all the persons in the sample were foreign-born. Table 6 indicates that most of the 105 immigrant workers in the *Who's Who* came from Germany or Austria (27 percent), Scandinavia (26 percent), or the British Isles including Ireland (18 percent). The largest number from any one country came from Germany, confirming the well-known influence of this national group in the early Socialist party. Surprisingly, only two of the German workers were skilled workers while fourteen were semiskilled. Eight of these immigrants were *petit bourgeois* or professional. Judging from the names of many American-born soldiers in the sample, second and third generation Irishmen were fairly well represented; but the small number of first generation Irish in the *Who's Who* compared to the number of immigrants from Great Britain suggests that foreign-born Protestants were more likely to become Socialist agitators than foreign-born Catholics. Unfortunately, it is impossible to confirm this suggestion, because the *Who's Who In Socialist*

29

America did not include religious information. However, the predominance of Protestants in the agitational elite of the SP is corroborated further by the proportionate dominance of native Americans in the sample as a whole (79 percent) and by the disproportionate absence of immigrants from the Catholic countries of Europe in the foreign-born sample (less than one-third of all Europeans). In fact, there were only eight "new immigrants" in the entire sample; the eight, three of them Jews, came from Russia and Eastern Europe. There were none from Italy or Greece. This supports the theory advanced by Paul Buhle that most foreign-born Socialists were "old immigrants" prior to 1914.[56] The "new immigrants" who flocked into the Party's foreign-language federations during World War I were converted to socialism in Europe; they were not exposed to the *Appeal* or to its Army of salesmen-soldiers. If they were converted to socialism in America, it was through the Party's foreign-language papers, like the *Jewish Daily Forward*.

TABLE 2-6
National Origins of Foreign-Born
Socialist Agitators, 1914

National Origin	%	(N)
Scandinavia	26	(27)
Germany	24	(25)
Britain, Wales & Scotland	15	(16)
Canada	13	(14)
Eastern Europe & Russia	7	(8)
France & Belgium	6	(6)
Ireland	3	(3)
Austria	3	(3)
Switzerland	3	(3)
Totals	100	(105)

The SP's failure to attract "new immigrants" before 1914 did not mean that Socialists failed to recruit "unskilled" manual laborers. Despite the fact that the Industrial Workers of the World were expelled from the Party in 1912 for advocating sabotage, one-third of the people listed in the *Who's Who* of 1914 were industrial proletarians (i.e., 160 of the workers, including those in extractive industries). The *Appeal to Reason* did have a "populistic" flavor that attracted readers on the farms and the small towns of the trans-Mississippi West, but its editors also devoted a great deal of attention to workers' struggles. Sensational headlines and detailed stories from *Appeal* reporters on the industrial battlefields of the United States attracted many working-class readers who could comprehend the weekly's colorful version of the English language. For example, in 1906 when William D. Haywood and two other leaders of the Western Federation of Miners were illegally arrested and put on trial for the murder of Idaho's anti-labor ex-governor, the *Appeal* gave the case sensational publicity. Outraged by the "frame-up," Eugene V. Debs published his revolutionary challenge "Arouse, Ye Slaves" in which he warned that a million workers would take up arms if Haywood and his comrades were "murdered" by the state.

The *Appeal's* vigorous coverage of the case provoked action against it by progressives as well as conservatives, according to David A. Shannon; this, he noted, was "an indication of the paper's influence." After reading Debs's threatening challenge, President Roosevelt sent a copy of "Arouse, Ye Slaves" to his Attorney General with this note: "This is an infamous article? Is it possible to proceed aginst Debs and the proprietor of this paper criminally? . . . please notify the Post-Office Department so that the paper may not be allowed in the mails, if we can keep it out."[57] The federal government did not succeed in silencing the *Appeal* for another decade, years in which Wayland's weekly developed a large readership in industrial cities across the land. Its coverage of the Haywood case in 1906 signaled the beginning of this development. Some of the salesmen-soldiers who worked in industry mentioned this *cause celebre* as a key event in their political development. For example, Robert E. King, a steel worker from Kansas City, Kansas, reported that he "converted to Socialism by reading the *Appeal* during the Haywood trial."[58]

At any rate, the strong representation of industrial workers as well as craftsmen in the top ranks of the *Appeal* Army indicates that the old Socialist party was built upon a solid working-class base. This factor is ignored by historians like Daniel Bell who suggests that the Socialists' "proletarian chauvinism" was absurd given the Party's middle-class leadership. Shannon made the same point when he wrote: "For an organization whose motto was 'Workers of the World Unite,' the Socialist Party had an extraordinary number of members who were not of the working class."[59] Like Bell, Shannon based this generalization largely upon an examination of the occupations of the Party's national leaders. This analysis, based upon nearly 500 biographies, suggests that most of the active Socialists in the United States were workers, including craftsmen who represented the artisan radicalism of the nineteenth century and laborers who represented the most class-conscious elements of the twentieth-century industrial proletariat.

Who were the other members of the *Appeal* Army? In addition to the 99 small farmers and tenants, there were 115 people represented who were not of the working class; they were divided almost equally into groups

31

of white-collar workers, professionals, and small businessmen, and they came largely from towns or little cities (see Table 4). Ministers outnumbered all other professionals. The white-collar employees were clerks or salesmen. The businessmen were mainly small shopkeepers, little commercial capitalists who felt that they, like the small farmers, were being crushed by corporate capitalists or "plutocrats." Unlike other members of their class who remained loyal to their party and supported William Howard Taft, William Jennings Bryan, or Woodrow Wilson, these Socialist businessmen were not seduced by the Progressives' trust-busting rhetoric. Like their working-class comrades, these middle-class radicals believed that the reformers of the "Progressive era" were really acting in the interest of the big capitalists. Taft and Wilson were the spokesmen of the financiers on Wall Street not of the pharmacists on Main Street.

For example, J.V. Kolachny, a druggist from Ft. Cobb, Oklahoma, was a Bryan Democrat in the 1890s, but after Debs attacked the Great Commoner in the presidential campaign of 1900, this small-town pharmacist became a Socialist. He joined up shortly after the Socialist Party of America was founded in 1901, and became an important leader and editor in his section of the state. As of 1914, he was a member of the town council and, after a decade of outspoken agitation on behalf of the *Appeal* and the Party, Kolachny said that "he never lost any business on account of Socialism."[60] Other small businessmen came out of the milieu Herbert Gutman described in Midwestern mining towns where the *petit bourgeois* people and the professionals often supported workers' struggles against the industrial capitalists who invaded their communities.[61]

In some cases, these proprietors were converted to socialism when they were workers, that is, prior to the time they achieved "social mobility." For example, David Laury, cook and proprietor of Debs Hotel in Colville, Washington, saw the socialist light while reading the *Appeal* during the Haywood trial; F.J. Henry, who owned a rug-making shop in Taunton, Massachusetts, was "converted to Socialism by hard knocks received as a machinist." Like these businessmen, Dr. J.A. Rice of Live Oaks, California, was converted while he was a worker. He joined the party "when fellow workers in the printing trade showed him the meaning of the class struggle and induced him to read the *Appeal.*"[62] But there were also professionals and proprietors of *petite bourgeoisie* origins who joined the SP; they became radicals because they were being oppressed by corporate capitalism, because they distrusted the new Progressives as well as the old party politicians, or because they sympathized with the struggles of the workers and farmers who were also their customers, clients, and patients.

These examples highlight the intriguing quality of the information the *Who's Who* provides about why people converted to socialism. This

32

unusual evidence must be interpreted with caution, however. In a social milieu strongly influenced by revivalism and evangelicalism, many persons longed to have a conversion experience, the more dramatic the better. As a result, religious and political converts often overemphasized or actually fictionalized catalytic events in their lives which brought them around to the true faith or the just cause. Furthermore, the similarities and connections between religious and political conversions can easily lead to a facile equation of two ideologically distinct experiences. If socialistic conversions were really the political equivalent of evangelistic conversions, we would expect to find many Socialist agitators who saw the light after witnessing moving events or listening to charismatic speakers. We would certainly expect to find this sort of thing in the Southwest where the Socialists actually held "protracted" encampments that were consciously modeled after revival meetings.[63] If this evidence could be discovered, it might add credence to Daniel Bell's psycho-religious theory that the Socialists were more inclined to be "chiliastic" crusaders than pragmatic political activists.[64] The evidence presented in Table 7 challenges this theory.

TABLE 2-7
Reasons Given by Appeal Salesmen for their
Conversion to Socialism

Means of Conversion to Socialism	%	(N)
Listening to Debates	.5	(3)
Listening to Speakers	3	(16)
Experiencing and/or Witnessing Political and Social Events	3	(17)
Reading along with those Means Listed Above	3	(16)
Observing and/or Experiencing Social and Economic Conditions	6	(32)
Discussion and/or Reflection	9	(46)
Reading Socialist Literature	74	(357)
No Information	1.5	(8)
Totals	100	(495)

Only a small percentage said that they were influenced by charismatic speakers, usually Eugene Debs or Big Bill Haywood.[65] The percentage converted by speakers was even smaller in the Southwest, despite the existence of the summer camp meetings and the presence of many preachers and former evangelists in the Party's agitational corps. The impact of dramatic events (like the Haywood trial of 1906) was also relatively unimportant as a source of conversion experiences. A large proportion of the salesmen-soldiers interviewed for the *Appeal Who's Who* said that they became Socialists by experiencing and observing conditions of life and labor in capitalist America. For example, two tailors in the *Who's Who* described their conversions this way: Max Oettel, a German immigrant working in Philadelphia, said he was "converted to Socialism by hard work, small income, and long hours" while Israel Barsky, a Russian immigrant working in Conneaut, Ohio, simply said that he was "converted to Socialism by the capitalist system."[66] Table 7 also shows that a significant number of top soldiers became Socialists by talking with Party members and reflecting on the things they had seen and heard. Many said that plain old "common sense" told them that capitalism had to go.[67] Thus, only one-quarter of the Socialist agitators in the *Who's Who* were converted by direct personal experiences, and those were rarely dramatic, let along "chiliastic." Contrary to Bell's theory, this evidence indicates that the most committed Socialist activists, indeed the most throughly converted agitators, came to socialism through rational rather than emotional experiences.

This hypothesis is strengthened by the fact that three-quarters of the sample converted to socialism by reading books, newspapers, and pamphlets. The influence of socialist literature may be somewhat exaggerated in this group, because its members were the leading newspaper hawkers and pamphlet hustlers in the country. And because 54 percent of the entire sample cited the *Appeal to Reason* as the cause of their conversion, it might be inferred that the importance of Wayland's weekly was also exaggerated. Reading in general was more important for these leading agitators than it was for the rank and file as a whole. A survey of 6,300 Socialist party members in 1908 revealed that 52 percent were converted through reading. But the fact that two-thirds of the Socialists who responded to this SP survey subscribed to the *Appeal* suggests that the influence of Wayland's weekly as a vehicle of conversion was not exaggerated by the agitators listed in the *Who's Who*. In fact, it was the only Socialist Party newspaper with a real national circulation in the years between 1901 and 1910 when exactly one-half of the *Appeal* Army activists converted to socialism. Indeed, Wayland's weekly was probably the most influential mass propaganda organ in the history of American radicalism[68] The influence of the *Appeal to Reason* was especially important in the early 1900s because a surprisingly small number of people in the sample (only 22 percent) had been members of radical parties in the nineteenth century (and 20 percent were nonpartisan). In fact, 64 percent were members of the Democratic party or the GOP when they converted to socialism.

In addition to those who heard and answered the "one hoss" editor's *Appeal to Reason,* 19 percent of the agitators listed in *Who's Who* said that they enlisted in the fight for the Cooperative Commonwealth after reading

34

pamphlets like "Servant in the House" and Oscar Ameringer's "Life and Deeds of Uncle Sam" or books like Bellamy's *Looking Backward* and Blatchford's *Merrie England* Marx's *Das Kapital* was not mentioned nor was Gronlund's *Co-Operative Commonwealth* which influenced important leaders like Wayland and Debs. These books were too inaccessible and often too dense for American readers. In any case, most Socialists could read popular translations of Marx, Engels, Kautsky, and Bebel in the *Appeal* along with interpretations and criticisms of ideas advanced by American "socialists." Wayland and his fellow editors took this task seriously. They felt that the *Appeal's* effectiveness as a vehicle for Socialist conversions depended in large measure on the success of their attempts to translate, edit, and interpret the "socialist classics." In any case, what stands out in these reports on conversion experiences is the importance of literacy, not only among professionals and self-taught craftsmen, but among factory operatives and manual laborers as well. There are too many histories of the Socialist party that focus on the movement's national leaders; this study has attempted to correct for that bias by studying the social origins and the political ideas of the rank and file agitators whose ideological development was every bit as important as that of the well-known organizers and the intellectuals in the Party.

In conclusion, the remarkable *Who's Who in Socialist America, 1914* accurately reflects the strengths and the weaknesses of the prewar movement. In the first decade or so, the Debsian Socialists were able to organize a strong national party which included its share of outspoken preachers, intellectuals, cantankerous farmers, and eccentric businessmen, but the SP's main source of strength was its working-class membership; it was a blue-collar backbone running out of the Mid-Atlantic states to the Midwest's industrial cities, railroad towns, and coal camps, and it included skilled craftsmen who were active in radical movements of the nineteenth century and industrial proletarians (largely Anglo-Americans, Germans, or Scandinavians) who were in the vanguard of labor militancy in the early twentieth century. At this time, the fact that there were more Socialist workers concentrated in the Middletowns of America than there were in the large cities was a strength rather than a weakness, because it enabled the SP's working-class base to work closely with discontented people from the petty bourgeois and professional classes. In the short run this was important because it extended the Party's agitational work and deepened its educational effectiveness.

These efforts in which the *Appeal* Army played a vanguard role advanced the Socialists' electoral activities impressively in the years before 1912, and, of course, elections were what the SP was all about. The successes of "gas and water" Socialists on a local level often resulted from alliances with leaders and financial backers from the professional and petty bourgeois classes; and this of course led to compromise. Later, it led some historians to brand urban socialism the left wing of progressivism. This label has frequently been applied to SP mayors like George Lunn of Schenectady, New York, a Presbyterian minister who acted more like a Progressive than a Socialist, according to his disillusioned secretary Walter Lippmann.[69] It is often forgotten that the twenty-three other Socialists elected with Lunn were all workers, half of them machinists.[70] Mayor Lunn, like most articulate Socialist leaders, received considerable publicity. Subsequently, he and other party politicians, like Victor Berger, received a great deal of atten-tion from historians. But the strength and the style of socialism in Schenectady was not determined by Reverend Lunn as much as it was by the unknown workers, like Walter Kruesi, who ran the city government. These machinists and other workers built the party by selling socialist literature, organizing locals, and conducting the campaign that put George Lunn in city hall. Most of them remained loyal to socialism after the mayor became a Democrat.

The strength of the *Appeal* Army among workers and nonworkers alike in the small country towns like Ft. Cobb, Oklahoma, and the coal camps like Russellville, Arkansas, in the small cities like Muncie, Indiana, and the medium-sized cities like Schenectady also reflected the SP's ability to use its working-class base as a means of achieving electoral gains. The Party was built not only upon the national leadership of discontented members of the petty bourgeois and professional classes, but also on the local, regional, and trade union leadership of articulate skilled workers and class conscious industrial workers. But this socialist strength was limited from the start. The problem was that nearly all of the agitators who strengthened the SP were native white males, or older assimilated immigrants. The weakness of the *Appeal* Army of 1914 in the large cities also reflected its weakness among the new immigrant proletariat of the time. In the short run, the SP responded by building a mass following in its foreign-language federations, for example, among Russian Jews in New York and Finns in Massachusetts, but the gains were short-lived, because these very groups formed the bases of strength for the new Bolshevik parties when they split from the SP in 1919. The absence of new immigrants in the ranks of the *Appeal* Army did not reflect a lack of SP electoral strength in cities (this increased dramatically after 1914, as James Weinstein shows), but it did reflect the lack of an organic connection between the Party's new immigrant members and the old rank and file in the towns and small cities of the heartland.[71] Less apparent at the time was the Party's weakness among the working women and black people who were moving into laboring positions in the cities. As Weinstein suggests, the Party did become more conscious of its general weakness among women and blacks. Although recruitment efforts across racial lines, such as they were, failed totally a significant number of women were brought in the Party in the early 1900s;[72] but like many of the new immigrants and most of the blacks, they were irrelevant to the SP's electoral strategy because they were disfranchised. While Anglo-American women played more important leadership roles in the SP than either the new immigrants or the blacks, their tiny representation in the *Appeal* Army also reflected an inorganic relationship to the movement's white male rank and file.

The "salesmen-soldiers" of the Army were, as Wayland boasted, the backbone of the Socialist propaganda effort; they effectively deepened the Party's bases of strength among farmers, townspeople, and workers, but these agitators, like their comrades in other lines of political work, failed to extend the SP's bases of strength from old immigrant workers in small industrial towns to new immigrant workers in larger cities or from unionized male wage earners to disfranchised black and female wage earners. However, like the Socialist party itself, the *Appeal* Army helped to radicalize many different kinds of American people, including farmers, artisans, and businessmen who were being eliminated by corporate capitalism as well as factory operatives, transportation workers, and wage earners in the extractive industries whose labor was essential to economic growth in the twentieth century.

And so Jimmie Higgins spoke to many angry people in his day. When he just gave a soapbox oration, his words were soon forgotten, but when he sold someone a subscription to the *Appeal to Reason,* the message kept coming through week after week. The remarkable effectiveness of Wayland's weekly depended as much upon its salesmen as it did upon its editors, just as the effectiveness of the Socialist party's work depended as much upon unheralded agitators of the rank and file, like the soldiers of the *Appeal* Army, as it did upon the administrators and intellectuals in the national and state headquarters.

NOTES

1. See David A. Shannon, *The Socialist Party of America, A History* (Chicago, 1967) and Daniel Bell, *Marxian Socialism in the United States* (Princeton, N.J. 1967). The interpretations of the class origins of progressivism can be found in Alfred D. Chandler, Jr., "The Origins of Progressive Leadership," in Elting Morison, ed., *The Letters of Theodore Roosevelt,* vol. 8 (Cambridge, 1954) pp. 1462–65, and Robert H. Wiebe, *The Search for Order, 1877–1920* (New York, 1967), pp. 111–95.

2. See Melvyn Dubofsky, *When Workers Organize* (Amherst, 1968); James Weinstein, *The Decline of Socialism in America, 1912–1925* (New York, 1967), chapter 2, pp. 29–52; and John Laslett, *Labor and the Left: A Study of Socialist and Radical Influences in the American Labor Movement, 1881–1924* (New York, 1970).
3. *Who's Who In Socialist America* (Girard Library, Kan., 1914) The copy I found was located in the Yale University Library. There are also copies at Duke University and the Wisconsin State Historical Society.
4. I would like to thank Paul Cullinane for helping with the tabulating and coding of this biographical information and also Cliff Romash for helping with the computer programming.
5. Howard W. Quint, "Julius Wayland, Pioneer Socialist Propagandist," *Mississippi Valley Historical Review* 35 (1949), 585–605, and Shannon, *Socialist Party of America*, pp. 28–34.
6. James R. Green, "Socialism and the Southwestern Class Struggle, 1898–1918: A Study of Radical Movements in Oklahoma, Texas, Louisiana, and Arkansas" Ph.D. dissertation, (Yale University, 1972), chapters 2–4.
7. Ibid., pp. 124–26.
8. See the helpful listing of Socialist periodicals in Weinstein, *Decline of Socialism in America*, Table I, pp. 94–103.
9. Ibid., pp. 53–62.
10. Mari Jo Buhle, "Women and Socialism" (unpublished paper presented at the 87th meeting of the American Historical Association, New Orleans, December 29, 1972).
11. *Who's Who*, p. 44.
12. Mari Jo Buhle, "Women and the Socialist Party, 1901–1914," *Radical America* 4 (1970), pp. 36–57.
13. Kate O'Hare pointed this out to her comrades when Oscar Ameringer and other Southwestern Socialists argued that the SP should recruit small farmers because they did not exploit hired labor. O'Hare argued that they did exploit their wives and children. *Proceedings of the National Congress of the Socialist Party* (Chicago, 1910), p. 233.
14. Quoted in "Economic Needs of Farm Women," U.S. Dept. of Agriculture, Rept. No. 106 (Washington, 1915), p. 49.
15. *Who's Who*, pp. 43, 53, 84, 38, 30.
16. For two first-hand accounts see Kate Richards O'Hare, "How I Became a Socialist Agitator," *Progressive Woman* 2 (October 1908), pp. 4–5, and Dorothy Day, *The Long Loneliness* (New York, 1952), pp. 41–82.
17. See Green, "Socialism and Southwestern Class Struggle," chapter 4.
18. Chandler, "Origins of Progressive Leadership."
19. This fact raises some questions about the alleged continuity some historians have found between populism and socialism in the US; they are explored in Green, "Socialism and Southwestern Class Struggle."
20. See Melvyn Dubofsky, "The Origins of Western Working Class Radicalism, 1890-1905," *Labor History* 7 (1966), 135–37.
21. David A. Shannon, "The Socialist Party Before the First World War: An Analysis," *Mississippi Valley Historical Review* 38 (1951), 281.
22. Green, "Socialism and Southwestern Class Struggle," chapter 1.
23. Ibid., p. 225. For Oklahoma City, see Garin Burbank's essay in this volume.
24. Shannon, "Socialist Party Before First World War," p. 280.
25. Bell, *Marxian Socialism in United States*, pp. 82–84, and Shannon, *Socialist Party of America*, p. 53.
26. Chandler, "Origins of Progressive Leadership," p. 1463.
27. Green, "Socialism and Southwestern Class Struggle," passim.

28. Chandler, "Origins of Progressive Leadership," p. 1463.

29. *Who's Who*, pp. 40—41, 45.

30. "List of Delegates to the Emergency Convention of the Socialist Party, 1917" (Socialist Party Papers, Duke University Library, Durham, N. C.) cited hereafter as SP Papers. I would like to thank Mari Jo and Paul Buhle for obtaining a copy of this document for me.

31. Shannon, *Socialist Party of America*, p. 94.

32. "Minutes of the National Executive Committee Meeting, April 10, 1909," *Socialist Party Official Bulletin*, April, 1909. An even higher percentage of the Socialists elected to public office between 1911 and 1914 were working class, 82 percent of those listed in a 1915 survey. "Elected Officials," ca. 1915, SP Papers. Most of the Socialist officials on this list were elected in various cities and towns. As a result, many farmers elected to county and township office on the SP ticket, (over 100 in Oklahoma alone) are not represented. For a partial list of Oklahoma Socialists elected in 1914 see "Oklahoma Socialist Party State Office Report on Elected Officials," Oklahoma City, 1914, SP Papers.

33. For example, Emanuel Hlavacek, an Austrian motorman, who was "converted to Socialism by experience gained in unions and in strikes," joined the Socialist party in 1906 after several active years "helping to organize the Carmen's Union in Philadelphia," *Who's Who*, p. 46.

34. "Elected Officials," ca. 1915, SP Papers.

35. See Laslett, *Labor and the Left*, chapter 5.

36. For an excellent case study of artisan radicalism among New England shoemakers see Paul G. Faler, "Workingmen, Mechanics, and Social Change in Lynn, Massachusetts, 1800—1860" (Ph.D. thesis, University of Wisconsin, 1971); also see Allen Dawley, "The Artisan Response to the Factory System in Lynn, Massachusetts" (Ph.D. thesis, Harvard University, 1971). Lynn was the leading shoemaking city in the nation during the nineteenth century.

37. As Thomas Wentworth Higginson put it, in Massachusetts during the 1800s "Radicalism went with the smell of leather . . . ." Quoted in David Montgomery, *Beyond Equality: Labor and the Radical Republicans, 1862—1872* (New York, 1967), p. 118.

38. See Laslett, *Labor and the Left*, chapter 3, and Henry F. Bedford, *Socialism and the Workers in Massachusetts, 1886—1912* (Amherst, 1966).

39. *Who's Who*, pp. 72—73.

40. This phenomenon remains to be studied in the United States. For a discussion in the British context see E.P. Thompson, *The Making of the English Working Class* (New York, 1963), pp. 183—85.

41. Robert and Helen Lynd, *Middletown* (New York, 1956) pp. 75—80.

42. *Who's Who*, pp. 13, 20, 31, 83, 8, 42, 39, 35.

43. Ibid., 85—86.

44. David Montgomery has argued that the "control struggles" of skilled workers in the late nineteenth century created a unique syndicalist form of American socialism. The argument is developed in an unpublished paper entitled "Trade Union Practices and Syndicalist Thought" originally presented at the Sorbonne, 1968.

45. Frederick A. Barkey, "The Socialist Party in West Virginia from 1898 to 1920: A Study in Working Class Radicalism" (Ph.D. thesis, University of Pittsburgh, 1971). A significant number of the workers studied were glass makers.

46. *Who's Who*, p. 72.

47. Ibid., p. 76.

48. Laslett, *Labor and the Left*, chapter 6.

49. The influence of Howat and Holt in building a Socialist movement among the coal miners is discussed in James R. Green, "Coal Miners and Southwestern Socialism, 1896—1916: A Study of the Relationship between Industrial Unionism and Agrarian Radicalism" (unpublished paper presented at the 86th meeting of the American Historical Association, New York, December 29, 1971.)

50. *Who's Who*, p. 47.

51. In the Southwestern coal fields most of the Socialist UMW leaders were Anglo-American or Franco-Belgian workers, and the precincts in which these miners predominated gave SP candidates their highest percentages, but by 1912 Italian, Slavic, and Afro-American miners were supporting the Party's candidates, especially in union elections. However, these "new immigrants" had very little representation in the leadership of the SP or the UMW. See Green, "Coal Miners and Southwestern Socialism."

52. Ibid.

53. Green, "Socialism and Southwestern Class Struggle," chapter 1.

54. Howard Quint, *The Forging of American Socialism* (Indianapolis, 1964), p. 199.

55. Faler, "Workingmen, Mechanics and Social Change," pp. 98–105.

56. Paul Buhle, "Debsian Socialism and the 'New Immigrant' Worker," in William L. O'Neill, ed., *Insights and Parallels: Problems and Issues of American Social History* (Minneapolis, 1973), pp. 249–77.

57. Shannon, *Socialist Party of America*, p..30. Also see Ray Ginger, *Eugene V. Debs, A Biography* (New York, 1962), p. 262.

58. *Who's Who*, p..54.

59. Bell, *Marxian Socialism in United States*, pp. 82–83, and Shannon, *Socialist Party of America*, p..53.

60. *Who's Who*, p..56.

61. Herbert G. Gutman, "The Worker's Search for Power," in H.W. Morgan, *The Gilded Age: A Reappraisal* (Syracuse, 1963), pp. 36–69.

62. *Who's Who*, pp. 45–46, 58, 81.

63. For descriptions of the Southwestern Socialist encampments see Oscar Ameringer, *If You Don't Weaken: The Autobiography of Oscar Ameringer* (New York, 1940), pp. 265–67, and Eugene V. Debs, "Revolutionary Encampments," *Southern Worker* (Huntington, Ark.), April–May, 1913.

64. Bell, *Marxian Socialism in United States*, pp. 6–8, 57.

65. *Who's Who*, pp. 17, 104, 106, 114.

66. Ibid., pp. 73, 10.

67. See S.O. Cable's statement in ibid., p. 20.

68. W.J. Ghent, "The 'Appeal' and Its Influence," *The Survey*, 26 (April 1, 1911), 24–28. See also Bell, *Marxian Socialism in United States*, p..58; and Quint, "Julius Wayland, Pioneer Socialist Propagandist," pp. 585–605.

69. Walter Lippmann to Carl Dean Thompson, New York City, Oct. 29, 1913, SP Papers. Lippmann wrote: "The temper of the progressives is to use any political machine that will serve them. In a city like Schenectady, both old parties are utterly hopeless, the Bull Moose is weak, and the Progressives are quite ready to turn temporarily to the Socialists if they feel they can trust them. The path is smoothed for them if the candidate of the Socialists is a man who moved from progressivism to Socialism a year or so before, a popular man whom everybody knows. But note what happens: the reformers are harder to hold on to than the Socialists. The whole campaign turns on keeping them in line. Everything is done to attract them, and the real Socialists stand around like a husband who is married to a flirt." He went on to say: "If Socialists are to make anything of political action, they have to keep themselves clearly distinguished from the progressives." [See Appendix.]

70. "Elected Officials," ca. 1915, SP Papers.

71. Weinstein, *Decline of American Socialism*, chapter 3; and Buhle, "Debsian Socialism, and the 'New Immigrant' Worker," pp. 249–77.

72. Weinstein, *Decline of American Socialism*, pp. 53–73; and R. L. Moore, "Flawed Fraternity—American Socialist Response to the Negro, 1901–1912," *The Historian* 32 (1969), 1-16.

SALLY M. MILLER

2. MILWAUKEE:
Of Ethnicity and Labor

Milwaukee, like other large American cities at the opening of the twentieth century, found itself lacking necessary municipal services, concerned
about a declining urban environment, and victimized by politicians and utility corporations. One result of its struggle to meet these and other problems of modernization was its acceptance of the leadership of Socialist mayors for more than three decades, making its history unique among the largest American metropolises.

Milwaukee emerged as an important center in the 1840s. Its location
on the western shore of Lake Michigan, where the Menomonee and Milwaukee Rivers flow into the lake, insured its commercial growth. Industrialization by the end of the century transformed the city and led to plants
strung out along the various waterways, with industry introduced to the
suburbs and the city simultaneously. A permanent concentration on heavy
industry dominated the local economy.

Milwaukee's expanding population, a basis of her economic growth,
led to preeminence in the state. From a population of 20,061 in 1850, the
first federal census after Wisconsin achieved statehood, Milwaukee's population spiraled to 285,315 in 1900. Civic leadership of this metropolitan complex, however, was absent, as the Democrats and the Republicans vied with
each other to avoid costly improvements and to promise lower taxes. With
the emergence of the Social Democratic party, embodying the idea of extensive municipal services, a multi-party system crystallized.[1]

A unique demographic composition from the start differentiated
Milwaukee among inland American cities. In 1850 two-thirds of her residents were of foreign birth, with German immigrants forming one-third of

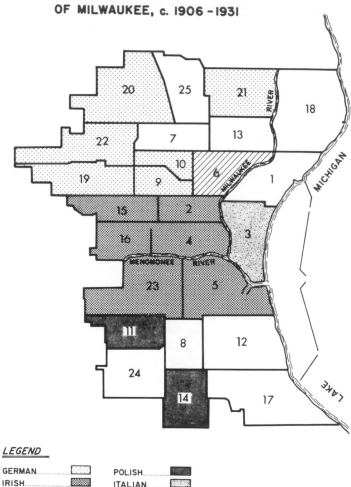

ETHNICALLY IDENTIFIABLE WARDS
OF MILWAUKEE, c. 1906 - 1931

LEGEND

GERMAN
IRISH
JEWISH and
BOHEMIAN

POLISH
ITALIAN
OTHER

the entire population and shaping the city's culture. In the last decade of the century, with 39 percent of her inhabitants born abroad Milwaukee was the most foreign of the twenty-eight largest American cities, with immigrants and their children making up more than half of the population.[2]

Germans found the Milwaukee region attractive as an area strikingly familiar in climate, soil, and crops. In addition, it offered a liberal franchise and lacked the public debts of eastern states with their internal improvements. Germans came in three waves, the first two dominated by farming folk and others whose traditional peasant-handicraft economy was experiencing dislocation due to modernization. The third wave was composed of industrial workers and skilled artisans, departing from a unifying Germany undergoing birth pangs. These workers assimilated into the Milwaukee version of the industrial order they knew and found their community life in the network of German institutions already established.[3]

The heart of German Milwaukee lay in the northwest side of the city where the German immigrants of the forties and fifties had settled just beyond the Irish neighborhoods. That residential pattern remained stable until economic and social mobility at the end of the century created internal class stratification. Thereafter, workers and shopkeepers maintained their ethnic enclave on the northwest side, especially in the ninth, tenth, nineteenth, twentieth, twenty-first, and twenty-second wards, while middle-class and well-to-do Germans dispersed, settling in the upward mobile areas to the east and in the suburbs. The vitality of the nationality was demonstrated in the emergence of a German vote, the existence of the German theater and social groups, and a vigorous German-language press. The cultural life of the Germans peaked at the turn of the century, and thereafter their influence in the city's political, economic, and social life became more diffuse and yet less Old World.[4]

Milwaukee's numerical share of the so-called new immigrants was relatively small. While more than ten different central and eastern European groups settled in Milwaukee prior to World War I, only the Poles were sufficiently numerous to attain any semblance of power. The Polish settled on the south side in the eleventh and fourteenth wards, living near their places of employment in heavy industry. Another enclave of Poles was situated to the north near the Milwaukee River, close to the tanneries and flour mills. In 1910 the Poles made up one-fifth of the foreign-born population of the city and had come to represent the swing vote in municipal elections.

The Poles and the other small nationality groups depended on their own institution building and positioning in the ethnic "pecking order." Residential segregation, occupational limitations, and social prejudice typically marked life's perimeters. All these immigrant groups were overshadowed by the German presence which most specifically affected them through

43

domination of the local labor movement.[5]

Germans played a distinctive role in the American labor movement, bringing to it a sense of class consciousness not characteristic of native Americans. Organized labor in Milwaukee after the Civil War was clearly German. Intermittently drawn to politics, German skilled workers in the strife-torn eighties founded a branch of the American Federation of Labor. The Federated Trades Council, a central labor organization formed in 1887 by the cigar makers, typographers, and molders, became the permanent embodiment of organized labor locally.[6]

Steady growth resulted in a membership of 20,000 in seventy locals by the end of the century. By then, the FTC was strengthened by the new Wisconsin State Federation of Labor. The unionists depended on three weapons in their efforts to improve their conditions: collective bargaining, lobbying, and, most crucial, an alliance with the Socialists of Milwaukee. The partnership of the Milwaukee skilled workers and Social Democrats essentially stemmed from the fact that personnel was drawn from a common pool. German workers formed the backbone of each organization. These workingmen, believing in labor solidarity, political representation, and social legislation, perceived the unions to be their economic arm and the Socialists their political arm. As a result, a kind of "interlocking directorate" came to exist between the two movements.[7]

A number of charter members among the brewers and the cigar makers were Socialists. In 1893 the FTC endorsed the socialist daily, the *Vorwaerts,* the only pro-labor newspaper in the state, and in 1897 it supported the Social Democracy, a new national political party. Two years later the FTC elected an executive committee composed exclusively of Socialists and endorsed the principle of nationalization of major industries. The Socialists, for their part, cautiously approached the unionists, anxious to avoid intimidating them. But by 1900, while each movement maintained its own integrity and identity, they cooperated in municipal politics and were broadly supportive of one another.[8]

The connection was mutually advantageous. The FTC benefited immeasurably from its relationship with the Socialists who played a significant role in labor's winning public acceptance in Wisconsin earlier than it did elsewhere. Through the Socialists, labor eventually gained access to public officials and to public office. Patronage and favorable administrative measures helped stabilize labor's local position. Within the labor movement itself, Socialist opposition to dual unionism was valuable, as was the party's encouragement of union membership among its own rank and file, its nomination of party unionists for public office, and its endorsement of union objectives. In return, FTC endorsement of and funding of various Socialist newspapers, its acceptance of collective ownership, and its general orientation enabled the Milwaukee Social Democrats to come to power in 1910.[9]

The history of socialist activity in Milwaukee formally began with the organization of a branch of the Marxist International Workingmen's Association in the mid-seventies, but it was not until the 1890s that party organization, media, and leadership began to assume permanence. From their labor base Milwaukee Marxists first moved toward the local Populist party but this thin coalition rapidly dissipated, and in 1897 Milwaukeeans played a prominent role in the founding of the Social Democracy of America and were chartered as branch number one.[10]

At that time, American Socialists were completing a series of organizational moves leading to a permanent party of national scope. The Social Democracy, founded by Eugene V. Debs of the American Railway Union and Victor Berger of Milwaukee, lasted only one year and was scuttled in favor of the Social Democratic Party. The new party was joined in 1900 by dissidents from Daniel De Leon's Socialist Labor Party, and together the various factions agreed upon political action, cooperation with organized labor, and an evolutionary route to socialist goals. In 1901 they founded the Socialist Party of America.[11]

In ideology, the Milwaukee Social Democratic Party agreed with the revisionist leadership of the national party. Socialism would triumph inevitably over capitalism without bloodshed as monopolies and trusts transformed industrial society. Propaganda and political action served to prepare the public and to introduce needed reforms. While socialism could not come on only a local level, such victories were important in building a foundation. In its Milwaukee application, revisionism was known as "the Wisconsin idea," which stressed local party autonomy and a partnership with organized labor. Milwaukee managed to incorporate the principle of local autonomy into the by-laws of the national party, maintaining its importance in enabling the party to build upon regional variables. Milwaukeeans acknowledged the right of the national organization to point direction, but little else. In regard to labor, Milwaukee Socialists assigned the trade unions a significant role in the advancement of society toward socialism. The unions served to organize workers in their occupational sphere, teach them solidarity, and thus educate them to their own interests. While theoretically it was deplorable that organized labor was restricted to the skilled, in practice the Milwaukee Socialists were comfortable with skilled German union men and scornful of unskilled new immigrants. The partnership they envisioned with labor was one of Germans and natives almost exclusively.[12]

Political action, important to the Milwaukee party initially, was emphasized increasingly. The original idea of the propaganda value of campaigns for public office became undermined as the possibility of victory loomed. And although national party policy prohibited campaign cooperation with bourgeois parties, the Milwaukee Socialists were accused of ignoring that principle in their zeal for ballot box progress. Charges of political opportunism were levelled at them continuously by party members to their left.[13]

Four leaders of the Milwaukee party not only dominated the local scene but also became figures of some importance in the national party. Victor Berger (1860–1929) epitomized the Milwaukee movement. Berger was an Austrian immigrant whose American career as a newspaper editor and publisher was in fact an appendage to his party activities. As one of the major leaders of the right wing of the national party, he carefully husbanded his control of the local movement. He served six terms in the House of Representatives, the first Socialist to enter the Congress, and came to glory in his public role while mildly denying his reputation of local party boss.[14]

Frederic F. Heath (1864–1954) was one of the few Yankees in the Milwaukee party and his role was instrumental in attracting the English-speaking. A founder of the national party, Heath campaigned on the local ticket several times and served as an alderman, a member of the Milwaukee school board, and as a county supervisor for a generation.[15]

Emil Seidel (1864–1947) and Daniel W. Hoan (1881–1961) served as Socialist mayors of Milwaukee. Neither shared Berger's flamboyance or aggressiveness and did not challenge his leadership. Seidel was a second-generation American woodcarver and patternmaker. He ran for several local and state offices, serving as alderman as well as mayor, and campaigned as Debs's running-mate on the national ticket in 1912. Hoan was also a second-generation German-American. He worked his way through law school and, already a convinced Socialist, was elected city attorney on that ticket in his first race for office in 1910. For the next generation, he was never out of office.[16]

The party over which these four men presided grew rapidly. Its membership rolls, activities, and spinoff organizations all expanded steadily, with Milwaukee County locals numbering more than sixty branches within a dozen years. Membership figures, which can only be conjectured, evidently reached toward 5,000 in the state as a whole with perhaps two-thirds of that total representative of Milwaukee County. The party's most important asset was the mini-publishing empire which Berger headed. It eventually included an English-language daily and German and Polish weeklies, as well as various broadsides printed at election times in the different local languages. The party sponsored various social activities such as carnivals, bazaars, card parties, and Sunday schools, which enabled it to shape the lifestyles of members' families in a manner unique among American political parties. In its community involvement, in fact, the Milwaukee organization operated in the image of the German Social Democrats, considered the most successful Socialist party in the world.[17]

In internal structure the Social Democrats also reflected the party in the Old Country. The bureaucracy and the discipline of the Milwaukee organization bore no comparison with American political parties. The control imposed on the membership enhanced its potential impact beyond its actual numbers, while the structured hierarchy of professional functionaries encouraged vested interests, conservative decision making, and the minimizing of direct democracy. Despite the thrust of party ideology toward opening social institutions to mass control, the party's own hierarchical structure bred oligarchic tendencies.[18]

The Milwaukee County Central Committee was the decision-making body and in this apparatus was located the power of the Social Democrats. The CCC controlled the budget, screened candidates for public office, and supervised those elected through systematized caucuses and undated resignations. Within that setting, organizational and propagandistic activity flourished. Party growth was based on its hold on the northwest side of the city, especially the residential areas of the German workers and shopkeepers whose votes gave the Socialists twenty-six of their first thirty aldermanic victories. In the party's maiden run for office in 1898, the Social Democrats won only 5 percent of the votes cast, but they began to gain confidence, and in 1904, the breakthrough occurred. With graft tainting the older parties, with Socialist campaign literature published in seven languages and distributed by the "bundle brigade" to each house in the city, the Socialists elected nine aldermen and several county officials. Berger's race for mayor had netted the party 25 percent of the total.[19]

TABLE 3-1
Socialist Mayoralty Election Returns[20]

1898	2,430	5.2%
1900	2,584	5.0
1902	8,457	14.4
1904	15,056	25.3
1906	16,784	27.5
1908	20,887	33.1
1910	27,608	46.4

The evolution of the platform serves as an index to the changing focus of the party and its gradual effort to appeal to a wider audience. In its first platform in 1898, the Social Democratic Party presented labor-oriented specific and immediate demands, such as municipal ownership of utilities, an equitable tax burden, public works, free legal and medical services, free school books, urban renewal, and social and cultural measures.[21]

This relatively modest list of reformist demands, preceded by a preamble stressing the class struggle and the ultimate goal of collectivism, remained the basic offering of the party. The specific and immediate demands provided ammunition to hostile Socialists anxious to prove that the Milwaukee comrades were opportunistic self-seekers. Even so, the Milwaukeeans were en route to a number of platform modifications which allowed greater leftist condemnation. The party had become aware that it must make inroads into the middle class and the professional class and, on the state level, reach the farmers if its appeal were to grow. Accordingly, the party minimized its hostility to the Catholic Church as its opening wedge to non-hardcore supporters. It was assumed that accommodating the less militant through moderating the party stance could win over untapped resources without disturbing the basic commitment to social transformation. It was precisely this crucial decision which made possible the desired party growth while diluting the thrust of its meaning. To be sure, party leaders reiterated their interest in the support of only true believers, but policies and platforms belied that rhetoric.

The party's major concession to potential middle-class support was the deletion of the platform plank prohibiting the granting of franchises to private utility corporations. The substitute measure granted such franchises under carefully delineated conditions. By this stroke, the Social Democrats moved dramatically away from basic socialist tenets. While two-thirds of a century of hindsight demonstrates that nationalized giant enterprises within a capitalist framework may not be of clear benefit to the public nor the nationalization of one or two industries alone, nonetheless, without encouraging key elements of the economy toward the state sector, a precondition of a socialist society is avoided.

Party leader Berger now maintained that major priorities were the attainment of home rule, government honesty, and modernization. The timing of the party's directional shift was acute for Milwaukee experienced then a crisis of confidence, and new sources of leadership were in fact sought. The fortuitous coincidence of old party atrophy and Socialist readiness during a national period of reform gave the Social Democrats their opportunity. Municipal corruption drove reforming activists and honest citizens into the arms of the graft-free Socialists.[22]

Between 1904 and 1906, a flurry of indictments were handed down against both Democratic and Republican local officials who had buckled before corporation pressure and bribes and were entangled in a web of graft. City newspapers headlined the various sensational charges, and irate citizens, led by the Milwaukee Municipal League, held mass meetings and spearheaded a reform-minded coalition. The Socialists issued propaganda and became the main beneficiaries of the upheaval. By 1906 the Municipal

League and the newly formed Voters League, and even the antagonistic Milwaukee *Journal,* proclaimed the need to elect honest officials without reference to political party. The Social Democrats had shed some of the alien taint they had worn, and Socialists found themselves winning endorsements from groups seemingly beyond their frame of reference. As distinctly graft-free, the Social Democrats were able to run on a platform promising a municipal housecleaning, the policing of private utility corporations, and the confronting of mushrooming urban problems.[23]

At the same time that the Social Democrats were approaching citywide success, they were creating a positive impression in the State Legislature. In the November general election of 1904, five party members were elected to the State Assembly and one member to the State Senate. For thirty years Socialists representing the Milwaukee area held seats in every session of the Wisconsin legislature, speaking on behalf of socialist principles and standing for various measures of social legislation. They often joined in legislative maneuvering with progressive Republicans and thereby had a chance to enact legislation. Some of their early measures enacted into law, all weighted toward labor, included the erection of safety devices at dangerous factory machinery, a Full Crew Bill to insure sufficient workmen on trains, an eight-hour shift for telegraphers, and a bill to investigate state unemployment. The peak of legislative achievement occurred in the 1911 session, the legislature in which the Social Democrats reached a high of fourteen representatives. The coalition of Socialists and Progressives enacted a comprehensive Workmen's Compensation act, safety legislation, regulation of women's hours, and child labor legislation.[24]

The coalition of the Socialists and Progressives was unlikely and yet logical. The Socialists believed that the centralization of modern industry led to the need to strengthen government through which the people collectively could regulate their own political and economic lives. Conversely, the Progressives, at least the rural-based supporters of Robert M. La Follette, saw such tendencies toward centralization as reprehensible and they hoped to utilize regulation as a means to eventual decentralization and limited government to insure the revival of individual opportunity within the capitalist system. Each used the other to secure specific reforms of the system at Madison. Otherwise, because of the geographic nature of their support, the Progressives dominated the state of Wisconsin until the eve of World War I and the Socialists were a force at that time in the city and county of Milwaukee. Neither achieved meaningful victories in the other's territory.[25]

In 1906 and 1908 the upward trend at the polls continued for the Milwaukee Socialists, even though they ran from a weakened position due to a new state law. Promoted by a coalition of Republicans and Democrats, the new law undercut Socialist voting strength by providing that the Common Council include twelve aldermen-at-large and one instead of two aldermen from each ward. Such legislation clearly handicapped a party with localized pockets of support. To offset that weakness, the Socialist municipal platform in 1908 carried a direct appeal to the middle-class voter who was advised that he would directly profit from the end of capitalist exploitation. In the election the Socialists won nine seats on the Common Council in place of the twelve they had held, but the mayoralty vote climbed again, Emil Seidel losing by only 2,000 votes to former Democratic mayor David S. Rose.[26]

The national media began to notice the Milwaukee movement.[27] In the April 1910 municipal elections Milwaukee Socialists won the largest victory Socialists ever registered in a major American city. Emil Seidel was elected mayor by a plurality, winning 27,608 votes to the Democrats' 20,530 and the Republicans' 11,346. The Socialists carried not only the German wards but also for the first time won votes in the Polish fourteenth ward on the strength of Polish-language propaganda and the muting of their anti-Catholic sentiments. To facilitate Seidel's work, the voters gave him a Socialist-dominated administration. The city attorney, city treasurer, and comptroller, twenty-one of thirty-five aldermen, and one-fourth of the school board were Socialists. In addition, the Social Democrats obtained a majority on the board of supervisors and, later that year, they elected two-thirds of the County's delegation to the State Legislature and sent Berger to Congress from the Fifth Congressional District, comprising the northern half of the city and suburban and rural areas. Exulting over their triumph, the Socialists yet assured themselves that theirs was essentially a working-class victory.[28]

The national press as well as friendly Socialist commentators covered the Seidel inaugural and watched the workings of the administration attentively. They heard Seidel promise in his address before the Common Council to fight doggedly to achieve humane ideals. He reminded the elected party officials of their principles and commitments:

In your policy, the promises contained in our platform should have a prominent part. Such measures as can be carried out under the provisions of our present charter should be taken up at once. Where the charter interferes, proper bills should at once be drafted to be presented to the next legislature.[29]

Formidable barriers lay in the Socialists' path. While the lack of home rule handicapped any municipal administration, one with an ambitious program was decidedly on the defensive. As recently as 1909, the

State Assembly had defeated a home rule measure, which had been framed by a charter convention and passed by the State Senate. Thus, despite the recent efforts of reformers, Milwaukee did not control its own destiny, especially in financial matters. Accordingly, many Seidel measures required unobtainable legislative approval. Statutory and debt limitations further handicapped the administration. At the same time, the Socialist majority on the Common Council fell short of the three-fourths necessary to sustain basic procedural changes. And as has been pointed out by historian Frederick I. Olson, the non-Socialist council minority was more powerful than its numbers due to its experience and political influence. Moreover, the Socialists were cautious about some of their proposed programs which would raise the tax rate and alienate the public.[30]

The most explicit changes were seen in the openness and efficiency with which municipal government functioned during this two year period. The Socialists streamlined city government and, in order to inform the public, sponsored free lectures and published a weekly, *Political Action*. The most far-reaching innovation was the establishment of the Bureau of Economy and Efficiency to survey and overhaul administrative procedures. Conceived by Councilman Victor Berger, who chaired the Committee on Legislation prior to assumption of his congressional seat, this reliance on government by experts was remarkably similar to the systematic and businesslike approach to municipal government of middle and upper-class reformers across the country. The noted economist, John R. Commons of the University of Wisconsin, who had served Governor Robert M. La Follette in such a capacity, headed the eighteen-month project. He inventoried the city's conditions, assets, and needs and introduced cost accounting, centralized purchasing, and uniform methods of disbursing funds and maintaining departmental records.

The fifty Socialist city and county public officials caucused weekly. Each Saturday they reviewed the proposals of Commons and his staff, and planned strategy and policy for the coming week. Commons, no friend to socialism, praised the dedication and discipline of simple "mechanics and trade unionists" whose goals, he wrote, were "Efficiency coupled with Service [sic] to the poor and the working classes of the city."[31]

In the two years of the Seidel administration, the Socialists clearly impressed the public with their honesty, independence from the "interests," fresh approach, and energetic record. They regulated industry and curtailed privilege, while catering to the cultural and social needs of the city as no earlier administration had done. The city credit rating improved, deficit financing ended. The administration pushed factory and building inspection, the implementation of anti-vice ordinances, and fire and crime prevention policies. For labor, this first pro-worker administration instituted

51

union wages and an eight-hour day for city employees, provided a free unemployment office, offered arbitration in major strikes, encouraged private companies to unionize, and forced the police to respect strikers' rights. On the other hand, the corporations were forced to comply with existing ordinances, and those with long-term utility franchises found themselves supervised and threatened by resolutions of expropriation. As its most applauded achievement, the city won a rate reduction from the notorious conglomerate, the Milwaukee Electric Railway and Light Company.

A housing commission and a harbor commission were appointed. Health measures, such as the establishment of a Tuberculosis Commission and a hospital for contagious diseases, were promoted. City beautification was encouraged and open space preserved as the Council and Seidel set up a land commission to plan parks and parkways, plant trees, and develop and enforce land use regulation of private property. In its cultural endeavors, the city offered recreational programs, free concerts, and a reorganized Milwaukee Public Library.

Beyond regulation and reform, the activist administration was perhaps more restricted than it had anticipated. State and charter regulations which precluded its ability to end the contract system, to institute direct purchasing or certain public works projects, and other measures which needed a large Council vote or state permission, all narrowed its scope. Rebuffed in appeals to the state to establish a municipal ice house, slaughterhouse, lodging houses, and markets, stripped of the mayor's position as official head of departments, the administration's goals became those of introducing reforms and maximizing service within the existing framework.[32]

The Socialists' program, both proposals and enactments, demonstrated a concern for the masses of the people. However, much of it, even ignoring external limitations, reveals an undue confidence. Their offerings did no more than touch upon the surface of life's realities, and the issue of the quality of life and the very fundamental dangers of the new, centralized urban-industrial order escaped them. The Social Democrats, blinded by their doctrine, harbored no doubts about the power of the state to serve the needs of the people and to be responsive to their wishes. Active government did not imply to them threats of coercion and regimentation of the masses or of possible loss of individual rights. Rather, greater power and efficiency in the hands of responsible government would end inequities and alleviate injustice. Nor did they question industrial and technical progress. To be sure, they wished to add amenities to the lives of working people, but the potential psychological dehumanization of fragmented lives in an increasingly industrialized order seemed not even to occur to them. They appeared content with material progress and merely wanted to assure, as far as they could, that the wealth accrued to those they considered its producers.

Left-wing Socialists attacked the Milwaukee administration for its general failure to differentiate itself from non-Socialist municipal reformers, such as Tom Johnson of Cleveland and Samuel Jones of Toledo. The Milwaukee Socialist administration and others too were castigated for misguided attempts to conciliate the middle class through moderate policies, such as, for example, minimizing labor's strike activities. William English Walling, one of the most influential of the party's intellectuals, supported some progressive reforms, but argued that it was nevertheless a contradiction in terms for Socialists to hold office without the power to apply Socialist principles. The Milwaukeeans were dismissed as opportunistically pursuing a meaningless form of state socialism. In fact, government ownership under a capitalist system would be state capitalism rather than socialism.[33]

Such harsh criticism was often ambivalent, for many of the critics actually supported municipal reform as the starting point of political action. Moreover, they could draw no clear line between political action for propaganda purposes and that for actual reform. The distinguishing mark between Socialists and reformers in public office was that the Socialists always had a further demand. Unlike middle class reformers whose platform was circumscribed, Socialists sought further changes leading to an alteration of the system, and this goal was shared by Socialists both in and out of office. Those outside office, of course, enjoyed the luxury of criticism.[34]

A most significant difference between Socialists and reformers in public office lay in Socialist opposition to the commission and manager forms of municipal government. Although a party survey of Socialists living under the commissioner system revealed some disagreement, party policy vigorously condemned these institutional reforms. The national party blasted the concentration of power and the at-large elections particularly. Also opposed was the short ballot, centralization of power in the mayor's office, and other reforms celebrated for their purported democratization of municipal government. Congressman Berger, stating the Socialist position, advised a constituent that such so-called popular reforms limited the power of the people and encouraged oligarchy.[35]

Neither of the major structural changes in city government came to Milwaukee. In May 1912, however, in the pattern of the legislation of 1907 which introduced the partial shift from ward to city-wide aldermanic elections, old party progressives and conservatives in the State Legislature, supported by the metropolitan dailies, especially the Milwaukee *Journal,* the prestigious City Club and other influential well-to-do Milwaukeeans from the upper-income northeast wards of the city, coalesced to introduce nonpartisan city elections. In the State Assembly every representative of the east side districts hugging the shoreline voted for the measure while not one Socialist Assemblyman supported it. Once more socialist strength was minimized.

As in other areas of the country, as demonstrated by historian Samuel P. Hays, professional and business groups in their pursuit of rationalized and systematized city government, sought to minimize the decision-making power of the lower-income segments of the population. The trend toward decreasing local and particularist roles in government, exemplified in the undermining of the ward system, was spearheaded by those groups anxious to dominate political power. In Milwaukee, they had no viable progressive power bloc to utilize. Hence, the Milwaukee version of the centralization movement to halt grass-roots influence relied primarily on the State Legislature's control over the city.[36]

The unlabeling of the Socialists came after the fact. In April 1912, an old party fusion ticket defeated the socialist administration. The Socialists had satisfied the public appetite for reform: graft had disappeared and there seemed no need to retain an administration that rumor held was costly, boss-ridden, and perhaps patronage prone. The Socialists won only 40.6 percent of the votes cast in 1912 as opposed to 47 percent in 1910. They retained their support in the northwest side wards and even prevented the fusionist candidate, former Health Commissioner Gerhard Bading, from winning the Polish fourteenth ward. Moreover, Seidel won almost 3,000 votes beyond his 1910 total, which the Milwaukee *Leader* celebrated as, in fact, a victory. Seidel claimed major achievements which, he said, at least left the city stronger than he found it, and the party emphasized having forced the old parties to admit their similarity: now the issue of capitalism versus socialism would be clearer to the public.[37]

That fall, all seven Socialist county administrators were defeated, the number of party members in the State Legislature halved, and Berger was defeated for reelection to Congress. Berger's two-year term of office had not meant any measurable strengthening of the local Socialist movement, beyond the propaganda level. His speeches and resolutions focused on national issues and, by his own count, only three percent of his voluminous correspondence came from local constituents. Thus, his congressional service was directed away from Milwaukee, and indeed his neglect of the local situation was believed to be a factor in his defeat.[38]

The reversal did not signify the decline of the Social Democrats, for despite the varied tactics utilized against them, their vote grew and their recapture of the mayor's office lay not too far in the distance. Yet, on the other hand, in a basic way, Seidel's brief two-year administration was the golden age of the Milwaukee Socialists. It marked the only period in which the Socialists controlled both the executive and the legislative branches of

54

local government. Moreover, they would never again have the same sense of momentum and confidence in the inevitable progress of the movement As in the national party, the period from 1910 to 1912 marked the peak of socialism's steady upward growth. While there was no precipitate decline at that point but rather what has been characterized by James Weinstein as a "patchwork pattern," Socialists in Milwaukee and elsewhere never regained that early buoyancy and enthusiasm.[39]

The Socialists marked time from 1912 to 1916. Their major asset in these years was their attractive young city attorney, Daniel Webster Hoan. Unlike their other city-wide winners of 1910, Hoan had been elected to a four-year term, and thus remained in office after the 1912 debacle. Reelected in 1914 on the strength of his policing of the privately owned utilities, Hoan came to epitomize struggle in the public interest against the local corporations. As city attorney, Hoan advised the Common Council and drafted legislation to win more autonomy from Madison, intervened with the Assessor's office to insure a more equitable assessment of the wealthier wards and, in the main, devoted his time to suits against corporations, especially the powerful railway and light company. He successfully pressed fare reduction and forced the company to sprinkle between the tracks and implement safety ordinances. Moreover, he saved the city money by forcing the company to pave along its tracks and to return city paving funds already expended. These and other popular measures won for Hoan the image of a dedicated public servant, a reputation which he rode into the mayor's office. His achievements weighed more heavily with the voters than did the red bogey that Mayor Bading raised.[40]

In this period the Socialists attempted to streamline their organization while retaining their membership and platform. In order to obtain the necessary 50 percent at the polls since a plurality would no longer suffice, the party resurrected the bundle brigade to insure widespread distribution of propaganda. The winning ticket of 1910 lost in 1914, except for Hoan and those aldermen running in the safest wards. Seidel won 44 percent of the vote compared with his 40.6 percent of 1912, and the *Leader* expressed confidence that 50 percent of Milwaukee would soon be committed to socialism. It chortled that the Nonpartisans had won the election but lost another battle. Two years later, Dan Hoan ran for mayor, campaigning more against the streetcar company than for socialism, and he won with 51 percent of the vote. He stood alone, however, for less than one-third of the Common Council were Social Democrats and all other city-wide offices were held by party opponents.[41]

At Hoan's assumption of office, old issues of graft and public need were obscured by the world war. The heavily foreign Wisconsin municipality, with its large German population and various Slavic ethnic groups, was

55

caught up in the war upon its outbreak, and by 1916 tensions and hostilities had developed. The world war was ingrained into the Milwaukee fabric years before American intervention.

Public opinion followed nationality lines. Bazaars and other fundraisers for the Central Powers were patronized by the German community, and even some English-language newspapers, such as the *Free Press,* were blatantly pro-German while others, such as the *Journal,* opposed ethnic political pressure groups. The Poles and others whose homelands were within the Austrian Empire played a muted role until the enunciation of Wilson's territorial settlement in the Fourteen Points. On the eve of American intervention, informal polls showed the Milwaukee area opposed to involvement, and the German community on the defensive. While hitherto German cultural life had been expansive, the German profile was to become diluted and the Americanization movement energized locally.[42]

The professed internationalism of the Milwaukee Socialists in a time of heated nationalism proved disruptive for them. The local party had always taken the Social Democrats of the Old Country as its example, and yet it had derided patriotism in favor of international brotherhood. The party condemned the war as capitalist-inspired and bemoaned the fact that most of their European comrades supported their nations' policies. Some of the Milwaukee party's German support was alienated by the Socialists' announced neutrality, and political rivals exploited that situation in the bitter November 1914 election campaign. Succeeding elections were all fought on the question of loyalties. To minimize its problems, the party quietly altered its name from the Social Democrats to the Socialist party. Its German image, however, persisted, complicating its wartime dilemma.[43]

The path of the national party set the parameters of the Milwaukeeans' difficulties. Initially the Socialist party condemned the war in Europe and, stressing American disinterest, adopted the slogan created by Berger's Milwaukee *Leader,* "Starve the war and feed America" and opposed the preparedness campaign. The party petitioned the Congress and supported Socialist Congressman Meyer London and those others in the House and Senate opposed to intervention. In April 1917, as the United States declared war, the Socialists met in emergency convention. A now militant party, dominated for the first time by its left wing, it condemned American intervention as unjustified and in its St. Louis Proclamation, promised vigorous opposition to the war effort, antimilitarist propaganda, resistance to possible curtailment of civil liberties, and continued pursuit of the class struggle.[44]

The Milwaukee Socialists were clearly unhappy with a party position which only intensified their discomfort. The Milwaukee organization, like the national party, was already weakened by personnel shifts and defections

Algie M. Simons, a longtime leader and fixture on the National Executive Committee, abandoned the party and his position on the *Leader*, and organized the still-born Social Democratic League. Winfield R. Gaylord, extremely popular in the Milwaukee area, also left the party. The two men played major roles in the Wisconsin Loyalty League and sought to convince local public opinion of Socialist disloyalty.[45]

Mayor Hoan trod a difficult path during the war. He avoided the party's convention and did not issue a personal war statement. When, in December 1917, he indicated reservations concerning the St. Louis Proclamation, party turmoil erupted, and only his participation in the writing of the local platform reaffirming the Socialist war position healed the wounds. But Hoan's official civil defense duties could not be ignored, and the County Central Committee agreed to his handling of war programs which fell to his office. Often his execution of these responsibilities succeeded in muting war emotions. For example, in July 1916, Hoan transformed demands for a preparedness parade into "A National Civil Demonstration." Later he chaired the local Bureau of Food Control, where the prevention of war profiteering became his special interest until his ouster from the supervisory body. At the same time, he used his office to assist the party in its campaigns for peace and civil liberties. He invited the convention of the People's Council for Democracy and Peace to Milwaukee but was rebuffed by Governor Emanuel L. Philipp, as earlier the Socialist mayor of Minneapolis had been blocked from hosting the convention by that State's governor. Hoan protested the jailing of dissenters and assisted Berger's *Leader* in its fight to prevent government curtailment of its operations. But nevertheless his ambivalent stand prevailed: in his reelection campaign of April 1918, Hoan condemned the war but assumed credit for Milwaukee's shouldering of its share of war work.[46]

The two main components of the party's support held during the war years, although each modified its position and underwent change. The German-dominated Federated Trades Council condemned the European war and rejected invitations from the Wisconsin branch of the National Security League to participate in the preparedness movement. After the declaration of war the FTC's path was a pale shadow of the Socialists'. While not officially opposing the war effort, it affiliated with the Socialistic People's Council rather than the AFL's rival organization, the American Alliance for Labor and Democracy. However, growing policy discontent within the FTC led it to cooperate with the County Council of Defense, spearhead patriotic mass meetings, and urge its membership to purchase war bonds.[47]

The other foundation upon which the Milwaukee movement had been built, the German community, rallied around the party at the ballot box in the elections of 1918. While some local Germans had criticized the

57

Socialists for a lack of German patriotism, once the United States entered the war, support for Socialist wartime dissenters became one way to protest against American policy. In the special election of March 1918 to fill an unexpired Senate seat Berger, on an antiwar platform, won 110,487 of the 423,343 ballots, the largest number of votes yet registered for a Socialist in Wisconsin. In April, in one of the stronger Socialist municipal victories, Hoan bettered his previous total and the Common Council became more than one-third Socialist. Finally, that November, Berger was returned to Congress after three successive losing races. The Socialist gains at the polls were complicated and yet aided by a number of actions by the federal government. Conspiracy indictments against the party's major candidates for state offices and denial of second-class mailing privileges to the *Leader* for its editorial position served to swell election totals as civil libertarians and war protestors joined the nucleus of German and Socialist voters.[48]

In these years the party on the national level experienced upheaval and schism. While old line leaders, including Milwaukeeans Berger, Hoan, and John M. Work, formerly executive secretary of the national party and currently editor of the *Leader*, sought to deflect the party from its antiwar position, the left became more militant. A few months after the Armistice, a left-wing faction organized within the party, which led to a schismatic convention at the end of August 1919. The left established the Communist party and the Communist Labor party, and the right retained control of remnants of the Socialist party. The Wisconsin State Executive Committee, originally fearful of a public confrontation, had advised against holding a convention but came to welcome fragmentation. Both Hoan and Berger had warned of a possible bolt by Wisconsin if the left captured the party. Eventually they looked forward to the chance, Hoan wrote, "to clear the deck for clean-cut political action." And, instead of avoiding the issue, Hoan even helped chair the rump convention. Wisconsin leaders blamed the birth of the Communist party on government persecution but, unthreatened by Bolsheviks in their tightly controlled Milwaukee organization, they came to rationalize the events as offering new opportunities for a radical democratic party.[49]

The war years had been an unwanted intrusion. When Hoan was first elected in April 1916, he spelled out a program for the city, including municipal planning, a city-owned lighting plant, harbor improvements, better sewage disposal facilities, reinstitution of centralized purchasing, and renewed pursuit of home rule. But such policies lost their inherent interest, and Hoan simply tried to take a liberal line on issues. Party platforms in this period, while referring to traditional concerns, underlined the need for freedom at home. Socialism was termed "the only genuine patriotism of

58

today." Although no headway toward either collectivism or even reform occurred, ballot box progress was made in each election during the war and in the first city elections thereafter. In 1920 the party gained an additional alderman, reducing the Nonpartisan majority to only three, and Hoan raised his percentage of the vote from 51 percent to 52 percent. He reversed his only clear wartime loss by winning the Polish fourteenth ward where his vote had fallen by half in 1918. But the Socialist party was on the defensive, unlike its first two decades.[50]

TABLE 3-2
Population: City of Milwaukee[51]

Date	Population	Percentage Foreign-born	Percentage German-born
1880	115,587	40	27
1890	204,468	39	27
1900	285,315	31	19
1910	373,857	30	17
1920	457,147	24	8
1930	578,249	19	7

The Milwaukee of 1920 offered a vastly different picture from 1900 in terms of demographic figures and public attitudes. Those of foreign birth residing in the city in 1920 made up 24 percent of its population as opposed to the 31 percent of 1900. That figure would drop further in the 1930 census to 19 percent. Within the overall figures, the percentage of the German-born slipped as well. While in 1900, 19 percent of Milwaukee residents born abroad were German, in 1920 the figure fell dramatically to 8.7 percent, and in 1930 the percentage was 7.2. The German cultural dominance of the city peaked in the 1890s, as has been indicated above, but the sharp decrease in new immigrants from the Fatherland hurried that decline beyond what might have been predicted.[52]

Only one facet of the changing scene was the diminished German immigration. Perhaps more important than reduced numbers was the effort to force assimilation. In cosmopolitan Milwaukee, the major foreign groups had successfully maintained the right of self-determination; Germans, Poles, and to some extent other groups had struggled with the public schools and the local churches for cultural autonomy. In the crucible of war, however, the dimensions of the battle altered. The local media, various patriotic organizations, and even the Catholic church encouraged the so-called Americanization movement. The campaign was directed at first by the Americanization Committee of the County Council of Defense under May Wood Simons, a former Socialist leader and the wife of A.M. Simons of the Wisconsin Loyalty League. The promotion of militant nationalism and a common

59

language was pursued through the public schools and through factory-based programs. The Milwaukee community offered a greater challenge than other cities, having resisted almost all prewar Americanization efforts, and local factories were less than cooperative about grafting assimilation campaigns onto their industrial welfare programs. Nevertheless, local Americanizers succeeded in undercutting and diluting Milwaukee's Old World atmosphere. Not only was the public school curriculum altered, but even private organizations, clubs, and theaters Americanized their names and their offerings. As a slight indication of the new ethos, especially the fear of forced assimilation, postwar platforms of the Socialist party insisted upon ". . . the unrestricted right to use any language in church services and also for the right to teach . . . any . . . language, in public or parochial schools, that the patrons may desire."[53]

In the local labor movement, too, gradual acculturation and artificial pressures brought modifications which served to loosen the ties between the FTC and the Socialist party. The German membership of the FTC found itself drawn into the American orbit as did other Milwaukee Germans, while simultaneously the FTC came to respond to the conservative influence of the AFL. In a concrete way, the FTC needed the Socialists less than it once had. While labor always appreciated a Socialist mayor as an asset, nevertheless it began to reward its political friends and punish its enemies rather than to depend upon one party only. The State Federation of Labor posted its own lobbyists in Madison in order to pressure and work with progressive Republicans and others. Clearly by the end of the twenties, despite a lingering relationship, the FTC and the Socialists were moving away from one another. As historian John Laslett argues, assimilation and other American political and economic factors meant a diminishing base of radical commitment within the German unions.[54]

The twenties were years of decline for the Socialist party nationally. Struggling merely to survive, the party shrank from the 104,822 dues-paying members of 1919 to 11,277 three years later and experienced a leadership vacuum as Debs, Berger, and other well-known figures died. A reversal of traditional policy was effected in 1922 in order to revive the party. With labor, the Non-Partisan League, Farm-Labor representatives, progressive Republicans and others, the Socialists supported Senator La Follette's presidential candidacy in 1924 on a reformist, non-Socialist platform. But the effort did not lead to the hoped for formation of a widely based third party with an autonomous Socialist faction.[55]

The Socialist party in Milwaukee, with all its weaknesses, seemed a center of vitality compared with the party nationally. While the Wisconsin movement was certainly not on the upswing, the Milwaukeeans were far better off than many of their comrades. Northwest side wards still provided

60

the strongest support for the party, while supplementary support sometimes came from the Polish wards to the south and increasingly from the
middle-income wards to the east, primarily in mayoralty elections. Labor,
despite its growing aloofness, offered the party votes and underwrote the
Leader.

These pockets of strength, however, were insufficient for Socialist
domination of city government. In order to govern effectively, party members found it necessary to coalesce informally with Nonpartisans on the
Common Council and to seek mutually advantageous arrangements with
Polish politicians. For example, Polish Nonpartisan aldermen cooperated
with the party in exchange for Polish appointees to office, such as the building commissioner and the chief of police. Not until such deals, fully six
years after Hoan took office, could he win Council acceptance of even one
of his appointments of a department head.[56]

TABLE 3-3
Socialist Percentages of Total Votes Cast in
Mayoralty Elections in Selected Wards[57]

	Ward	1912	1914	1916	1918	1920	1924	1928
Wards at least	9	46%	49%	56%	64%	64%	67%	67%
50% German stock	10	52	51	60	69	71	74	72
	19	38	41	49	56	51	58	62
	20	71	61	64	69	69	73	70
	21	51	53	61	68	65	67	57
	22	41	42	48	57	53	62	62
Wards at least	11	58	65	71	67	67	66	65
50% Polish stock	14	52	59	68	28	51	41	45
City totals		41	44	51	51	52	56	58

Hoan retained his mayoralty position by increasing percentages with
victories in as many as three-quarters of the wards; Berger spent three terms
in Congress, and Socialists, though in decreasing numbers, remained on the
Board of Supervisors, the school board, and in the legislature. Common
Council elections between 1920 and 1926 saw Socialists hold approximately 45 percent of the seats, and thereby they were able to offer Hoan strong
support. In 1928, an easy Hoan victory, the Socialists were cut down to
six seats from their previous total of eleven, apparently due to membership
losses during a time of pronounced conservative ethos nationally.[58]

The platforms and resolutions of the party during the twenties are
clear indices of concerns and direction. While the Milwaukee Socialist party continued to focus on immediate social reforms and appeals to diverse
groups, it virtually disavowed pursuit of its major goal: the collective ownership and management of the means of production and distribution. In

1926 the Socialist platform announced that the object was "to merge Capitalism gradually into Socialism." However, in a historical declaration, the party recognized that such a transformation involved national reorganization and, therefore, it was solely a matter for the national party. Further, the Milwaukeeans asked that the National Executive Committee delete the word "revolutionary" from the preamble of the national constitution. Thus, it can be argued that in 1926 the Milwaukee Socialists abandoned their purported reason for existence. Thereafter, the Socialists were barely distinguishable from Progressives, except for their consistent contempt for regulatory commissions and their concomitant espousal of municipal ownership. Otherwise, the party endorsed home rule, protection of and expansion of labor legislation, farmer cooperatives, old age pensions, conservation, and other ameliorative legislation comfortable to Progressives.

Throughout the decade, the party acknowledged its loss of spirit and members following what it called "the war madness." Of those whose loyalty it still retained, some turned to the party only because of their traditional social ties. Seeking to strengthen itself in Wisconsin, the party was less acerbic toward the state's Progressive politicians, and did not oppose Senator La Follette in his final senatorial campaign in 1922. But in 1924, the Milwaukeeans were initially hostile to the national Socialist party endorsement of La Follette's independent presidential race, fearful of undercutting some of their own support at home. Similarly, the party was wary of any political alignment unless it was clearly in the name of the American worker. The Milwaukeeans were concerned about their shrinking base locally and nationally, and yet their anxieties paralyzed them and prevented a wholehearted partnership in the national party's effort to find allies. Thus Milwaukee conducted no more than a holding action, without militancy, ambition, or socialist goals.[59]

In the executive branch of city government, at least, the party continued to retain leadership through Mayor Hoan. Hoan was the dominant figure in the local party as, following Berger's death in 1929, he became Milwaukee's major national figure. However, Hoan's ambitions were not national in scope. He apparently wanted no more than to retain control of his elective office, and as mayor, he harbored no long-range socialist goals. His interests lay in providing the city with an honest and efficient administration; he depended on merit appointments drawn especially from experts and technicians, and sought to achieve home rule and to expand municipal functions, in order to insure the public welfare and to reduce the costs of living. His only nods toward socialism were in his dedication to the idea of municipal ownership of utilities and in his devotion to labor.

Despite Nonpartisan opposition, Hoan succeeded in establishing or implementing a municipal stone quarry, street lighting system, sewage

62

disposal plant, water purification plant, and the first low-cost cooperative
housing project, the Garden Homes, to be built by any American municipality. A major failure in this area was his inability to move the city into
municipal marketing.

Hoan reintroduced central purchasing, a major hallmark of the first
Socialist administration in Milwaukee. He initiated improved budgeting
and long-range financial planning, resulting in Milwaukee's becoming the largest American city to approach solvency. Most important was the creation
of a debt amortization fund in 1923, enabling the city to accumulate its
earned interest in a trust, working toward the elimination of Milwaukee's
bonded debt. He encouraged health and safety measures, harbor improvements, city planning and zoning, and community recreation. Many of
these steps were achieved with the help of outside lobbying which the may-
or encouraged in order to supplement his minority support on the Common
Council.[60]

By the end of his first dozen years in office, Milwaukee had come to
look on Hoan as a fixture. Not until the New Deal would he have effective
opposition in an electoral campaign. His increasing support came from
erstwhile opponents, such as the Milwaukee *Journal* and professional and
business groups which were satisfied with Hoan's efficient and orderly government and fearful of any change. The national media by then applauded
Milwaukee as a forward-looking city under a model mayor. A favorable
article signalled him out as one-tenth Socialist and nine-tenths businessman.
Indeed, national criticism for Hoan came only from other Socialists who,
more than ever, sneered at Milwaukee's "sewer socialism." But the thrust
of their comments was true. Hoan's biographer is correct to discuss his
work in terms of municipal progressivism, for his vision went little beyond
that. The zeal of the early party was gone, and with the introduction of
the only municipal measures possible without home rule, no real goals remained.[61]

The crisis of the Depression inspired the Socialists. Economic dislocation reinvigorated the party, and with a burst in membership, the elections of 1930 and 1932 were encouraging. The Socialists increased their
numbers in the State Legislature and, improving their county showing,
elected a sheriff. In the 1932 city election, Hoan won by a landslide of 63
percent, his highest percentage of votes in his eight mayoralty campaigns.
For the only time, he carried with him other city-wide candidates, as the
party elected a city treasurer and city attorney, and won twelve of twenty-
seven seats on the Council. But despite the apparent party revival, Hoan
was unable to meet the economic crisis. Lacking a Council majority, he
could not implement his social proposals of municipal marketing and bank-
ing or the substitution of the unemployed for automation in the Public

Works Department. Also unimplemented were his more prosaic proposals of departmental reorganization, city-county consolidation, the reduction of city wages, and a short work week to stimulate employment. Milwaukee's solvency disappeared in the crisis, leading to an attempted recall of Hoan by a taxpayers group. The city, like others across the nation, ultimately depended on the federal government to resolve the Depression.[62]

The national party briefly became revitalized and optimistic in the throes of the Depression but dissension and factionalism soon divided it among an Old Guard and various militant sects. The pattern in Milwaukee was not altogether different: defensiveness toward the New Deal, local factionalism, and finally coalition and virtual extinction in 1935. The umbilical cord to the FTC was finally severed in these years. Labor deleted all references to socialism in its constitution and, to underline the break, moved its headquarters out of Brisbane Hall which it had shared with the Socialists for more than twenty years. The split with labor led to the loss of the Milwaukee *Leader*, long dependent on FTC financial support. Simultaneously, the growth of the Communist movement in Milwaukee began to gut the party. The Socialists vetoed a policy of united action and attempted to protect their locals from front organizations. But increasing factionalism, including conversions, harmed the party.

For survival purposes the Socialists grasped at a straw which ironically led to their demise. In the pattern of the previous decade, the party sought strength in coalition with local progressive elements. In 1935 the Farmer-Labor Progressive Federation was born. The Socialists abandoned their electoral column in return for Federation endorsements of public ownership and cooperative farm marketing. They retained their right to designate candidates in Milwaukee but, with a ticket only half Socialist, the city elections of April 1936 were a rout. Hoan scraped through in confrontation with a formidable candidate but for the most part the Socialist slate was wiped clean. This election, fought on Mayor Hoan's record rather than on traditional principles or policies, foreshadowed Hoan's defeat of 1940. By then, the coalition was recognized to have been a disastrous error. The Socialists tried to resurrect their organization the next year, but their era was long buried.[63]

The Socialist Party of America never took real interest in municipal socialism. The party acknowledged that local reforms could mitigate the worst evils of the capitalist regime, and therefore the idea of Socialists in local offices was supportable. However, arguing always that socialism could not be implemented in one city alone, the party only absentmindedly came to draw up a municipal program for the guidance of its locals. At its 1912 convention the Socialist party resolved to establish a permanent committee on municipal and state matters and a legislative bureau to act as a clearing-

64

house of information for Socialists in public office. The party's municipal program, designed by a committee chaired by Carl D. Thompson, former Wisconsin State Senator, was in the Milwaukee image, containing measures such as municipal ownership, home rule, city planning, public health, and other social legislation. Once enunciated, it apparently was worth no further attention by the national party.[64]

In Milwaukee, where American Socialists had their clearest opportunity to explore whatever application socialism might have to a municipality, party activists operated in a vacuum and their record has to be viewed in isolation. Enjoying the backing of the leading ethnic group of the city in combination with the support of organized labor, the democratic Socialists proceeded to exercise considerable influence in Milwaukee after the turn of the twentieth century. Between 1900 and 1932, they averaged 25 percent of all votes cast in the various municipal elections, and even in presidential elections in that period, Milwaukee gave 23 percent of its votes to the Socialist candidates. The apex of the movement was reached on the eve of World War I, and thereafter the lingering decline of the party gave it another fifteen years of visibility if not viability. Years later, in 1948, Frank P. Zeidler, as a ghostly reminder of a dynamic past, became the third Socialist mayor of Milwaukee, but his twelve-year term of office bore only his Socialist tag as a link to the earlier generation.[65]

Socialists in public office were differentiated from others who sought reforms by their belief that government was not an evil but rather an instrument of public service. Willing to use its potential power, the Socialists of Milwaukee, assisted at times by the grudging support of the Nonpartisans, speeded the introduction of modern government to the city. They stressed honesty and efficiency, and utilized technicians and experts to confront the problems of the urban-industrial order. They vastly expanded governmental responsibility while redefining its goals and humanizing its thrust. In systematizing and expanding municipal government, their pattern was not unlike that of non-Socialist reformers elsewhere. But listening to a different drummer, they couched their efforts in an ideological frame of reference which resulted in a broader pursuit of reform. However, their distinct goals of social transformation remained unachieved. Perhaps their greatest contribution toward a changed social structure was in drawing labor into the public arena as a legitimate interest group. As early as the Seidel administration, labor in Milwaukee came to assume a place in the public dialogue. But except for the introduction of a few municipally owned utilities, the clearly Socialist side of the ledger was barren.

Ironically, the Socialist-labeled administrations of Milwaukee achieved success in implementing the goals of reformers rather than revolutionaries. Despite themselves, the Socialists epitomized progressive municipal reform more boldly than those who bore the name.

65

NOTES

1. H. Yuan Tien, ed., *Milwaukee Metropolitan Area Fact Book, 1940, 1950, 1960* (Madison, 1962), p. 21; Gerd Korman, *Industrialization, Immigrants, and Americanizers: The View from Milwaukee, 1866–1921* (Madison, 1967), pp. 17–21; Bayrd Still, *Milwaukee: The History of a City* (Madison, 1948), pp. 329–37, 484; Roger David Simon, "The Expansion of an Industrial City: Milwaukee, 1880–1910" (unpublished Ph.D. dissertation, University of Wisconsin, 1971), p. 62.

2. Tien, p. 23; U.S. *Census, Eleventh, 1890, Vital and Social Statistics*, vol. IV, 346; U.S. *Census, Twelfth, 1900, Population*, vol. I, pt. 1, p. cxc; Still, pp. 574–75. Of the 285,315 residents of Milwaukee in 1900, 235,889 were first or second generation Americans.

3. Still, pp. 111–13; Albert Bernhardt Faust, *The German Element in the United States with Special Reference to its Political, Moral, Social and Educational Influence* (Boston, 1909), I, 473; Carl Wittke, *We Who Built America: The Saga of the Immigrant*, rev. ed. (Cleveland, 1967), pp. 198, 205; Marcus L. Hansen, "The Revolutions of 1848 and German Emigration," *Journal of Economic and Business History* 2 (1930), 634–35.

4. Still, pp. 127, 264–65; Simon, pp. 44–45, 77–81, 86–91; Carl Wittke, *The German-Language Press in America* (Lexington, 1957), pp. 197–201; Korman, pp. 42–43. While it is possible to speak of a German position in politics, the German community divided its votes among Republicans, Democrats, and Socialists, and the Socialists never had the support of a majority of the Germans in Milwaukee.

5. Simon, pp. 81, 98–103; Still, pp. 268–72, 274–78; Korman, pp. 42–43. For a discussion of the experience of one peasant immigrant group in Milwaukee, see Theodore Saloutos, "The Greeks of Milwaukee," *Wisconsin Magazine of History* 53 (Spring 1970), 175–93.

6. Robert Ernst, *Immigrant Life in New York City, 1825–1863* (New York, 1949), pp. 100, 112; Edwin Witte, "Labor in Wisconsin History," *Wisconsin Magazine of History* 35 (Winter 1951), 85–86; Still, pp. 287–95; John R. Commons, *The History of Labour in the United States* (New York, 1918), II, 273; Thomas W. Gavett, *The Development of the Labor Movement in Milwaukee* (Madison, 1965), pp. 27, 47, 59–65, 77.

7. Gavett, p. 77, 114; Marvin Wachman, *History of the Social-Democratic Party of Milwaukee, 1897–1910* (Urbana, 1945), p. 40. It was Victor Berger who encouraged the analogy of an economic arm and a political arm. See Milwaukee *Leader,* December 16, 1911.

8. Wachman, pp. 11, 20, 34–36; Frederick I. Olson, "The Socialist Party and the Unions in Milwaukee, 1900–1912," *Wisconsin Magazine of History* 44 (Winter 1960–61), 111–13; Gavett, pp. 91–98. Frank J. Weber, an officer of the FTC for over thirty years, was a prominent local Socialist.

9. Olson, pp. 111–16; Gavett, p. 31.

10. Wachman, pp. 9, 13–16; Still, pp. 289, 296; Korman, pp. 56–57; Frederic F. Heath, ed., *Social Democracy Red Book* (Terre Haute, 1900), pp. 55–56.

11. For the preunity era on the national scene, see Howard H. Quint, *The Forging of American Socialism* (Columbia, South Carolina, 1953).

12. On the inevitability of socialism see Socialist Party, *Proceedings* of the 1908 National Convention, p. 227; *Social-Democratic Herald*, April 29, 1905, September 25, 1909; Milwaukee *Leader*, December 7, 1911; on local autonomy, see Socialist Party *Proceedings* of the 1908 National Convention, p. 13, and *Proceedings* of the 1910 National Congress, p. 242; Victor Berger to Morris Hillquit, November 24, 1903, April 8, 1905, Morris Hillquit Collection, State Historical Society of Wisconsin; on the partnership with labor, see Socialist Party *Proceedings* of the 1908 National Convention, pp. 38–39, and Berger in *International Socialist Review* 10 (January 1910), 598; on racism in the Milwaukee party, see Socialist Party, *Proceedings* of the 1910 National Congress, pp. 118–21, and Victor Berger, "What is the Matter with Milwaukee," *Independent*, April 21, 1910, p. 841.

13. *Social-Democratic Herald,* April 15, 1905; Socialist Party, *Proceedings* of the

1908 National Convention, pp. 241–42; Socialist Party, *Proceedings* of the 1910 National Congress, p. 276.

14. Sally M. Miller, *Victor Berger and the Promise of Constructive Socialism, 1910–1920* (Westport, Conn., 1973), pp. 22–32.

15. Frederic F. Heath, "How I Became a Socialist," *The Comrade* 2 (April 1903), 154–55; Wachman, pp. 12–13, 53, 67.

16. For Seidel, about whom little has been written, see Frederick I. Olson, "Milwaukee's First Socialist Administration, 1910–1912: A Political Evaluation," *Mid-America* 43 (July 1961), 197. For Hoan, see "Socialists Again Elect Milwaukee's Mayor," *Survey* 36 (April 15, 1916), pp. 69–70; Joseph P. Harris, "Our American Mayors," pt. 17, "Daniel W. Hoan of Milwaukee," *National Municipal Review* 18 (September 1929), 549–50.

17. For an overview of operations, see Wisconsin Social Democratic Party, *Proceedings* of the 1910 State Convention. Frederick I. Olson, "The Milwaukee Socialists, 1897–1941" (unpublished Ph.D. dissertation, Harvard University, 1952), pp. 57–58, 74–79, 82; *Socialist Woman* I (July 1907) offers examples of socialist activity aimed at various age levels and interests. See Sarah C. Ettenheim, ed., *How Milwaukee Voted, 1848–1968* (Milwaukee, 1970), for the most convenient listings of election figures. There is a paucity of information on membership figures. Peter J. McCormick, former Coordinator of General Materials and Services of the Milwaukee Public Library reports that no hard membership data is extant. His extensive researches in this area are much appreciated by the author.

18. See Carl E. Schorske, *German Social Democracy, 1905–1917: The Development of the Great Schism* (New York, 1955), chapter V, for the application of the Weber-Michels sociological analysis of bureaucracy to a Socialist party. It offers insights applicable to the Milwaukee bureaucracy, although the Milwaukee organization was less imposing and far simpler than the German.

19. "Socialist Control of Public Officials in Milwaukee," typed statement in Municipal File, no date, internal evidence suggests 1911, Socialist Party of America Collection, Duke University; Carl D. Thompson, "How the Milwaukee Socialists Distribute Literature," State and Local Collection, Wisconsin File, 1898–1920, Ibid.; Daniel W. Hoan, *City Government: The Record of the Milwaukee Experiment* (New York, 1936), pp. 76–78; Olson, "Milwaukee Socialists," pp. 1, 55–66; Ettenheim, p. 124; Wachman, pp. 43, 47, 52–53.

20. Ettenheim, p. 124; Wachman, p. 82.

21. Party platforms may be found in State Party Conventions and Constitutions File, Milwaukee County Historical Society Collections. The earliest such records here, however, date from 1907. For earlier documents, and for municipal platforms and constitutions, party newspapers must be examined. Wachman is the best secondary source available on the evolution of party policies. Party measures such as free monthly symphony concerts and additional public baths pinpoint most clearly the vision of expanded services which differentiated Socialist platforms from those of the two older parties.

22. Wachman, pp. 58–59; Victor Berger, as quoted in Still, pp. 377–78. On the softening toward organized religion, see Socialist Party, *Proceedings* of the 1908 National Convention, pp. 202–04. Gilbert H. Poor, a former minister, was hired specifically as an organizer to spread Socialism among churchgoers. See Gilbert H. Poor, *Interesting Sketches: Blazing a Trail, The Story of a Pioneer Socialist Agitator* (no place, 1911), p. 84.

23. Still, pp. 359–72, 310–11; Wachman, pp. 46–51; David P. Thelen, *The New Citizenship: Origins of Progressivism in Wisconsin, 1885–1900* (Columbia, Missouri, 1972), pp. 164–67, 278–81. Thelen traces the origin of the Wisconsin progressive movement to the state-wide ramifications of the Milwaukee street railway struggle. (See below).

24. See Ethelwyn Mills, *Legislative Program of the Socialist Party: Record of the Work of the Socialist Representatives in the State Legislatures 1899–1913* (Chicago, 1914); Fred L. Holmes "Socialist Legislators at Work," *Independent* 70 (March 23, 1911), 592–94; Carl D. Thompson, "Social Democratic Program in the Wisconsin Legislature," *American Political Science Review* 1 (1907), 457–465. Prominent Socialists who won legislative seats included Frank J. Weber,

Winfield R. Gaylord, state organizer and perennial candidate in the Fourth Congressional District of Wisconsin, and Carl D. Thompson, who headed the Information Department of the party's National Office. See also *The Party Builder,* August 30, 1913, for legislative activities.

25. Herbert F. Margulies, *The Decline of the Progressive Movement in Wisconsin, 1890–1920* (Madison, 1968), pp. 152–56.

26. Ettenheim, p. 124; Wachman, pp. 60, 64–67.

27. Herbert N. Casson, "Socialism, its Growth and its Leaders,"*Muncy's Magazine* 33 (June 1905), 295–98; Socialist Party, *Official Bulletin,* February 1910, for an example of the symbiotic relationship in this particular area with the national party. In additional to nationally known socialists such as Debs, other prominent leaders who participated in Milwaukee campaigns included Karl Liebknecht of the German Social Democratic party and Keir Hardie of the British Labour party. For such appearances, see *Voice of the People,* November 5, 1910, Milwaukee *Leader,* July 3, 1912. The intense drive at the polls of the Social Democrats can be illustrated by a letter from Berger to Hillquit in which he states that minor elections cannot be ignored; Socialists must be a familiar sight to the voters in every campaign. Berger to Hillquit, March 29, 1909, Morris Hillquit Collection, State Historical Society of Wisconsin.

28. Victor Berger to inquirer, November 26, 1910, Social Democratic Collection, Milwaukee County Historical Society; *Political Action,* July 23, 1910; Mary E. Marcy, *International Socialist Review* 10 (May 1910), 990–91; Ettenheim, p. 124; Olson, "The Milwaukee Socialists," pp. 200–01. Several times the party ran strong races in the Fourth Congressional District but was never able to capture that seat.

29. Emil Seidel Inaugural, April 19, 1910, Emil Seidel Collection, Milwaukee County Historical Society. Berger also felt it necessary to remind his fellow office-holders that they were Socialists first; see *Social-Democratic Herald,* May 28, 1910. Examples of national press coverage, generally sympathetic, are Frederic C. Howe, "Milwaukee: a Socialist City," *Outlook* 90 (June 25, 1910), 411-21; "Victor Berger, the Organizer of Socialist Victory in Milwaukee," *Current Literature* 49 (September 1910), 265–69; George Allan England, "Milwaukee's Socialist Government," *American Review of Reviews* 42 (November 1910), 445–55; John Collier, "Experiment in Milwaukee," *Harper's Weekly* 55 (August 12, 1911), 11.

30. Still, pp. 376–78; Olson, "The Milwaukee Socialists," p. 204. Olson, "Milwaukee's First Socialist Administration," pp. 200–02.

31. The pages of *Political Action* offer the best guide to the work of the Seidel administration; see, for example, December 17, 1910. John R. Commons, *Myself: the Autobiography of John R. Commons* (Madison, 1963), pp. 150–53; Frederic C. Howe, *Wisconsin: An Experiment in Democracy* (New York, 1912), pp. 48–49; Olson, "The Milwaukee Socialists," pp. 206–08.

32. *Political Action,* September 10, 1910, October 29, 1910, December 17, 1910, February 11, 1911, March 18, 1911; Gavett, pp. 111-12; Still, pp. 515–20. The free employment office served as an example to states and even to foreign governments which used the Milwaukee office as a model. See discussion in Don Lescohier, *Working Conditions, Vol. III* of *History of Labor in the United States,* ed. John R. Commons (New York, 1935), pp. 195–96.

33. *New Review,* 1 (December 1913), 930; William English Walling, *Socialism as It Is: A Survey of the World-Wide Revolutionary Movement* (New York, 1912), pp. 179, 184, 196, 208; Walling, "Government Ownership," *International Socialist Review* 12 (April 1912), 652.

34. Walling, *Socialism as It Is,* p. 180; James Weinstein, *The Decline of Socialism in America, 1912–1925* (New York, 1967), pp. 109–13.

35. Socialist Party, *Proceedings* of the 1912 National Convention, Appendix C, "Report of Committee on Commission Form of Government," pp. 184–87; Victor Berger to inquirer, May 25, 1911, Social Democratic Collection, Milwaukee County Historical Society.

36. Milwaukee *Journal,* May 4, 1912; Milwaukee *Leader,* May 4, 1912; Samuel P. Hays, "Reform in Municipal Government," in *The Urbanization of America: An*

Historical Anthology, ed. Allen M. Wakstein (Boston, 1970), pp. 292–95. See also James Weinstein, "The Small Businessman as Big Businessman: The City Commission and Manager Movement," in *The Corporate Ideal in the Liberal State* (Boston, 1968).

37. Milwaukee *Leader,* April 3, 1912; Ettenheim, p. 125; Weinstein, *The Decline of Socialism,* p. 111; Emil Seidel, "Milwaukee's Achievements," *The American Labor Year Book,* 1916, I, p. 117; Emil Seidel, "Fighting for the Nation's Cities, *American Socialist,* March 20, 1915. Assessments of the Seidel administration include Albert J. Nock, "Socialism in Milwaukee," *Outlook* 107 (July 11, 1914), 608–12; Ted Mueller, "Socialist Movement of Milwaukee," in typescript, no date, internal evidence suggests 1936 or 1937, Milwaukee County Historical Society; Henry Pelling, "The Rise and Decline of Socialism in Milwaukee." Bulletin of the International Institute of Social History 10 (1955), 96–97; Olson, "Milwaukee's First Socialist Administration," pp. 205–07.

38. Berger's Congressional record is found in Social Democratic Party, *Milwaukee County Campaign Manual,* Fall, 1912, Milwaukee County Historical Society; Socialist Party, *Proceedings* of the 1912 National Convention, p. 234, in which Berger described his approach to office and the way he allotted his time; Elizabeth H. Thomas to Victor Berger, July 14, 1911, Social Democratic Collection, Milwaukee County Historical Society; Ettenheim, p. 105; Frederick I. Olson, "Victor Berger: Socialist Congressman," *Wisconsin Academy of Sciences, Arts and Letters* 58 (1970), 33–34.

39. Weinstein, *The Decline of Socialism,* p. 115.

40. Hoan, pp. 58–59; *The Party Builder,* September 20, 1913; England, "Milwaukee's Socialist Government," p. 453; Frank P. Zeidler, "Dan Hoan, Successful Mayor," *Historical Messenger* 17 (March 1961), 23–24; Still, pp. 517, 522; Olson, "The Milwaukee Socialists," p. 276.

41. Olson, "The Milwaukee Socialists," pp. 276, 304–06; Still, pp. 521–23; Milwaukee *Leader,* April 8, 1914; "Socialists Again Elect Milwaukee's Mayor," *Survey* 36 (April 15, 1916), 69–70; Wisconsin Social Democratic Party, *Proceedings* of the 1914 State Convention.

42. Still, pp. 455–58; Francis Hackett, "How Milwaukee Takes the War," *New Republic* 6 (July 17, 1915), 272–73; Karen Falk, "Public Opinion in Wisconsin during World War I," *Wisconsin Magazine of History* 25 (June 1942), 395; Korman, *Industrialization, Immigrants, and Americanizers,* pp. 167–73. For a general overview, see Clifton J. Child, *The German Americans in Politics* (Madison, 1939)

43. *American Socialist,* November 14, 1914; Milwaukee *Leader,* October 31, 1914, October 30, 1916; "Victor Berger Reproaches His German Friends," *Current Opinion* 59 (August 1915), 80; Oscar Ameringer, *If You Don't Weaken* (New York, 1940), pp. 305–06.

44. Milwaukee *Leader,* August 21, 1914, February 16, 1917, February 17, 1917, February 27, 1917; Miller, pp. 121, 124–26, 145–48, 165–68.

45. Milwaukee *Leader,* May 3, 1917, May 25, 1917; Miller, pp. 120, 172, 202–03. The Socialists in the Wisconsin legislature introduced resolutions of American neutrality.

46. Miller, p. 203; Robert C. Reinders, "Daniel W. Hoan and the Milwaukee Socialist Party during the First World War," *Wisconsin Magazine of History* 36 (August 1952), 48–52; Mueller, p. 31; Olson, "The Milwaukee Socialists," pp. 346–49, 377. Berger publicly blasted what he called Hoan's wobbling yet Berger also bragged about his own war work during his trial for conspiracy. See Milwaukee *Leader,* December 28, 1917.

47. Gavett, pp. 126–31; Milwaukee *Journal,* June 19, 1919.

48. Miller, pp. 204–06; Ettenheim, pp. 106, 125; Ameringer, p. 315; *The Eye Opener,* April 13, 1918, March 9, 1918; Milwaukee *Leader,* October 13, 1917, February 25, 1918, March 28, 1918, April 20, 1918; Charles D. Stewart, "Prussianizing Wisconsin," *Atlantic Monthly* 123 (January 1919), 103–05. Stewart at the time observed that mobs disrupting Socialist campaigns and also government indictments were responsible for the protest vote. Also see "Why Milwaukee Insists on Berger," *Literary Digest* 65 (January 30, 1920), 19–20.

49. Daniel W. Hoan to Thomas Van Lear (Socialist mayor of Minneapolis), July 5, 1919, Social Democratic Collection, Milwaukee County Historical Society; Hoan telegram to Representative James R. Mann quoted in Milwaukee *Journal*, January 6, 1920; Socialist Party, *Proceedings* of the 1919 National Convention, pp. 128, 317; Victor Berger to Morris Hillquit, August 20, 1919, Hillquit Collection, State Historical Society of Wisconsin; *Commonwealth*, May 3, 1919, August 9, 1919, September 6, 1919. The evolution of the Socialist party at this time can best be traced in David A. Shannon, *The Socialist Party of America* (Chicago, 1967), pp. 126—53.

50. Wisconsin Socialist Party, *Proceedings* of the 1918 State Convention. P. 7 contains relevant platform material. Still, pp. 523—24; Olson, "The Milwaukee Socialists," pp. 353, 393.

51. U.S. *Census, Tenth,* 1880, *Compendium,* pp. 540, 544—46; U.S. *Census, Eleventh,* 1890, *Abstract,* p. 34; U.S. *Census, Twelfth,* 1900, *Population,* vol. I, pt. 1, pp. cxc, clxxvii, 800—03; U.S. *Census, Thirteenth,* 1910, *Abstract,* pp. 65, 210; U.S. *Census, Fourteenth,* 1920, *Abstract,* pp. 378—79; and with some adaptation from Still, pp. 574—75.

52. Tien, p. 23.

53. Korman, *Industrialization, Immigrants, and Americanizers,* pp. 167—75, 191—94. Korman shows the extent to which Americanizers were interested in minimizing labor unrest. Still, pp. 461—63. See Wisconsin Socialist Party, *Proceedings* of the 1924 Convention for a platform response to forced assimilation.

54. Gavett, pp. 146—51; John Laslett, *Labor and the Left: A Study of Socialist and Radical Influences in the American Labor Movement, 1881—1924* (New York, 1970), pp. 44—46.

55. Socialist Party, Membership Reports, Socialist Party of America Collection, Duke University; Shannon, pp. 163—84. For the 1924 campaign, see Kenneth C. MacKay, *The Progressive Movement of 1924* (New York, 1947).

56. Gavett, p. 147; Pelling, pp. 98—99; Harris, "Our American Mayors," p. 552.

57. Ettenheim, pp. 125—27, for mayoralty returns.

58. Olson, "The Milwaukee Socialists," pp. 415, 433, 437—38.

59. Wisconsin Socialist Party, *Proceedings* of the 1922, 1924, 1926, and 1928 Conventions; Olson, "The Milwaukee Socialists," pp. 464—65. Home rule supposedly was achieved in 1924, but without charter revision it proved to be a hollow victory. Self-government still was not a fact.

60. Olson, "The Milwaukee Socialists," pp. 415, 420—22, 475; Still, pp. 525—28, 545—47; Hoan, pp. 121—79.

61. Harris, "Our American Mayors," p. 549; Reinders, "Hoan and the Milwaukee Socialist Party," p. 55. Morris Hillquit, hardly a flaming militant, in 1932 derided the pragmatic Socialists of Milwaukee who "believe in building modern sewers and showing results right away." Hillquit as quoted in Shannon, p. 217.

62. Ettenheim, p. 126; Olson, "The Milwaukee Socialists," pp. 478—85, 491; Still, pp. 528—29, 540, 560. The party's 1932 platform indicative of its depression policies is conveniently reproduced in Hoan, pp. 333—38.

63. Shannon, pp. 204—50. Gavett, pp. 171—73; Olson, "The Milwaukee Socialists," pp. 520, 524—36, 565—70. National membership rose from 9,560 on the eve of the Depression to 20,951 in 1934, its high mark since the era of World War I; it fell to 6,500 after the November 1936 election. The Milwaukee Socialists, in party infighting, remained with Norman Thomas rather than walking out with others of the Old Guard. Milwaukee County membership shrank to 1,200 by the end of the 1930s.

64. See "Report of Committee on Municipal and State Program," Appendix K of the Socialist Party, *Proceedings* of the 1912 National Convention, pp. 214—17. The few other Socialist publications on municipal matters tended to stem from Milwaukee sources, for example, Emil Seidel, *Which Must Go?* (Milwaukee, 1923) a pragmatic argument in favor of public ownership; and Daniel W. Hoan, *The Failure of Regulation* (Chicago, 1914) stressing the emptiness of Wisconsin's regulatory efforts and the implicit need for municipal ownership as an alternative.

65. Ettenheim, pp. 2–3. Milwaukee gave far fewer of its votes to Thomas than it had given to Debs. On Zeidler, see Milwaukee *Journal,* March 17, 1948. Zeidler joined the Socialist party in 1933 at the age of twenty-one.

KENNETH E. HENDRICKSON, Jr.

3. TRIBUNE OF THE PEOPLE:
George R. Lunn and the Rise and Fall of Christian Socialism in Schenectady

During the pre-World War I era the Socialists of New York State achieved their greatest electoral success in November 1911, when a Socialist administration swept into power in the city of Schenectady. The party gained control of the mayor's chair and the Common Council, elected eight of thirteen aldermen, a number of district supervisors, and also sent the Socialist party's first member to the State Assembly. Its success came on the wave of an intensive campaign against municipal graft and corruption led by the Reverend George R. Lunn, Pastor of the First Reformed Church of Schenectady. Lunn was a social crusader and he began his work long before he affiliated with the Socialist party. His brand of reform, however, fit the desires of the party for office and the wishes of the people for clean government. Thus, large numbers of voters were willing to support him and would have done so regardless of his party affiliation. Lunn was never a true Socialist in the Marxian sense, but nevertheless, his administration represented an important, if brief, triumph for the party. For this reason it is worthy of note by students of the American Socialist movement, as well as students of the general history of urban development and municipal reform.

The city which elected the first Socialist administration in the state of New York was a rapidly growing one. In the first ten years of the twentieth century the population of Schenectady increased nearly 130 percent from 31,682 to 72,826. This increase was caused by the expanding operations of two great industries located in the city: General Electric and American Locomotive. In 1910 the former employed some 16,000 persons, while the latter employed approximately 10,000.[1] Schenectady claimed a higher average wage than most industrial cities of comparable size, and the unions were fairly strong. On the eve of the municipal election of 1911, the Socialist party in Schenectady was organized according to party tradition as a Central Local surrounded by a number of foreign language branches. It had no more than 250 active members, and even this estimate may be exaggerated. The makeup of the regular membership is difficult to determine with any sort of precision; however, many of the leaders were of Irish descent as indicated by the fact that most of the Socialist candidates for alderman during this period bore Irish names. As for electoral support, it seems clear that skilled, organized labor gave the party its heaviest vote. In the thirteenth ward, for example, where the population was largely native born and skilled, Lunn was victorious in both the elections of 1911 and 1913. The fact that a heavy majority of workers in this ward were machinists indicates that Mayor Lunn and the Socialists were popular with this group. Conversely, in the third ward, where the population was largely immigrant and unskilled, Lunn's vote was relatively low in both 1911 and 1913. Between these two extremes were areas such as the second ward where the population was a mixture of middle class and professional people. Here, Lunn won in the three-way race of 1911, but lost to the fusion candidate in 1913. It should be noted, however, that the Socialist party never succeeded in building a permanent base of support in Schenectady such as it did in other cities—Milwaukee and Reading, for example. In Schenectady, the rise and fall of socialist political fortunes can be traced directly to the party's brief affiliation with George R. Lunn and his reformist zeal.[2]

Lunn, whose activities were essential to socialist success in Schenectady, appears to have been a born leader as well as a dedicated reformer. He was reared and educated in the Midwest until the year 1897 when he migrated east to study in the Divinity School at Princeton. He was in his first year of study when war broke out with Spain, and he immediately volunteered for military service. For the duration of the war he served with the Third Nebraska Volunteers under William Jennings Bryan, but he saw no combat.

After the war Lunn returned to Princeton to complete his studies, but he did not remain long before deciding to go to New York City. There, he enrolled in Union Theological Seminary and served simultaneously as assistant rector of Lafayette Presbyterian Church in Brooklyn. During this period also, he married, and in 1903 was granted the degree of Bachelor of Divinity. In November of the same year he was called to Schenectady to become Pastor of the First Presbyterian Church.[3]

Lunn was a true Christian Socialist, a man endowed with an unbridled faith that the gospel in action could solve man's problems. He came to his

73

first pulpit in Schenectady's most substantial congregation resolved to fight for a better social order; to preach the gospel of life and also to have a hand in doing real things. He was prepared from the beginning to eschew traditional religion but, since at first he spoke only in generalities, his congregation was not disturbed. Problems did not arise until he began to translate his vision into action.[4]

The pastor first attracted attention as a result of his crusade against the city's street railway company, which aroused public ire by increasing fares. Until 1907, the street railway system of Schenectady was owned by General Electric. It was operated more for the convenience of employees than for profit, gave good service, and sold tickets at a rate of six for a quarter which was considered quite fair. In 1907, however, the New York Central—Delaware and Hudson lines of the Vanderbilt Traction Syndicate moved to secure control of trolley traffic in the Mohawk Valley. What one official described as "refined compulsion" was put on G.E. to sell the trolley system in exchange for a promise by the Vanderbilts to purchase $3,000,000 in electrical supplies.

Franchises in Schenectady were perpetual and required no payment to the city; however, there were certain incidental privileges desired by the new owners which required ratification. When these were presented to the Common Council in the spring of 1907, the management of the Vanderbilt subsidiary, the Schenectady Railway Company, was asked to define its policy. The citizens were particularly anxious to know whether the six-for-a-quarter tickets, popularly known as the "red tickets" were to be continued.

The managers of the company issued a public statement on May 14, 1907, in which they begged the question, saying that while they desired to provide the best and cheapest possible service, they could not guarantee that the "red tickets" would be continued. This statement caused little complaint, however, because it was commonly believed that verbal assurances had been given the Common Council that six-for-a-quarter tickets would remain. And indeed, they did remain for a year; but then, on March 1, 1908, the company withdrew "red tickets" and raised the trolley fare to a flat five-cent rate. The change came, unfortunately, during the slack time of a business depression, the panic of 1907, when an estimated 7,000 men in Schenectady were out of work. Thus, it brought a real hardship on a significant portion of the population, and to make matters worse, many believed they had been deliberately tricked by the company. Pastor Lunn agreed, and even though the general manager of the company was a member of the finance committee of his church, Lunn volunteered to lead a citizens' committee of protest.

The committee called first upon Horace E. Andrews, president of the

Schenectady Railway Company. He attempted to convince them that five cents was a normal rate; that no transit company could make money at six tickets for a quarter; that businessmen rather than working men were most affected by the change; that only one small dividend had been paid since the property was acquired; and that only by raising fares could he fulfill his sincere desire to improve service. This explanation did not satisfy Lunn. He pressed the issue by making inquiries into the financial condition of the company, but succeeded only in driving the general manager of the S.R.C. out of his congregation. This was the first major development in a long series which eventually led to a split in the church, but it did not slacken Lunn's determination and his committee went on with its agitation.[5]

The trolley car controversy might never have altered Lunn's career as a minister or brought about his eventual union with the Socialists, but it was not an isolated incident. Lunn's Christian Socialist philosophy compelled him to seek the most effective way to put the teachings of his faith into action. And so, he went into politics.

In his first major activity in the arena of political reform, Lunn turned his attention upon the county supervisors. By the autumn of 1908, in the minds of many citizens, the operations of the county board had become so intolerable that a committee was formed to demand action. It was a prestigious group, including in its membership four bankers, the chief local officials of G.E. and American Locomotive, a number of merchants, two lawyers, a former judge, and several other prominent citizens.

In 1908, at a time when the Schenectady County Board of Supervisors was controlled by the Republicans, the State Comptroller was Democrat Martin H. Glynn. Glynn sent in a team of five special examiners who found numerous irregularities and submitted their findings to the Comptroller. Since he was to be succeeded in 1909 by Charles H. Gaus, a Republican, Glynn hastened to issue a preliminary report on December 31, 1908, in an effort to make certain the investigation would continue. Most of this report dealt with the financial transactions concerning repairs to a number of county buildings including the Court House and jail. It revealed major irregularities.

None of these irregularities was probed in detail by the preliminary report, but it was promised that a more lengthy discussion would follow. The final report, however, never came. Gaus, the new Comptroller, quashed the inquiry, and the Citizens' Committee dissolved for reasons never made clear. Dr. Lunn (he was granted an honorary doctorate by Union College in 1905), however, did not intend to let the matter die, and he read the full text of the preliminary report from the pulpit. Subsequently, the matter was considered by a Grand Jury, but the majority voted against indictments. Nine outraged members of the Grand Jury minority then sought the advice of Lunn, who counseled a direct appeal to Governor Charles Evans Hughes. Hughes, in turn, acted immediately by appointing Deputy Comptroller Virgil Kellogg as a special attorney to conduct a more thorough investigation, and his work eventually led to indictments against the supervisors.[6]

Dr. Lunn's extraministerial activities caused predictable friction in his congregation of Schenectady's "best people." Many of his parishioners viewed the social gospel approach as a direct assault upon religion as they understood it; while for others, like the manager of the Schenectady Railway Company, the results were even more immediate and material. Some were fond of saying that Lunn talked and acted like a Socialist and that if he was one he ought to be in jail instead of in the pulpit preaching to them. Thus, it was probably inevitable that a break with his congregation should come. In the spring of 1909 the congregation debated Lunn's fate with vigor and then, surprisingly, voted to retain him by the wide margin of 269 to 101. Nevertheless, he submitted his resignation and it was accepted by the consistory by the vote of seven to one. On Sunday, April 25, 1909, Lunn announced his decision to leave the church effective January 1, 1910. The pastor declared again his belief that the inequalities of the American industrial system placed obligations for action upon all Christian ministers. Since a large minority of his congregation obviously disagreed with that view he said a continuation of their relationship was impossible.[7]

It was apparently Lunn's intention to leave Schenectady after January 1, 1910, but this was not to be. Shortly after the announcement of his resignation he was presented with a petition signed by some 1,500 citizens asking him to stay and become the leader of a "Peoples' Church." He agreed and soon after leaving First Presbyterian began the operation of the new church in a downtown theater. This Peoples' Church merged with the First Congregational Church to form the United Peoples' Church, providing slightly greater financial backing for the venture, and also giving Lunn a church building once more. He frequently preached in the First Church on Sunday mornings and in the downtown theater at night.[8]

Unfortunately, the union was in effect only a short time before further trouble erupted. Under the original merger agreement, Lunn and the former pastor of the First Congregational Church, the Reverend Mr. George F. Prentiss, were to be co-pastors of the United Church. Lunn was to handle the preaching and Prentiss was to handle parish work and serve as Minister of Music. This arrangement did not work out. Prentiss felt he was called upon to do too much, and he and his friends were also disturbed by the fact that Lunn drew the higher salary. Thus after several weeks of indecision, Prentiss decided to resign leaving Lunn in full control of the

76

church and all its properties. The latter soon brought in another young Christian Socialist, Robert Bakeman, to serve as his assistant minister. For a time all went well. Within another two years, however, this arrangement also began to deteriorate as the congregation became more and more disturbed by Lunn's socialist preaching.

Early in 1913 a group of parishioners in the United Church attempted to rid themselves of Lunn by means of an appeal to the Church Body in New York City questioning the validity of the earlier merger. It was ruled that the merger had been improper and thereupon the Old Church congregation voted Lunn out of office. The Congregationalists even went so far as to appoint a committee to occupy the church building in order to prevent Lunn from taking it over. The pastor, however, used his powers as mayor to bring the police into the case and force the committee to vacate. Following this the Congregationalists went to court and received an injunction barring Lunn from the church. When at length the entire matter was referred to the courts for final decision, however, the pastor and his followers were victorious and they remained in control.[9]

While Lunn preached the social gospel in his new church, he also added another dimension to his crusade by founding a newspaper. On May 7, 1910, he announced to his congregation that he intended to begin publication of a weekly paper which would be devoted to the advocacy of clean government and Christian ethics. He promised that his paper would give particular attention to the investigations of special attorney Kellogg and would not rest until the grafters were undone and adequate county government restored.[10] The first issue of Lunn's paper, *The Citizen,* appeared on May 20, 1910, and true to his word the first front-page editorial proclaimed that *The Citizen* would fill the city's need for a "fearless weekly newspaper whose primary purpose is to stand for the great silent majority."[11]

At first the paper was a one-man operation. Lunn operated from a small downtown office and the *Schenectady Gazette* did his printing. In just two months, however, *The Citizen* became so popular that Lunn decided to expand. He rented larger office space and purchased a linotype machine on credit. He also inaugurated a job-printing business to help pay expenses and despite intense competition his popularity continued and he was able to survive.[12] Lunn continued to press the issue of graft and corruption in county government in the pages of his paper, but he heightened the controversy by suggesting that the district attorney and several other officials had been "derelict" in their duty for not discovering the evil-doers earlier. He hinted at collusion asking, "Did you gentlemen know of the graft and corruption that is costing the people thousands of dollars or not? The people want an answer."[13]

The harried officials did not answer, but the Albany *Telegram* did respond by jumping to the defense of the district attorney. "Mr. Briggs," protested the *Telegram* writer, "is a lawyer of repute and a man of high standing in the community . . . who has a record of never having found an indictment that was set aside. It is evident to a good many people that Lunn has been carried away. . . ."[14]

Lunn countered in his next issue. In an editorial entitled "Graft Cannot Live," he declared that *The Citizen* was not vindictive. "This paper deplores the fact that men of this county must be punished for mishandling public funds. . . . The time has passed when politicians contemptuously ignoring the public trust can debauch the treasury of the people and escape unscathed after a purse vending term in office."[15] By this time, however, the Kellogg investigation had resulted in the indictment of several county officials and the crusade was in decline.

Another major issue, however, was very much alive. The trolley car fare dispute had never been settled, and Lunn began to apply more pressure beginning with the first issues of *The Citizen*. By December 1910, the Citizens' Committee, with Lunn still in the lead, had induced the Common Council to ask for intervention by the Public Service Commission. This was achieved, and the commissioners held hearings, but a controversy arose as to whether or not they had enforcing powers; and as a result nothing was done. The dispute dragged on for many months and eventually, after Lunn was elected in May, the Socialist party sent Morris Hillquit from New York City to handle the case on behalf of the Citizens' Committee. In the court battle which followed, the plaintiffs lost and thus the "red tickets" disappeared from Schenectady forever.[16]

Shortly after *The Citizen* appeared, Lunn took up another crusade, and in this he was more successful. "The people of Schenectady demand a lower gas rate," he proclaimed. He argued that the rate of $1.50 per thousand feet charged by the Mohawk Gas Company was exhorbitant by comparison with rates in other cities. "*The Citizen* will lead in a fight to protect working men and merchants from paying tribute," he wrote. "The Mohawk Gas Company is owned by General Electric and the fact that thousands of gas consumers are employees of the G.E. Company is still a bigger reason why the price of gas should be as low as possible." At Lunn's instigation a petition demanding cheaper rates was circulated and submitted to the New York State Public Service Commission. Eventually, the commission agreed to investigate the matter but before a ruling could be issued the gas company gave in to pressure and voluntarily reduced its rates.[17]

Lunn continued his search for evil. He criticized the city administration unmercifully claiming that prominent officeholders had for sometime been cooperating with a "paving ring" to bilk the city through padded contracts. In June 1910, he pointed out that the city was without playgrounds for its numerous children, and he demanded that steps be taken to remedy that defect at once. In December he demanded free textbooks for all Schenectady's school children, pointing out that a municipal ordinance required that books be provided even though it was not done in practice. Soon after, he recommended the establishment of a municipal lighting plant, and followed that with more charges of graft and corruption in the administration concerning first, the construction of an addition to one of the city's high schools, and second, the operations of the "paving ring."[18]

If Lunn's actions reflected his reforming zeal, his sermons reflected his Christian Socialist philosophy and even though he had made no direct overtures to the Socialist party as yet, he was clearly drawing very near to them in his thinking. As early as the spring of 1908, for example, in a sermon which must certainly have shocked his staid Presbyterian congregation, he declared that private ownership carried with it certain obligations to society. If these obligations were not met, then private ownership could not be justified. "The resources of this country are sufficient for all the people of this fair realm," he said. "These resources have been given to the people by their eternal God, but certain sons of privilege have preempted the valuable portions and surrounded them with the gatling guns of private property rights. If you listen, you can hear them cry, 'This is mine; am I my brother's keeper?' "[19]

By the summer of 1910, Lunn's editorials in *The Citizen* also began to reflect an apparent desire to identify with the Socialists. He suggested to his readers that both the Republican and Democratic parties were decadent and asserted that they were devoted to the vested interests. He also began to quote Socialist writers, particularly the German Social Democrats, and it all seemed calculated to elicit an invitation from the Socialists that he join them.[20] If he was partially motivated by a desire for office, and the indications are that he was, then the Socialist party was virtually his only available avenue. His alienation from the two major parties was all too obvious; he could not expect support from them. The Socialist organization, on the other hand, represented a ready-made springboard to success, particularly since they had no record to defend whereas the old party leadership had much to hide.

The press began to speculate about Lunn's intentions. " . . . Things are taking an unusual turn in the hotbed of peculiar politics [the Socialist party] . . . . Dr. Lunn still declares that he had not given the Mayoralty rumor a moment's thought. But . . . his friends are emphatic in their statement that he will be the next Mayor of Schenectady." That "peculiar turn of events," of course, was the rumor that Lunn would run for mayor on the Socialist ticket with the possible support of the Progressives. This would indeed have been highly unusual since Lunn was not a member of the party, and the Socialist constitution required a two years' membership for anyone to run for any office under party endorsement. Also, it was against the rules for the party to endorse a candidate on any other ticket. Nevertheless, it was clear that the Socialists were very interested in Lunn. "It is true," said one party official to a reporter for the *Knickerbocker Press,* "that the party would never endorse the nominee of another party, but Dr. Lunn is so well known and the desire to see him Mayor is growing so strong that it is hard to tell so far ahead what might occur."[21]

Meanwhile, Lunn, as reflected in *The Citizen,* drew closer and closer to the party, and in December 1910 he joined the Socialists. Immediately thereafter, he was besieged with questions by reporters from the local dailies, and his response to the *Union* man was typical:

Yes, I have joined the Socialist party. The emblem of the uplifted torch will be mine hereafter. I do not think either of the great parties hold out promise for the problems that confront us. I believe that the Socialist party does. I did not join the party with the hope of immediate political success, although it will all come in time. Socialism is growing. I was an enrolled Republican last year but I have never been a hidebound member of any party . . . . I have always been associated with the Republicans but more as an independent than anything else, although I have supported Bryan. In the past my Republicanism can be explained by the fact that I had to affiliate with some party and so far as its tenets went the Republican party made the larger appeal to me.[22]

Subsequently, *The Citizen* became for all practical purposes a socialist propaganda tract. In January 1911, an article signed by Herbert Merrill, secretary of the Socialist Local, appealed to "all socialists and trade unionists" to support *The Citizen,* inasmuch as it had ". . . worked for a better city and proclaimed in no uncertain voice the emancipation of labor and the era of equal opportunity for all." In February, Charles W. Noonan, organizer of the Schenectady Local proclaimed, "Conscious of the vast value of *The Citizen* as a medium for propagating Socialism and desirous of seeing its circulation increased to the place where its publication will not be a financial burden to its publisher, the week of February 20 shall be known as *The Citizen* week." During this period, said Noonan, the party would make concerted efforts to increase circulation. In May the paper was incorporated with Lunn as president, Noonan as vice president, and socialists Hawley B. Van Vechten, Rueben L. Knapp, and Ben S. Henry as manager, secretary, and treasurer respectively. Thus *The Citizen* was transformed from the private property of Lunn into a cooperative venture controlled by the party.[23]

Lunn's personal activities in behalf of the party and reform intensified. His weekly editorials continued to harp on local issues of graft, corruption, dishonesty and inefficiency. In addition to his duties at the paper and in the pulpit, Lunn accepted numerous speaking engagements offering to debate the merits of socialism with all comers.[24] In June he made a three-week tour of the Middle West, stopping in Milwaukee where he was feted by the local Socialist organization and given an opportunity to study their administrative techniques.[25] On September 29, 1911, after receiving a special dispensation from the party, he accepted the Socialist nomination for mayor of the city of Schenectady, and officially opened his campaign.[26]

Most observers called it the most exciting, and in many ways the most vicious local campaign in many years. Lunn, as might have been expected, continued to hammer away at the issues and problems he had been publicizing for some time.[27] Meanwhile, the Republicans and Democrats, throughly alarmed at the possibility that Lunn might ride to victory on the wake of his immense prestige, left little undone in their efforts to discredit him. The Republicans nominated Alderman William S. Herron, an employee of General Electric, and attempted to sell him to the electorate as a "workingman's candidate." Herron and his managers declared that while he could point to an official record of consistent effort on behalf of the workers of the city, Lunn's program was only talk. Furthermore, the Republicans cautioned city residents to beware of giving away the controls of municipal government to the "untried and untrustworthy" Socialists. In one less than subtle attack, Walter Briggs, speaking on behalf of Herron declared, "This city is dependent upon two industries, and if their confidence in Schenectady were shaken (by the election of a Socialist municipal government) retrenchment would be inevitable."[28]

In another diatribe, a certain Mr. J.F. O'Curtain suggested that Lunn was exceedingly dangerous as a Socialist and that the directors of General Electric would "not appreciate" his election. It was of basic interest to the working men of Schenectady, concluded O'Curtain, to support the Republicans or "even the Democrats."[29]

The current administration of Mayor Duryee was a Democratic one and so that party was forced to spend most of its energy in the campaign defending itself against Lunn's attacks. In his newspaper and in numerous streetcorner appearances, the pastor accused the administration unmercifully of graft and inefficiency. He challenged Democratic candidate Charles H. Benedict to a public debate on the issues, claiming that he could cite facts and figures to prove his charges. But the Democrats, while constantly protesting their innocence, refused to accept the challenge.[30]

By election day, excitement in Schenectady reached fever pitch. Few who were actively interested in the campaign slept that night and when it became apparent that Lunn was to be the victor, pandemonium reigned. The streets of the city were jammed with his gleeful sympathizers. For the moment it was forgotten that no one, not even the Socialists themselves, had expected a Socialist triumph, and that they were ill-prepared to take over the reins of government.[31]

Lunn was elected overwhelmingly and carried a majority of the Common Council with him. In addition, Herbert Merrill was elected to the assembly and became the first Socialist in New York history to achieve that distinction.[32] Lunn carried nine of the thirteen wards, while Benedict carried two and Herron only one. In one ward Lunn and Benedict tied.[33] More significantly, Lunn ran far ahead of his ticket, his personal plurality of 2,000 votes unmatched by any other Socialist candidate.[34] *The Schenectady Gazette* was probably not far from the truth when it declared editorially, "The campaign was hard fought and decided on local issues and it cannot be called a Socialist victory. Many Lunn votes came from non-Socialists who believed Lunn's allegations concerning the conduct of city government by the two old parties."[35] The fact that Lunn drew a balanced vote throughout the city, coupled with the fact that he ran so far ahead of all other Socialist candidates, justifies the conclusion that he was personally responsible for the party's victory.

It must here be emphasized that many believed Pastor Lunn to be no true convert to socialism, but merely an "opportunistic reformer,"[36] and thus every person in Schenectady possessed of the least shred of political awareness eyed the mayor-elect with keen interest awaiting his announcement regarding appointments. It was well known, of course, that the party would expect all offices to be filled with Socialists, but Lunn indicated he might travel far afield from both party and city to find the people he wanted for each post.[37]

The party leadership, Noonan, Merrill and company, intended to dictate appointments, and to handle this problem they established a Committee of Thirteen to study the records and backgrounds of various candidates, and make recommendations to Lunn. The press began to speculate that a controversy would result since Lunn was expected to take a "determined position," and insist that only "men of demonstrated ability" be appointed regardless of party affiliation.[38] During the following weeks the daily press was not made privy to the intra-party debate and thus could do no more than speculate. Meanwhile, *The Citizen* attempted to make it appear that mere "discussions" were under way between Mayor Lunn and the Committee of Thirteen, and that no real difficulty existed. Finally, on December 22, it was reported that most of the important appointments had been made and that the party membership endorsed them.[39] This was not entirely true, however. While the major appointees were Socialists, Lunn did step outside the party to select Democrats W.T. Wooley and Frank Cooper for the posts of city engineer and corporation counsel, respectively, and there were objections from members of the party.[40] It was the first round of a battle which was to plague Lunn and the Socialists throughout the period of their ascendency in Schenectady, and would only be resolved with the eventual expulsion of Lunn from the party. On this occasion Lunn simply refused to heed the demands of Local leaders Noonan and Merrill, and the matter was quickly appealed to the State Executive Committee. When they refused to take jurisdiction the dispute was temporarily quieted.

Some of Lunn's appointees deserve specific mention. Among these are Walter Lippmann, a dedicated Socialist at this stage of his career, who was named the mayor's personal secretary, and Charles A. Mullen, a well-known paving expert, who was imported from Milwaukee to serve as Commissioner of Public Works. In addition, Walter E. Kruesi, originally of Schenectady, was called home from Boston to become Commissioner of Charities, while Dr. Charles P. Steinmetz, the great electrical genius, became president of the Board of Education, and Hawley B. Van Vechten, a local party hack, became city clerk. In addition, Morris Hillquit of New York City was named special counsel to the city. These men were all Socialists tried and true; and each of them later became an enemy of Lunn when the dispute within the Local intensified.[41]

His inaugural address, delivered before the Common Council on January 8, 1912, was Lunn's declaration of faith. He stated flatly that no Socialist administration could establish all the principles of socialism overnight. "We know," he admitted, "that we cannot abolish the capitalist system in Schenectady, but we can and will demonstrate to all the spirit of Socialism and the application of Socialist principles insofar as possible with the handicap of laws framed to establish and sustain capitalism." The new Mayor promised that his administration would work to guard and promote public health, improve education, establish economic security and make city government more efficient and economical. To accomplish these goals he would begin with a milk inspection program, and the construction of more parks and playgrounds. He promised a broadening of the educational system to include adult education programs, lectures, amusements and other cultural attractions. He promised to inaugurate a study of the problem of economic security in the city and to work toward a solution to this problem through the Board of Charities. To modernize city government he proposed the introduction of the unit cost system and the abolition of unnecessary jobs. He concluded by declaring that he favored public ownership of utilities, but was handicapped in this regard by laws which did not permit it.[42]

Lunn set out at once to make good on his promises and in so doing he provided Schenectady with one of its most interesting and controversial administrations. It began when the administration announced its intention to expand municipal services at once by selling ice to all residents at cost.

In January and February of 1912 the Department of Public Works filled an ice house on the banks of the Mohawk River with approximately 2,000 tons of ice using striking boilermakers from the American Locomotive Company for labor on the project. The intention of the administration was to give the ice to the poor and sell it at cost to those who could afford to pay. Lunn publicized the project as a part of his plan to aid in the improvement of the health and lifestyle of the city's low income groups. Unfortunately, the local ice dealers took a dim view of the plan and immediately challenged it in the courts where they secured an injunction enjoining the city from either selling or giving ice away. Lunn and his associates thwarted the injunction, however, by acting as individuals and securing more ice from new out-of-town sources. They then continued their deliveries as if there were no injunction. Their major source was the Shaughnesy Ice Company of Troy, which soon found itself under pressure to withdraw support from the Socialist icemen. In August, one J.M. McDonough who claimed to represent the Interborough Ice Company of New York City, approached the Shaughnesys and attempted to secure an option to buy all the ice they could produce. When they refused, the Shaughnesys were threatened with loss of credit by their bank, but since their financial position was strong they could not be intimidated. Later, it was discovered that no such company as the Interborough Ice Company existed and the plot was traced back to the Schenectady dealers themselves. Subsequently, there were other efforts to halt the distribution, but it continued for about one year. The expense, however, caused it to be discontinued with the net loss figured at $1,462.00.[43]

Lunn and his advisers also undertook to sell coal to the residents of the city at cost. They purchased some 5,000 tons on a city contract even though the estimated needs of the municipality were only 3,000 tons. The surplus was to be sold to the public. Orders were placed at the municipal grocery store and buyers were required to pay in cash. Then, a truckman employed by the city would deliver directly from the car on the siding to the customer. The price was approximately fifty cents per ton lower than that of the retail coal dealers, and they, like the ice dealers, sought the aid of the courts. They secured an injunction which prohibited the sale of coal by the city, but once again Lunn and his advisers foiled a judicial proscription by incorporating as "George R. Lunn and Associates" and continuing to do business in private until the end of Lunn's first term of office. "George R. Lunn and Associates" operated with private funds although it did its purchasing through city contracts. This was a questionable procedure and later, when a state board of examiners investigated the municipal projects of the Lunn era in Schenectady, it offered the opinion that all of the projects were probably illegal. However, no court proceedings were

84

ever inaugurated.[44]

Other municipally sponsored projects also experienced mixed success, but at least they were not challenged by the courts. One of these was the municipal grocery store, which began operations shortly after the inauguration. It was a small affair located in the basement of the City Hall Annex, and was designed primarily to provide groceries to the poor at cost or less. The Socialists were very proud of the fact that Keir Hardie, during a visit to the United States, came to Schenectady and praised their store. However, it was not an overwhelming success in attracting customers, and was eventually forced to go out of business. Between May 20 and December 1, 1912, the city expended $7,433.76 on inventory while realizing sales to the public of only $3,477.08. Since these losses could not be sustained, and since the store proved generally unpopular even with the poor, the remainder of the inventory was given away and the store was closed.[45]

Another project was the establishment of a municipal employment bureau which was organized as an administrative subdivision of the Department of Public Works. This agency, headed by Jacques Mengh, was very active during certain periods, as for example the first six months of 1912, when it handled some 825 applications for temporary and permanent employment.[46] Later, when the labor market improved there was much less need for such an agency and it was dropped.[47]

The case of the municipal lodging house and farm was much the same. The former was established to provide shelter for itinerant workers who had formerly been put up in the jail. In exchange for housing, the men were expected to put in a certain amount of time tilling the fields of the municipal farm. All produce from this farm was to be sold to the residents of the city at cost. The project, however, did not attract adequate support. While indigents were quite happy to avail themselves of the facilities offered in the lodging house, they were loath to labor for the city on the municipal farm, and as a result the success of both institutions was quite limited.[48] The Socialists also founded a "school of social science," patterned after the Rand School, for the dissemination of socialist theory, but it was not a permanent success. Inaugurated in the spring of 1912, it began operations with seventy-seven students and a staff of four local Socialists, but grew little during its brief lifetime. It closed at the end of Lunn's first term of office.[49]

Despite the fact that much of the program initiated by the Lunn administration was unorthodox, the mayor was continually criticized by party regulars who complained bitterly that he was much too conservative. This attitude was first publicly articulated by Walter Lippmann who resigned his post as the mayor's secretary after only four months in office. Upon leaving, Lippmann declared that while he had no quarrel with the progressive attitudes of the Lunn administration, they could certainly not be termed socialistic. The Socialist movement in Schenectady, said Lippmann, was "unripe and immature," unable or perhaps unwilling to avail itself of the great opportunity to advance the cause of socialism which had come with the sudden acquisition of political power. In short, concluded Lippmann writing in the New York *Call,* power had come to the Schenectady Socialists too soon.[50]

There are plenty of people in this country bothering about playgrounds and dental clinics. These things are worth having. But why not let the "progressives" do them? With the Socialists outside criticizing, hammering and insisting, the "progressive" will do all, perhaps more, than we, in the line of "efficiency" and "uplift." He will be kept alive by the pins we stick into him.

But when the Socialists become reformers there ceases to be an organized party of genuine radicals to keep the reformers alive. I have often thought of the slashing articles the Socialists in Schenectady would write about the present administration if they weren't responsible for the administration. As it is, they have to pretend that what they are doing is wonderful, epochmaking and beyond criticism. Reform under fire of radicalism is an educative thing; reform pretending to be radicalism is deadening.

Lippmann, upon his resignation, also wrote a long letter to Carl D. Thompson complaining of the lack of radicalism among the Socialist leaders of Schenectady. He argued here at length (some twenty-four pages) that Socialists could not hope for real political success until they had successfully prepared men's minds for the revolution. Thus, the party should curtail its efforts to elect people to office and concentrate on the educational propaganda work necessary to sow the seeds of socialism in America.[51]

That autumn Lippmann wrote his second book, *A Preface to Politics.* Here he repeated his charges against the Schenectady Socialists. They had sought "obvious success," he complained, and they won office with the support of voters not indoctrinated with socialism. Lunn's reforms were imperfect because they had to pass "the judgment of men who did not see life as the city officials did." "To me," he wrote, "it always seemed that we were like Peer Gynt struggling against the formless Boyg—invisible yet everywhere—we were struggling with the unwatered hinterland of the citizens of Schenectady."[52]

Curiously, Lippmann, who at this stage of his career seemed more radical than Lunn and his associates, soon found himself drifting away from socialism altogether. After roasting the Schenectady leaders in *A Preface to Politics,* he went on to list his objections to most of the generally held tenets of the socialist creed. By the time he had finished he was ready to reject socialism and to become a progressive.[53]

Although he never mentioned the subject, Lippmann was probably no more pleased by Lunn's activity in the arena of industrial-labor relations, where the pastor-mayor also attempted to act out his Christian Socialist ethics. There were two incidents of note which occurred during his first administration. The first came in the autumn of 1912 when a strike broke out in the nearby textile town of Little Falls. It was a classic confrontation between the forces of labor and industry. The local authorities sided with the owners and the strikers and pickets were subjected to harrassment and violence. Lunn was horrified by the news which reached him from Little Falls, and, along with his wife, Robert Bakeman, and a number of others, he journeyed to the beleagured city to demand that the strikers be accorded the basic freedoms of speech and assemblage. Almost immediately Lunn was arrested and placed in jail by the local authorities who took a very dim view of his efforts. He remained incarcerated for four days until he was parolled subject to further action and allowed to return home.

Meanwhile, the opposition press in Schenectady had a field day, accusing Lunn of crusading in distant towns while ignoring his local responsibilities, and at the same time humilating the city. *The Citizen* naturally responded with arguments about how the persecution of labor was everyman's responsibility, how the Bill of Rights had to be defended, and how much attention the mayor was paying to home affairs. Eventually, the uproar died down and later Lunn's conviction for disturbing the peace was set aside.[54]

Nearly a year later, during the lame duck period of Lunn's first administration, a local dispute erupted at General Electric. The problem centered not around any question of wages and hours, but rather was triggered by the layoff of two active union leaders, Frank Dujay and Mable Leslie. Plant manager George E. Emmons declared publicly that the firing of the two leaders was not an act of reprisal, but merely a part of necessary retrenchment caused by falling profits. Union officials countered with the charge that Emmons was a liar and they cited as evidence figures which showed that General Electric made $1,000,000 more in November 1913 than in November 1912. Though AFL officials advised the workers not to strike, they ignored this advice and walked off the job on November 26, threatening to stay idle for as long as it took to obtain justice for Dujay and Miss Leslie. A committee representing the local union was dispatched from the city to seek financial aid in other areas, and Mayor Lunn declared his sympathy for the workers. He also issued a public statement saying no one would suffer from lack of food or clothing as long as he remained in office.[55]

Four days later the strike ended at a meeting in the Mayor's office when a compromise agreement was reached between the contending parties with Lunn serving as arbiter. Under this agreement all workers, including Dujay and Miss Leslie, were permitted to return to work. All parties also agreed that if retrenchment was necessary, men from out of town and those with no families would be placed on part-time, and no one would be laid off unless absolutely necessary. The mayor was acclaimed a hero for his part in the agreement and according to the press, at least, all parties admitted that no accord would have been possible in so short a time without his intercession.[56]

Meanwhile, trouble brewed in the Socialist Local. Lunn's great popularity made it inevitable that many of his adherents would follow him into the party, and the size of the Local was increased to an estimated 750. At the same time two mutually antagonistic factions were created which constantly battled for control. On the one hand were the regular Socialists led by Charles W. Noonan, Herbert Merrill, and Robert Bakeman, who soon broke with Lunn. On the other hand were the conservatives led, of course, by Lunn himself. Antagonism was present from the very beginning, as evidenced by the patronage difficulty, but it burst into full view once more in April 1913, when the Noonan faction suggested that all Socialist office-holders should share their salaries with the party.[57] Lunn's refusal drew nationwide attention in the press, and brought at least one inquiry to the National Office from a comrade in far-off Cowan, Montana, who wrote:[58]

This attempt practically to apply the principles of the party is interesting to outsiders and the resistance offered by those who would lose by the transaction is equally interesting. Socialists after all seem to have about as much human nature as other people which is precisely the reason that most people think Socialism impracticable. Please give the facts in this case and oblige.

Carl D. Thompson, director of the Information Department of the National Office in Chicago, wrote immediately to his friend Charles Mullen for an explanation, and Mullen replied directly to Cowan, sending a carbon of the letter to Thompson.[59]

This story is built upon the fact that a few Socialists thought it would be a good idea to have all the Socialist officials pay their salaries into the Socialist Local and then have the Local pay the officials what they thought they were worth. It was admitted even by those who by the way were very few in number, that none of the Socialists were [sic] being overpaid.

We have things similar to this brought up by Socialists who are more interested in dreaming than in doing work for this city and the capitalist papers are making the best of these vagaries of some of our Comrades.

Another dispute broke out in late 1913 over the question of purchasing park sites. Here, although intraparty antagonisms showed up in bold relief, Mayor Lunn found himself in a rare posture of agreement with the instructions of the Local. The question turned on the matter of which park sites should be purchased. The nonpartisan park commission which had been appointed by Lunn, submitted a list of recommendations. The Socialist Local directed by a vote of 83 to 82 that these recommendations should be accepted, and the mayor agreed. Noonan, however, objected saying that certain members of the Common Council had speculative interests in the land involved. He, along with four other Socialist aldermen, voted against the ordinance declaring that the vote of the Local was so close that it could not be construed as an instruction. Eventually the ordinance passed, but the breach in party harmony remained open.[60]

Intraparty feuding was temporarily quieted during the campaign of 1913 which brought defeat to the Socialists. The Socialists held their nominating convention on the night of August 2, 1913, and despite the existence of tensions within the Local, Lunn was unanimously renominated for mayor. Charles Steinmetz, who had served on the school board during the first term was also unanimously nominated for president of the Common Council. There was, however, opposition to the renomination of Comptroller John Meyers who was considered by some to be incompetent and an embarrassment to the party. Yet Lunn pleaded eloquently for his renomination arguing that it would be difficult to explain his removal to the public. His entreaties carried the day and some 75 percent of the delegates gave their assent. The Socialists viewed their completed ticket with satisfaction and confidence. Despite the inclusion of a few candidates such as Meyers whom they considered weak or questionable, there was widespread optimism among the Socialists that the great popularity of Lunn and Steinmetz would see them through. Thus, even though they were certain the old parties intended to fuse, they looked forward to the reelection of Lunn and another two years in control of the city.[61]

The record upon which Lunn and his associates prepared to stand for reelection was a fairly strong one. Of course, as Lunn predicted in his inaugural, they had not brought socialism to Schenectady. But, on the other hand, they had striven with some success to bring good, clean, honest, efficient government to the city. In addition to the controversial projects which have already been discussed, the Socialists also upgraded the efficiency of city government by overhauling the filing system in the offices at City Hall, increasing the salaries of city employees, instituting a new purchasing and record keeping system, caring for the streets efficiently under the expert guidance of Charles Mullen, increasing the number of parks, improving the sewer system, improving garbage collection, and improving the water system with new piping and the installation of water meters.

True, Socialists who believed in the arguments of Walter Lippmann would scoff at these accomplishments as "sewer socialism" at its worst. It is also true that the political opposition charged the Socialists with overspending. Nevertheless, the fact remains that the Socialist administration gave Schenectady two years of honest, progressive government, made as many improvements as could reasonably be expected, and did so at reasonable cost.[62]

The record, however, could not prevail against fusion. Despite the fact that he polled more votes than in 1911, the mayor lost to J.T. Schoolcraft who ran on the combined Republican, Democratic, Progressive ticket. In analyzing this election it is interesting to compare the 1913 Socialist vote in Schenectady with that of 1911. In 1913 Lunn carried only three wards, the ninth, tenth, and thirteenth, but in the city at large he polled 7,402 or nearly 900 more than in 1911. Furthermore, his vote actually increased in seven additional wards by comparison with the 1911 returns. Clearly then, he did not lose his city-wide base of support. It was fusion which defeated him and his Socialist colleagues. It might also be noted that many of the other Socialist candidates received more votes in 1913 than in 1911 even though they too were defeated by fusion. For example, in the race for comptroller John Meyers polled 6,825 votes, and Philip Andres polled 6,752 for treasurer. Finally, the party was able to reelect four aldermen in its strongholds, the sixth, ninth, tenth, and thirteenth wards, while many of the other aldermen, though defeated, polled more votes than two years previously. The party was out of power, but by no means dead politically.[63]

Defeat did not remove Lunn from the political scene. He devoted much time to *The Citizen* and its crusades and he also strove to cement his control of the Socialist Local. It will be recalled that soon after Lunn's election in 1911, a dispute arose when the radicals demanded the right to dictate appointments to the mayor. Now this point was raised again when Lunn introduced an amendment to the state constitution of the Socialist party which specifically denied this power to Locals.[64] By this time Lunn had built up a substantial majority in the Schenectady Local and had been elected Organizer. He was able to push through acceptance of his proposed amendment and led an instructed delegation to the State Convention at Rochester on July 4, 1914, where after some debate the amendment was tentatively approved by a vote from the floor.[65] Returning to Schenectady in a somewhat stronger party position than he had occupied previously, Lunn was determined to fulfill his ambitions by reorganizing the Local.[66] His plan called for party business to be conducted by an Executive Committee rather than in open meetings, and presumably, Lunn intended that the committee would be controlled by his own followers. In any event, when the matter was broached at the last meeting of the Local in November 1914, pandemonium broke out. Lunn and former City Assessor Richard Ver Hagen, a leading member of the radical faction, exchanged shouted insults and nearly came to blows, whereupon Lunn walked out of the meeting threatening to quit the party.[67]

This threat implied the possible destruction of the Socialist organization in the city because of Lunn's great personal popularity and also because he controlled a majority of the Local. So serious was it considered that State Secretary Usher Solomon came up to Schenectady and prevailed upon the ex-mayor to return to the fold. Lunn did so at the December sixth meeting, and was immediately reelected to the chair by his followers. For a short time Solomon was pleased to witness a harmonious business meeting. Shortly, however, Lunn began to criticize the Noonan faction for their opposition to him, and once again disorder broke out, to be quelled only after a very emotional episode. After the restoration of order, Lunn's reorganization plan was voted upon and approved, thus administering another severe defeat to the radicals.[68] Lunn maintained control of the Local virtually unchallenged for several months thereafter, despite constant outbreaks of disharmony. He was able to weather even the violent episodes such as occurred in May of 1915 when the radicals introduced a resolution opposing war. Debate on the measure was heated, with Lunn (who opposed the resolution) and Noonan almost coming to blows.[69]

Lunn's power was temporarily diluted in August, 1915, Noonan introduced an amendment to the constitution of the Local which provided the organization with the power to issue policy instructions to all Socialist officeholders by a majority vote. Despite the fact that the amendment was unanimously rejected by the Executive Committee, it was debated on the floor and approved by the membership. While this development is difficult to explain, there are at least two probable causes which might be cited. One is that lethargy may have set in among the conservatives. This view is partially substantiated by the size of the vote on the recommendations of the Executive Committee, which was noticeably smaller than previous votes of the Local had been. The other, and more probable view is that resentment of Lunn's autocratic methods began to mount, and whittle away his majority.[70] At any rate, this action placed control of the Local in the hands of the radicals for the first time since shortly after Lunn was elected mayor in 1911. Immediately afterward, Lunn resigned as Organizer of the Local and rashly declared that he would not accept the Socialist nomination for mayor again even if it were offered to him. This caused immediate speculation that he might run as an independent, in which case his great general popularity would give him a very good chance for election.[71]

Once again it appeared likely that Local Schenectady might disintegrate, and once again the state organization sent in representatives charged with the responsibility of ironing matters out. State Secretary Solomon and State Committeeman Algernon Lee appeared in the city on August 10, 1915, declaring that both sides in the controversy had acted hastily. They suggested a compromise proposal which they hoped might reunite the warring factions. It provided that only elected officials might be instructed by the party, whereas the Noonan amendment included all officeholders. It also provided that instructions could be given only in a meeting called specifically for that purpose, and then only on matters dealt with in platforms or resolutions adopted by subdivisions of the party.[72] These pleas of Lee and Solomon for harmony were followed by over three hours of debate which at times became highly emotional, but finally, the substitute amendment was adopted by a vote of 76 to 72.[73]

Meanwhile, Lunn assumed a modified position from which he could move in any direction. He declared that he had by no means given up Socialism simply because he had resigned as Organizer of the Local, and that his only objection was on the matter of instructing officials. He retracted his previous statement, declaring that he would be perfectly willing to accept the Socialist nomination for mayor if it were offered him. But in reality Lunn's next move was primarily dependent upon the question of whether or not the radicals could maintain control of the Local. Their hold was somewhat weakened by the adoption of the substitute amendment, but the question still hung in the balance, and would be decided at the time the Local adopted a platform for the coming municipal election.[74]

Lunn succeeded in rallying his supporters for the meeting which assembled on August 26, 1915. It was the largest in the entire history of the party in Schenectady, and it brought overwhelming success to the conservatives. Their platform was adopted by a vote of 165—43, and Lunn was nominated for mayor by the astonishing vote of 236—74.[75]

Lunn's chances for election were excellent, for his general popularity remained intact. Furthermore, on this occasion there was to be no union of Republicans, Democrats, and Progressives, since that experiment had apparently pleased none of the fusionists. The Progressive organization was by now nearly extinct, while the two major parties announced after some hesitation that they would both run their own candidates, and that neither of them would support Mayor J.T. Schoolcraft, the fusionist candidate of 1913.[76]

Once again *The Citizen* poured forth its barrage of accusations, and once more the plea went out to the people to vote Socialist and return honest government to City Hall. Most of the criticism was directed against Republican candidate Horace Van Voast who had served a previous term as mayor. *The Citizen* even went so far as to charge that Van Voast had used public funds to purchase beer in 1902.[77]

Lunn was elected with a large plurality, polling 6,069 votes to 5,041 for Van Voast and 3,435 for Democrat Henry Buhrmaster, but it was not a party victory. For the third time Lunn received balanced electoral support from throughout the city, and it is of great interest to note that despite intraparty bickering, the mayor did exceptionally well in those wards which were the traditional Socialist strongholds. This would indicate that not only did his overall popularity remain high, but also that large numbers of party members and adherents were still willing to follow him. On the other hand, the vote for the Socialist ticket in general dropped by some 2,000 votes compared to 1913. Steinmetz was the only other Socialist elected, with the exception of two aldermen in the tenth and thirteenth wards.[78]

When he took office on January 7, 1916, Lunn was accompanied by what *The Citizen* was pleased to call "A group of very competent, experienced city officials." His problems as far as the Socialist party was concerned, however, were not over. Within days after he assumed office a dispute arose over his appointment of several Republicans and Democrats to office. Usher Solomon again made his way up to Schenectady to confer with Lunn and his antagonists. After two days of talks he left the city without issuing any formal statement. Lunn also declined to comment except to say that the implied threat of expulsion from the party which hung over him was of no concern.[79]

After Solomon returned to New York City the State Executive Committee asked Lunn to come down and take part in hearings regarding his appointments. He agreed to do so and went to New York accompanied by two members of the opposition (probably Noonan and Bakeman) to state his case. After brief consideration of their findings, the SEC issued a report on January 18, 1916, which demanded that Lunn remove at least one of the objectionable appointees or "the trouble for him would begin." Lunn replied decisively:[80]

I will absolutely refuse to comply with the request to declare the post . . . vacant, on the ground that I deny the right of the committee to act on the premises. I would rather be read out of the party than have my appointments dictated by a minority group.

After some weeks of hesitation the SEC carried out its threat. They revoked the charter of Local Schenectady on grounds that it had violated the party constitution through its failure to discipline Lunn. Usher Solomon journeyed North once more to undertake the task of reorganization.

These proceedings took place on the night of March 28, 1916, when about 200 members of the radical faction appeared before Solomon to apply for reinstatement and a new charter. Another 100 Socialists who continued to support Lunn renounced the party and declared their intention to form a new organization in the city to be known as the Social Democratic Club. Yet another group, much smaller, gave no immediate indication of their factional preference and Solomon decreed a period of fifteen days during which they were to apply for admission to the new Local or lose their status as Socialists. Mayor Lunn announced that he viewed the reorganization of the Local as tantamount to his formal expulsion from the party, but he declared that he had no thought of leaving politics, and in fact, seemed almost pleased with the outcome of his dispute with the radicals. His formal statement seemed to indicate that perhaps he had desired to be expelled all along:[81]

Solomon contended that no man can be elected to office under the Constitution without the consent of the SEC. I made my appointments knowing the SEC would not endorse them. The condition for entering the new organization which Solomon perfected last night was an unreserved pledge to abide by the principle of party control. The committee should have made its protest inasmuch as I said that if elected I would administer my office in behalf of all the people and not at the dictation of any group.

Thus, the Socialist party of Schenectady was "purified." But without the charm and personal magnetism of Lunn, it rapidly passed from the scene as an effective political force in the city, and the decline can be clearly seen in the statistics for the elections immediately following the war. In 1919 Lunn ran for mayor as a Democrat having made the transition while still in office during his second term. He polled 12,356 votes to win while Charles W. Noonan of the Socialists polled only 2,517. The pastor-mayor was reelected in 1921 with 12,546 votes as against 2,865 for John C. Billingham, his Socialist opponent. Clearly, the Socialist party was now dead politically although the Local remained in existence for many more years.[82] As for Lunn himself, he resigned as mayor during his fourth term in order to become lieutenant governor of the state of New York under Al Smith. He remained active in the Democratic party and eventually completed his career by serving as Public Utilities Commissioner from 1931 to 1942. He died in 1948.

The foregoing study of socialism in Schenectady leads to the following conclusions. First, is the obvious fact that the Lunn administration was hardly Socialist in the literal sense of the word. Nothing was done to threaten the capitalist system in Schenectady. There were no heavy tax burdens placed on industrial property, for example; and the few public ventures can

94

hardly be said to have been more than progressive or reformist in nature.

As for Lunn himself, it is clear that although enamored of the Socialist party, he did not become a permanent convert to any shade of Marxist doctrine. In fact, it seems justifiable to say that Lunn and the Schenectady Socialists used each other very much for their own purposes. Lunn desired office. He attacked and alienated the entrenched Republicans and Democrats, and then drifted almost naturally into the waiting arms of the Socialists. Lunn won office. He also won and temporarily held power within the Socialist organization. But he accomplished both of these objectives largely because of his great personal popularity, and because he was a reformer. When the mayor was expelled from the party he associated himself with the Democrats quickly and with apparent ease. As we have seen he went on to rather substantial accomplishments in the realm of politics while associated with that party.

The Socialists, on the other hand, at first found in Lunn a natural candidate. His refreshing personality and his reforming zeal seemed to suit their purposes admirably. Yet, in Lunn, the Socialists found they had a tiger by the tail. He was his own man and consistently refused to submit to the dictates of the Local. The result of these factors, of course, was the spectacular rise and fall of the Socialist party in Schenectady, which was occasioned largely by the activities of one man: Lunn.

There is another point which should be emphasized, however. The Schenectady affair is important as a case study of the activities of the American Socialist party at the local level. In broad outline the problems encountered by the Schenectady Socialists might very well be applied to the Socialists in general, for dissension and factionalism were certainly endemic within the movement. From the national level to the local level, these were perhaps the greatest problems which beset the American Socialist party and brought on its ultimate demise.

NOTES

1. Department of Commerce, U.S. Census (1910) Vol. 1, 86. Livy S. Richard, "Democracy in Religion," *The Survey* (July 2, 1910), 535.
2. See: Schenectady *Union Star,* November 5, 1913. The tabulated results in the alderman's election indicate that in ten of the thirteen wards the Socialist candidates bore Irish names. In the sixth, ninth, tenth and thirteenth wards, the successful Socialist candidates were all Irish. See also ibid, Nov. 8, 1911. Here the returns indicate that of the nine successful candidates for alderman all bore Irish names. See also: U.S. Department of Commerce, *Bureau of the Census,* Thirteenth Census of the United States, 1910; Population, Vol. 11, 862. The census indicates a population of 1,355 persons born in Ireland. Of the total foreign-born population in Schenectady only the German was larger (3,428). The

question will arise, of course, as to why the nucleus of the Socialist movement in Schenectady was Irish. This question cannot be answered precisely from existing documents or statistical data. The newspapers of the period give no indication of local anti-Irish nativism, and census data indicate that the Irish population was not clustered in any particular part of the city. Therefore, the most nearly explicit conclusion which can be drawn from existing data is that the nucleus of Socialist leadership in Schenectady was Irish, but that the heaviest electoral support for the party came from organized labor. See: *Schenectady County Census Records, Enumeration of Inhabitants*, 1915, Wards 2, 3, and 13.

3. "Mayor Lunn's Five Cent Start," *Literary Digest* 44 (February 24, 1912), 386–88.

4. Richard, "Democracy in Religion," p. 535.

5. Ibid., pp. 536–37.

6. *Schenectady Gazette*, undated clipping; *Fulton County Democrat*, May 4, 1910; Richard, "Democracy in Religion," pp. 538–39. The preliminary report showed that of the bills examined, more than half were not legally itemized. Neither did there appear to have been any competitive bidding for the work. Further, it appears that members of the board had sold goods to the county and then audited the bills themselves. Further investigation revealed more. During 1908 the county employed a Superintendent of Construction and Repairs whose duty it was to issue monthly reports to the supervisors regarding bills for day work. It was discovered that fully 90 percent of these bills differed in regard to the time charged by the contractors and time reported by the superintendent. It was also found that the board had indulged in questionable fiscal practices. For many years they had attempted to preserve the fiction of a low tax rate and had failed to levy sufficient taxes to pay current expenses. To hide the deficit they borrowed money and in turn covered these loans with funds from current operating expenses. When funds available for this purpose were finally exhausted, they floated $200,000 in bonds to pay the loan, an act in violation of the municipal code.

7. *Schenectady Gazette*, April 26, 1909; Richard, "Democracy in Religion," p. 541.

8. "Mayor Lunn's Five Cent Start," 388; *The Citizen*, November 11, 1910.

9. *Schenectady Daily Union*, February 14, 1911; *Schenectady Gazette*, May 17, 1911; *Schenectady Union-Star*, January 28, 1913; *New York Times*, January 26, 1913; *The Citizen*, January 17, 1913; *Knickerbocker Press*, December 30, 1917.

10. *Fulton County Democrat*, May 8, 1910.

11. *The Citizen*, May 20, 1910.

12. Handwritten MSS of Hawley B. Van Vechten, later associate editor of *The Citizen*, and city clerk in Lunn's first administration. The MSS was prepared in 1952 and is now located in the office of the City Historian, Schenectady, New York. There is no evidence that Lunn had financial backing from the Socialist party at this stage, but it is certainly possible that he did.

13. *The Citizen*, June 10, 1910.

14. *Albany Telegram*, June 12, 1910.

15. *The Citizen*, June 24, 1910.

16. *The Citizen*, June 3; September 6, October 7; December 2, 16, 19, 23, 1910; *Knickerbocker Press*, December 30, 1917.

17. *The Citizen*, July 22, 29; August 5, 19; October 7, 21; November 18, 1910. Also see: *State of New York, Sixth Annual Report of the Public Service Commission, Second District*, 1912, 1, 898.

18. *The Citizen*, June 10; December 16, 1910; March 10; April 28; June 9; July 28; August 11, 1911. Also see: files of *The Citizen*, September and October 1911. On April 28, 1911, Lunn declared in a news editorial that the heating and ventilating plant soon to be added to the Nott Terrace High School could be constructed for at least $20,000 less than the proposed figure of $57,000. Under pressure brought to bear by Lunn, the city called in an engineer to study the plans and he recommended certain revisions. In spite of this, the Common Council, after prolonged debate, accepted the original plans. Unabashed by this defeat, Lunn then attacked the Union Paving Company for overcharging in work performed for the city, and also for performing work of substandard quality. He continued to belabor this and other issues throughout the fall months as time approached

for the municipal elections.

19. Quoted in Richard, "Democracy in Religion," p. 540.

20. *The Citizen,* July 15, 19, 1910.

21. *Knickerbocker Press,* December 4, 1910.

22. *Schenectady Union,* December 9, 1910.

23. *The Citizen,* January 11, 1911; February 17, 1911; June 2, 1911.

24. For example see: *The Johnstown Republican,* May 12, 1911, which reports a debate between Lunn and Attorney J.W. Forrest of Albany on the subject, "Socialism v. Progressivism."

25. *The Citizen,* June 9, 1911. Emil Seidel, Socialist, was elected mayor of Milwaukee in 1910.

26. Ibid., September 29, 1911.

27. See the files of *The Citizen,* August, September, and October, 1911.

28. *Schenectady Union-Star,* October 27, 31, 1911.

29. *The Citizen,* October 6, 1911.

30. Ibid., October 27, 1911.

31. W.B. Efner, MSS, office of the City Historian, Schenectady, New York. No pagination. According to Efner, Lunn continued to declare until the end of his life that he had not expected to be elected mayor of Schenectady in 1911.

32. *The Citizen,* November 10, 1911.

33. *Schenectady Gazette,* November 8, 1911.

34. *Schenectady Union-Star,* November 8, 1911. In addition to Lunn, Philip J. Andres was elected city treasurer, Russell Hunt became president of the Common Council, John L. Meyers became comptroller, and Stephen Schwartz and Richard J. Verhagen became assessors. The party also elected nine aldermen including Matthew Dancy, 1st, William Turnbull, 6th, Charles W. Noonan, 7th, Thomas Folan, 8th, Harvey A. Simons, 9th, William C. Chandler, 10th, Thomas F. Fahey, 12th, and Timothy W. Burns, 13th.

35. *Schenectady Gazette,* November 8, 1911.

36. *Schenectady Union-Star,* January 29, 1913.

37. *Knickerbocker Press,* November 9, 1911.

38. *Schenectady Gazette,* November 10, 1911.

39. *The Citizen,* December 1, 8, 15, 22, 1911.

40. *Knickerbocker Press,* December 30, 1917.

41. *The Citizen,* January 8, 1912.

42. *Proceedings of the Common Council of the City of Schenectady, New York,* January 8, 1912.

43. ———, *Municipal Journal,* August 1, 1912 (Vol. 33), 159; *The Citizen,* July 5, 19, 1912; Charles Mullen to Carl D. Thompson, August 17, 1912; Mullen to Max Huider, January 21, 1914; Socialist Party Collection, Duke University Library, Durham, North Carolina, hereinafter cited as SPC, Duke. C.A. Mullen, "Schenectady's Fight Against Ice Combine," *The Coming Nation,* August 17, 1912 (No. 101 New Series), 7, 13.

44. *The Citizen,* September 13, 27, 1912; *Knickerbocker Press,* December 30, 1917; Mullen to Thompson, December 19, 1912; Mullen to Clinton R. Woodruff, August 16, 1913, SPC, Duke. Clyde J. Wright, "Schenectady's Socialist Attitude," *The Coming Nation,* December 28, 1912 (No. 120 New Series), 6.

45. *The Citizen,* April 12, 1912. Also see: Report of the Municipal Grocery Store for the period May 20 to December 1, 1912, SPC, Duke.

46. Mengh to Mullen, July 2, 1912, SPC, Duke.

47. *Knickerbocker Press,* December 30, 1917.

48. Walter F. Kruesi to Carl D. Thompson, August 28, 1912, SPC, Duke.

49. Mullen to Robert J. Wheeler, Allentown, Pa., October 20, 1913, SPC, Duke. Also see: *The Citizen,* February 9, 23; March 15; June 7, 15; August 16, 1912.

50. *New York Call,* June 9, 1912.
51. Lippmann to Thompson, October 29, 1913, SPC, Duke. (See Appendix.)
52. Quoted in Charles Forcey, *The Crossroads of Liberalism* (New York, 1961), p. 106. Also see: Walter Lippmann, *A Preface to Politics* (New York, 1914), pp. 182–83.
53. Forcey, *Crossroads of Liberalism,* p. 107.
54. *Knickerbocker Press,* December 30, 1917.
55. *New York Times,* November 26, 1913; clipping, source unknown, December 20, 1913, SPC, Duke.
56. *New York Times,* November 30, 1913.
57. Ibid., April 27, 1913.
58. John D. Cowan, Secretary, Socialist Party Local, Cowan, Montana, to Carl D. Thompson, June 13, 1913, SPC, Duke.
59. Mullen to Cowan, July 8, 1913, SPC, Duke.
60. *Knickerbocker Press,* December 2, 1913.
61. Mullen to Thompson, August 3, 1913, SPC, Duke; *The Citizen* August 3, 1913.
62. Mullen to Lunn, December 24, 1913, SPC, Duke. Also see: *Proceedings of the Common Council, City of Schenectady, New York,* 1913, p. 467. This document indicates that the budgets for the two years of the Socialist administrations equalled $985,149 for 1912, and $1,157,581 for 1913. For purposes of comparison it should be noted that the previous administration had budgets of $932,480 and $947,156 for 1910 and 1911, and tax rates during those years were $1.92 and $1.91, respectively.
63. *Schenectady Union-Star,* November 5, 1913.
64. *Knickerbocker Press,* May 14, 1914.
65. *New York Call,* July 5, 1914.
66. *The Citizen,* November 20, 1914.
67. *Knickerbocker Press,* December, 1914.
68. *Schenectady Gazette,* December 7, 1914.
69. Ibid., May 15, 1915.
70. *Schenectady Union-Star,* August 4, 1915. *Knickerbocker Press,* August 4, 1915. The Executive Committee of the Local voted unanimously to reject the amendment. After debate on the floor, however, the Local voted 60–56 to reject the recommendations of the Executive Committee. Shortly after, the Local voted 64–59 in favor of the amendment.
71. *Knickerbocker Press,* August 5, 1915.
72. Ibid., August 11, 1915.
73. *Schenectady Gazette,* August 14, 15, 1915.
74. *Knickerbocker Press,* August 14, 15, 1915.
75. *The Citizen,* August 27, 1915.
76. *Knickerbocker Press,* August 29, 1915.
77. *The Citizen,* October 15, 22, 1915.
78. Ibid., November 5, 1915; *Schenectady Union-Star,* November, 1915.
79. *New York Times,* January 19, 1916.
80. Ibid., January 19, 1916.
81. Ibid., March 29, 1916.
82. *Schenectady Union-Star,* November 5, 1919; *Schenectady Gazette,* November 9, 1921. The increased size of the total vote compared to previous elections cited is accounted for by the fact that New York passed a woman suffrage amendment in 1917.

GARIN BURBANK

4. SOCIALISM IN AN OKLAHOMA BOOM-TOWN: "Milwaukeeizing" Oklahoma City

In 1910 the victory of Socialist party candidates in the Milwaukee city elections and the election of Victor Berger to Congress heartened S.P.A. members across the country. Socialists in Oklahoma especially savored the prediction of Carl D. Thompson, Milwaukee's Socialist city clerk, that Oklahoma would be the first state to elect a Socialist government.[1] No one was more encouraged than organizers and speakers who had been travelling the length and breadth of Oklahoma to speak at country schoolhouses where impoverished farmers had gathered to hear explanations of their difficulties and proposals for relief. In these meetings the air hung heavy with bewilderment and frustration. Thousands of farmers had been among the hopeful who had rushed into Oklahoma after the opening in 1889 only to find that this belated frontier yielded poverty and despair far more often than it provided families with plenty and contentment.[2]

Among the country people Socialists attempted to transform suspicion of town businessmen into a political consciousness of the local and regional class structure. The distribution of power, prestige, and income severely limited the economic choices of farmers who had that oldest of American ambitions: to be hard-working producers and providers on a small farm of their own. Main Street professionals, merchants, and middlemen controlled not only land and its uses, but sources of supply, credit, and services. From the ranks of the more prosperous town businessmen came the leaders of the state's "progressive" Democratic party.[3]

Many farmers in Oklahoma, either mired in tenancy or barely clinging to their own farm, responded with increasing skepticism to the antimonopoly appeals of "progressive" Democrats. It was to a Socialist party which assailed "Bryan Democracy" as a political myth designed to obscure class privilege that impoverished farmers looked for a defense of their interests. The "farmers program" of the Socialist party of Oklahoma was nothing if not fiercely agrarian radical in character and purpose. By various devices the Socialists proposed to provide land for the landless and services and credit to all farmers at cost. Socialists aspired to give dignity and hope to the poor farm families whom "progressive" and enterprising townspeople often despised as backward, indolent, shiftless, and morally derelict.[4]

With only two years of serious agitation and organization behind them, the Socialists were already in 1910 attaining majority votes in many country precincts in southern and western Oklahoma. The political prowess of their rural organization greatly encouraged Socialists, but the more astute among them could see all too clearly that even large majorities in the country precincts could not prevail against the heavier majorities which Democrats won in the more populous county seat towns and small cities of Oklahoma.

The absence of significant support in the cities was a troublesome fact which Oscar Ameringer, one of the Party's best organizers, confronted upon his return to Oklahoma City in November 1910, after taking part in Berger's Wisconsin campaign. An Austrian immigrant who arrived in the United States in 1886 at the age of sixteen, Ameringer had previously worked as a union organizer in Illinois and Louisiana. He joined the Socialist party soon after its formation. His experience had persuaded him that a gradual and persistent struggle at the ballot box would eventually produce a socialist America. A firm opponent of "revolutionary" tactics, Ameringer worked to create a strong state executive committee which would give the correct ideological and tactical direction to the movement. In matters of tactics and doctrine he often found himself embroiled with agrarian Socialists in Texas and Oklahoma who were distrustful of centralized authority and, at times, sympathetic to the syndicalism of the I.W.W.[5]

In the Oklahoma *Pioneer*, the official Party newspaper, Ameringer undertook to explain, in a prominently displayed article, the electoral success of the Milwaukee Socialists. "In the first place," he wrote, "Milwaukee has the clearest proletarian movement in the country." Iron, steel, and more than 3,000 brewery workers, organized in cohesive and politically active trade unions, provided a core of strength for the Milwaukee Socialists. Ameringer approved the tactics of the Milwaukee comrades; they avoided abstract, theoretical arguments, kept out "short-haired women and long-haired men," and always "pushed the bread and butter question in the forefront. . . ."[6] To be sure, Oklahoma's Socialists had created a superior "rural movement," but what they needed now, Ameringer concluded, was a more disciplined organization which would address primarily state and local issues as well as make special efforts to win the political support of trade unions.

Socialists in Oklahoma City hardly needed Ameringer's encouragement, for they had long since adopted, with a headlong and perhaps heedless enthusiasm, the Socialist government of Milwaukee as their inspirational model of the future. They ceaselessly trumpeted the "achievements" and "progress" of Milwaukee. The Oklahoma *Pioneer* frequently compared the working conditions and the public administration of the two cities.[7]

The Socialists were especially persistent in their opposition to the strenuous efforts of businessmen, working through the Chamber of Commerce and a "Good Government" League, to replace the city's council government elected by wards with a commission government elected by a citywide vote. Businessmen, they argued, would find it easier to win citywide elections, would be accountable to no specific groups of voters, and would not be constrained from serving their own class interests. Thus Socialists advocated either the retention of wards or the introduction of proportional representation to ensure working class districts and minority parties some voice in city government.[8]

If the voters of Oklahoma City would only "Milwaukeeize," the *Pioneer* implored, economic security, efficient government, and better living conditions would soon be theirs. The Socialists assumed, almost to the point of enchantment, that the Milwaukee appeals and tactics would be an appropriate and effective means to achieve power in their own city. The stakes were high, the challenge formidable but exhilarating. "The winning of the city means the winning of the state," proclaimed the *Pioneer* in the weeks before the municipal election of May 1911.

Try as they would, the Oklahoma City Socialists proved unable to duplicate even the limited success of their Milwaukee brothers. In retrospect, the Socialist attempt to "Milwaukeeize Oklahoma City" was foredoomed. Oklahoma City, after all, was not Milwaukee. Tactics and programs suitable to a long-established, industrialized, and polyglot city like Milwaukee proved to be of marginal political utility in a recently settled southwestern boomtown whose native-born, largely white Anglo-Saxon population typically worked in small-scale trade and service enterprises. The combination of German ethnicity and working-class interest which formed the basis of Socialist reform politics in Milwaukee and St. Louis was hardly to be found in Oklahoma City.

If the new, mushrooming city of Oklahoma was not Milwaukee, neither was it Butte, Centralia, or Goldfield. In the towns which sprouted near the extractive industries of the Far West, workers often became militantly interest-conscious and a minority among them became native Ameri-

101

can revolutionaries. The workers drawn into the rapidly industrialized western mining and timber operations were subject to the often uncompromising exactions of distant corporate managers and the wearisome monotony of socially-isolated camp quarters.[9] But Oklahoma City had neither those extractive industries nor the discontented and angry workers they produced.

Between 1889 and 1910, 64,000 people moved onto the Canadian River Valley site which became the city. Nearly 75 percent of these people were native-born whites with native parents. The foreign-born and native-born whites with at least one foreign parent comprised approximately 15 percent of the population; Negroes comprised about 10 percent. There were 3,214 foreign-born whites, a mere 5 percent of the city's population. Somewhat more than 25 percent of these (947 immigrants) were of German or Austrian origins. Mexican, English, and Canadian immigrants were the next largest groups. Although there were 2,122 foreign-born males of voting age (9 percent of the total number of voters), only 848 of these men were naturalized citizens. Only 14 percent of the city's population had been born in the territory or state of Oklahoma. Although the migrants came from many states in the Midwest and South, slightly more than 50 percent of the city's population claimed eight southern and southwestern states as their birthplace.[10]

Oklahoma City was merely a new and struggling commercial center whose development was years behind such centers as Dallas, Kansas City, and Wichita. Its "manufacturing" enterprises were embryonic and typically produced only light goods. Only 1,400 wage earners and 800 salaried employees and managers were engaged in manufacturing. Thus the ratio of proprietors and managers to workers was much greater than in cities where industrial production was more highly developed and conducted on a much larger scale. Indeed half the "manufacturing" workers of Oklahoma City worked in printing shops, bakeries, and lumber mills, activities which may fall within the definition of manufacturing adopted by the Bureau of the Census, but which would hardly look like "manufacturing" in Milwaukee, Chicago, and Pittsburgh.[11] Lacking anything that might reasonably be called a factory or a mill, Oklahoma City was altogether an unlikely place for Socialists to expect the emergence of a "proletarian movement."

There was a fairly well-organized trade union movement in Oklahoma City. Approximately 3,600 men were reported as union members in 1910, the majority of them members of the building trades, printing crafts, and railway crafts.[12] The 3,600 organized workers comprised about one-eighth of the eligible voters in the city (24,700).[13] If one could assume a high degree of political consciousness on the part of union men, the organized workers would obviously constitute a substantial number of votes. But at the

102

same time it would surely be delusive to regard Oklahoma City's union members as a *bloc* of voters, given the diversity of trades, the dispersed character of enterprise, and the scattered work locations. The active support and votes of trade unionists did not confer any decisive advantages in Oklahoma City politics.

The organized crafts of Oklahoma City, unlike the cohesive unions of German brewery workers in Milwaukee, had no tradition of support for Socialism. The leaders of the small and recently organized craft locals in Oklahoma City were content to follow Samuel Gompers's program of "bread and butter" unionism. Immediate gains and preservation of their unions were the pressing concern of local union leaders. Except for one brief period of control by Socialist insurgents, the city's Trades Council was dominated by admirers of Gompers and antagonists of the Socialist party. The local labor newspaper, *The Labor Unit*, was owned, managed, and edited by leaders in the Printing Unions. The *Labor Unit* professed nonpartisanship in politics, ceaselessly called for "more" in the true Gompers spirit, and unrelentingly attacked Socialists as agents of "disruption" and deluded "political" dreamers. Its editorial identification box carried the motto, "A Clean, Conservative, Independent Nonpartisan Newspaper for the Home."[14]

The Socialist *Pioneer* replied that the editors of the *Labor Unit* and the leaders of the Oklahoma Federation of Labor made a lie of their professed nonpartisanship by their persistent support of the Democratic party in local and state politics. For Socialists the "hypocrisy" of the trade union leaders was confirmed when city and state Democrats took antilabor actions only to have the *Labor Unit* and OFL leaders continue their steady criticism of Socialist insurgents within unions and steady support of Democrats at election time. This strategy was misleading workers by encouraging them to vote for a party dominated by the business and professional men of Oklahoma's towns and cities.

It is certainly true that the OFL worked within the Democratic Party to secure passage of legislation favorable to working men. The Democrats were easily the majority party in the state and they controlled both houses of the legislature with overwhelming majorities. Experience had seemed to recommend reliance upon Democrats. The Democrats had a large majority in the state's Constitutional Convention held in 1906--1907 and the Constitution which emerged from the sessions contained provisions for an eight-hour day for miners, mine safety inspections, and prohibition of child or woman laborers in the mines.

Workers throughout the state were supposed to benefit from safety inspections of factories and railroads and from the elimination of the fellow-servant doctrine in cases of industrial accident. To the labor reformer

103

the "fellow servant" doctrine was a pernicious legal device which enabled employers to avoid liability for industrial accidents. The doctrine rested on the dubious argument that the injured employee shared responsibility because he was obliged to acquaint himself with the unsafe work habits of his "fellow servants." In the first state legislature, enabling legislation for factory and railroad safety inspections was passed, along with a bill requiring the eight-hour day for state, county, and municipal employees. "Yellow-dog" contracts were also outlawed.[15]

Such success had prompted the *Labor Unit* to proclaim Oklahoma a "working man's state." When President Taft slurred Oklahoma as "a zoological garden of cranks," the *Labor Unit* replied that at least Oklahoma had banished "the snakes of capitalism which squeeze the life out of the people." Capitalists would not accept a Constitution which provided for the initiative, referendum, and trial by jury in cases of contempt for violation of judicial injunctions.[16]

It was not until after the 1910 state election that discontented union leaders and members would have a plausible alternative to the OFL's reliance upon the goodwill and support of Democratic politicians. When the Socialists polled 11 percent of the statewide vote in that year, with much larger Socialist percentages being recorded in the rural areas of southern and western Oklahoma, they established themselves as a credible political threat to the Democrats. And when the *Pioneer,* heartened by success in the countryside, began addressing issues of immediate concern to Oklahoma City labor, it gave working men their first real opportunity to compare socialist prescriptions with the preachments of the Gompersites and the performances of Democrats holding state or city offices.

Angry strife between businessmen and organized workers erupted in Oklahoma City during the Spring of 1911, severely testing the political tactics of the trade union leadership. In late February the Oklahoma Street Railway Co. discharged motormen who were trying to organize a union and placed aboard the cars both nonunion motormen and armed guards. A strike, labor boycott, and ensuing street demonstrations near the car barns halted streetcars for six days. Downtown business and professional men, exasperated by the inconveniences and business losses attending the strike, formed a vigilante group of 1,000 armed deputies who took direction from the County Sheriff. The rifle-bearing deputies lined the routes of the streetcars in the downtown area and threatened to shoot any demonstrators who attempted to stop the cars. The motormen's union, acting on advice from the President of the OFL, accepted a compromise which provided for no discrimination against union members but which fell far short of the original strike demand: recognition of the union.[17]

Among trade unionists, devotees of Gompers's methods and the

Socialists differed sharply in their explanations of the results. The Socialist *Pioneer* emphasized that the state's Democratic governor, after meeting secretly with Oklahoma City businessmen, had almost sent troops to the city to prevent crowds from stopping cars. This, to the city's Socialists, was confirmation of their basic contention that the two major parties were dominated by business interests who would serve themselves at the expense of labor.

Clearly reluctant to cast aspersions on old political allies, OFL leaders focused upon the immediate events and issues of the strike and avoided the broader strategic questions raised by Socialists. The president of the OFL reported in the *Labor Unit* that he had been told by the Democratic mayor in early March that the city government would be compelled to put policemen aboard the streetcars (the President did not say whether the mayor had given any reasons for feeling "compelled"). Negotiating for the streetcar men, the president had accepted the "compromise" settlement because he believed that the company would keep its pledge not to dismiss union members and he feared that a continuation of the strike would lead to bloodshed between police and strike supporters. The OFL leader admitted that he did not know whether the mayor had acted with prior knowledge of the company's intentions. The *Labor Unit* tried to present the agreement ending the strike as a full victory for labor and published the comment of the Democratic State Commissioner of Labor, who said that, in his opinion, the agreement signified the Company's recognition of the union.[18]

During the strike the actions of the crowds, presumably composed in large part of working people, bespoke a militance equal to that displayed by the businessmen who suppressed the demonstrations. It was this discontent and anger which the Socialists tried to shape to their political advantage in the two months before the city elections. Their thundering denunciations of the repression of the strike won attention which otherwise would not have been available to them. Socialists could lambast Democratic office-holders for their support of the business community while the conservative trade unionists felt constrained to distinguish "pro-labor" Democratic businessmen from the businessmen who aided the streetcar company. Socialists suggested that the reluctance of trade union leaders to criticize the Democrats sprang from the fact that Mont R. Powell, president of the Trades Council and a leading member of the Printer's Union, was running for a Democratic nomination for city commissioner. Naturally the *Labor Unit* endorsed Powell, saying that "a more conservative man . . . could not be found among the several candidates aspiring for the place."[19]

On March 9, amid the uproar of the streetcar strike, the city's voters had approved a charter revision providing for commission government.

105

The conjunction of the strike and the charter election was regarded as fortunate by the Socialists and unfortunate by the trade unionists. Their responses further illustrate the divergence between the socialist and trade union methods of defining and defending the interests of working people. For nearly two years businessmen had been agitating without cease for the abolition of ward government. In May 1910, a charter amendment supported by the Chamber of Commerce and the major daily newspapers was narrowly defeated, 2,147 to 2,247, with the highest percentage of "no" votes being found on the "south side," an area which local political reporters described as "working class."[20]

On the eve of the 1910 charter election the *Labor Unit* had been no less vigorous than the Socialists in denouncing the dangers of "centralized" commission government under the aegis of businessmen. Arguing that the ward system had effectively represented diverse neighborhoods, the *Labor Unit* asked whether it would be easier for the worker "to travel from Capitol Hill [far south-side] to Main Street . . . than it is to step across the street and visit the ward representative?"[21] However, by October 1910, and for reasons not apparent, the *Labor Unit* was approving the formation of a "Progressive Labor Club" whose purpose was to work towards a genuinely "progressive" form of commission government, including the initiative, referendum, and recall, city-owned utilities, and the eight-hour day on municipal work. The trade union sponsors of a labor list of candidates for the Board of Freeholders which was to be elected to write the new charter included one business and one professional man and emphasized that theirs was a ticket for all the people.[22] None of the labor or Socialist candidates for Freeholder was elected. Almost all of the endorsees of the Good Government League and the Chamber of Commerce won the voters' approval to create a new charter.[23]

And so when the new charter was presented to the voters in March 1911, it did not reflect the "progressive" spirit that the *Labor Unit* had envisaged the previous Fall. The *Pioneer* was quick to observe that the charter required the signatures of 35 percent of the voters before a recall election could be held, a requirement which effectively nullified the possibility of a recall. And the *Pioneer* attacked provisions which seemed to guarantee the current municipal utilities franchises. To Socialists these devices only proved that the public utilities were seeking an "elective municipal monarchy" which would permit them to plunder the people without constraint.[24]

At this juncture trade union leaders, confronted by a militant business community, were not at all critical of the commission government proposal. The *Labor Unit* published no analyses, spoke not a single editorial word, and reported in a one-inch story that the Trades Council, after an

106

"interesting" debate, was "pretty evenly divided" on the merits of the commission government proposal. The Council declared its neutrality and urged union members to vote as they saw fit. After the election, in a brief editorial blurb, the *Labor Unit* mocked those who claimed that the city was run by "pirates" and "monsters" and that its citizens were the unwary victims of lies spread by the "major newspapers."[25] Very obviously these remarks served to caricature the stand of the one newspaper consistently and uncompromisingly opposed to the commission government proposal: the Socialist *Pioneer.*

President Zeigler of the OFL was reported to have said, "This is certain, the charter cannot become mixed in the labor trouble, or the labor troubles in the charter election."[26] From these remarks it would appear that Zeigler either feared that the strike would endanger the charter, since it was the child of the businessmen whom union laborers were then fighting, or that opposition to the charter from labor leaders might make the businessmen more obstinate in their support of the Street Railway Company on the strike issues. Perhaps he feared both.

TABLE 5-1
"No" Vote on the Commission Government Amendment, March 1911
(May 1910 results in parentheses)

Precinct	Percent	Total Vote	Total Population	Turn-out Percentage Increase/Decrease
Ward 1	15 (50)	632 (528)	6,642	+ 20
2	22 (53)	703 (561)	8,320	+ 25
3	36 (53)	1,013 (729)	12,705	+ 39
4	61 (77)	467 (610)	6,336	− 25
5	21 (62)	959 (453)	7,875	+112
6	19 (28)	414 (738)	9,400	− 44
7	10 (31)	1,046 (516)	8,195	+103
8	56 (69)	350 (259)	4,732	+ 35

The charter election results, no less than the defeat of the streetcar strike, were remarkable testimony to the organizational activities of the businessmen and to the intensive propaganda of the major daily newspapers, the *Times* and the *Daily Oklahoman.* The city-wide vote was 4,098 "yes" and 1,486 "no," making a total of 5,584 votes, an increase of nearly 1,200 from the May 1910 election.[27] The greatest numerical increase occurred in the "silk stocking" seventh ward on the north side, 1,046 voting in March 1911, where only 516 had voted in May 1910. The coefficient of correlation between the opposition votes at the two elections was a significant .65. The working-class fourth and eighth wards continued to vote strongly against "Good Government," though even in these wards there

107

was some erosion of the opposition. But the sharp shift in ward five and the heavy turn-out in the northside seventh ward gave the victory to the advocates of "business" government. The sharp decline in the sixth ward was probably due to the disfranchisement of Negroes by the Oklahoma "grandfather clause," approved as a constitutional amendment in August 1910. The results merely confirm the basic fact that the two wards most frequently identified as working class neighborhoods and the seat of union labor sentiment had lower populations than the other wards. Those other wards must have contained many people who "worked," but who, in the eyes of the local political reporters, were not associated with labor unions and the "working class."[28]

There were working men and leaders who were impressed by the Socialist party's criticism of the trade union leadership in the aftermath of the streetcar strike and the commission government election. One important man in the top leadership of the OFL even changed his political allegiance. The *Labor Unit* itself was forced to admit that it was the "most sensational" incident of the year when J. Luther Langston, secretary-treasurer of the OFL, declared that he was a Socialist. The *Pioneer's* jubilant banner proclaimed "Langston for Socialism."[29] In the past Langston had been critical of the Democrats and had considered but dismissed the possibility of forming a labor party. Now he found an alternative in Oklahoma. In his statement of "conversion" he argued,

Yes, it has been my privilege, and seeming pleasure to help 'reward our friends and punish our enemies.' For instance, I helped 'lick' Bill Murray and elect Lee Cruce governor of Oklahoma. And, before Lee Cruce had thoroughly 'warmed' the gubernatorial chair, he [Lee Cruce] called out the troops to shoot me and my kind down like so many dogs, if need be, to DEFEAT the Carmen's Union in its struggle against the Oklahoma Railway Company. The troops didn't come, but Lee Cruce called them just the same—at the request of about a dozen 'eminently respectable' businessmen . . . . Lee Cruce did all this, mind you, without even so much as intimating that he would like to have labor represented in the secret conference that took place before the troops were called out.[30]

Langston concluded that the governor had been loyal to *his* class and he regretted the error of workers, himself included, who had chased "old party rainbows" instead of electing men from their own class. Predicting that a labor party would not be possible for another twenty-five years in Oklahoma, Langston urged workers to disregard the frequently-repeated charge that there were too many "cranks" in the Socialist party. Enter the party, he advised, and make it effective in the struggle for the "full social value for the workers."

Luther Langston had found himself a political home from which he would not depart for nearly a decade and the conservative trade union leaders in Oklahoma City found themselves hard-pressed to discount Langston's defection and rebut his attack upon the Democrats. But as the campaign for election for the mayor and city commissioners became increasingly heated, the *Labor Unit* once again could be found attacking the Socialists, not the Democrats. The editors gave cautious approval to Democratic candidates, whose advertisements on different pages promised "a Business Administration by Businessmen using Business Methods." Not only would "efficiency" be attained, these Democrats suggested, but there would be, as a result, more work, higher wages, and lower taxes. Among the Democratic candidates for commissioner was one union man to whom the *Labor Unit* gave special praise and promotion. This praise revealed the degree to which conservative trade unionists had absorbed business values. The editors knew that "a man getting the bulk of his education and training in a newspaper office is better fitted to fill a position of this kind than a former streetcar conductor, whose principal duty to the company he worked for was to see that the correct number of fares were [sic] collected . . . and also that he turned in a proper amount each night."[31] This would seem at first glance a most impolitic argument to make in a city where two months previously businessmen had suppressed a streetcar strike, but it may well be that praise for a candidate's "business" abilities was persuasive in a town of small enterprises and independent-minded craft workers. Perhaps only a hard-core of discontented workers objected to "business" government and "business" unionism.

The Socialists certainly objected. They tried hard to persuade the city's voters that their Party had given Milwaukee its first "Honest, Progressive, and Competent administration. . . ." The Socialist program for the city included municipal ownership of all public utilities (there was no significant support outside the Socialist party for "gas and water socialism"); permission for city employees to form labor unions; issuance of operating licenses only to those businesses which paid a "living" wage; and provision for city-owned houses which would be rented cheaply to working people (real estate sales and rentals were a major business activity in the growing city). In addition, the *Pioneer*, with another streetcar strike impending, challenged the Democrats who were campaigning as "friends of labor" to match Oscar Ameringer's pledge that, if elected mayor, he would not permit police to protect strike-breakers hired by the company.[32]

The Socialists and the conservative trade unionists held separate "mass" meetings in which they vied for the votes of working people in the last week of the election campaign. Luther Langston spoke for the Socialists and implored his listeners to study the lessons taught by recent events

109

in the city. "I have given the best years of my life to the trades union movement and have learned through bitter experience that the economic movement is not sufficient to emancipate the working class. We must vote as we strike," he concluded. The main speaker at the Socialist meeting was Theodore Melms, president of the Milwaukee City Council, who urged the audience to scrutinize the claims of conservative trade unionists that they did not mix their politics and unionism. Melms suggested that this merely covered their own political activities in the major parties. The *Pioneer* headlines claimed that "4,000 voters" had indicated their readiness to vote Socialist.[33]

A reporter for the hostile *Daily Oklahoman* commented upon the German accents of the Socialist speakers, as if to imply that the audience ought to have been suspicious of speeches not delivered in the familiar southern drawl. He did acknowledge, though, that the crowd was very much "with" the speakers.[34]

Unfortunately the *Labor Unit* did not carry a report on the "mass" meeting called by the local trade union leaders. However the last preelection issue of the *Labor Unit* repeated the familiar themes of conservative trade unionism: that Socialists would vote for a union man *only* if he were a Socialist party member; that Socialists and Republicans had consummated an unholy marriage to defeat the Democrats; and that the Democrats would do more for labor.[35]

TABLE 5-2
Socialist Percentages in May 1911 City Election and "No" Votes on Commission Government, May 1910 and March 1911

		Socialist	"No" May 1910	"No" March 1911
Ward	1	10	50	15
	2	22	53	22
	3	34	53	36
	4	31	77	61
	5	14	62	21
	6	26	28	19
	7	8	31	10
	8	47	69	56

In the city election held on May 9, 1911, 8,260 voters cast ballots. Oscar Ameringer received 1,876 votes (23 percent) for mayor and the other Socialist candidates ran fairly close to him.[36] Predictably the Socialists did better in the working-class wards on the south side of the city than they did in the middle-class wards on the north side. The "silk stocking" seventh ward gave the Socialists only 8 percent. But in the four precincts of the working-class "eighth" on the far south side of the city Ameringer won slim majorities at two boxes, a plurality at a third, and came in second in the fourth box, for a total of 47 percent in the ward. In wards three and four Ameringer polled 34 and 31 percent respectively.[37]

The *Labor Unit* interpreted the election results as a vindication of the city's trade union leaders. An editorial suggested that "Mont R. Powell and other level-headed union men . . . were exonerated on last Tuesday when four Democrats were elected to commissionerships."[38] Another comment suggested that although only one union man was elected, the other men were "friendly to organized labor." The *Labor Unit* had accused Socialists of shunning all labor candidates except those who were Socialists as well. The response of the *Labor Unit* suggests that "nonpartisan" unionism meant virtually predetermined if not obligatory support for anyone who called himself a Democrat, be he banker or union laborer.[39] Significantly, the *Labor Unit* merely noted the unprecedented size of the Socialist vote and then headlined an article attacking insurgency in unions, "Radicalism must be checked." The article, reprinted from the Worcester, Massachusetts *Labor News,* said that the cause of insurgency was "no more nor less than a desire on the part of a faction, which in the main is dominated by Socialists, to change the present policy of trades unionism to one of more radicalism."[40]

Socialists were pleased with the progress of "insurgency." The election results inspired the *Pioneer* to predict that the Socialists would win the state in 1912. These exhilarated hopes soon gave way, though, to a more sober estimate of the situation of Socialists in the city. The Socialist vote had come almost exclusively from organized workers, the *Pioneer* editors argued, but even if all organized workers were sympathetic to socialism they "could never develop [sic] the numerical strength required for a political victory."[41] The Socialists would have to seek the support of unorganized workers and professional people as well.

But a Socialist victory in Oklahoma did not come to pass. The Party built up strong support in the rural areas of Oklahoma, winning 17 percent of the statewide vote in 1912, 21 percent in 1914, and 16 percent in 1916. Oklahoma City was never "Milwaukeeized" because the hope was merely an illusion founded upon a largely inappropriate comparison of the two cities. The city election of 1911 was the *only* one in which Socialists polled more than a negligible vote. Socialists were not even able to hold the "working-class" vote after the emotions aroused by the streetcar strike had subsided.

In part, the Socialist hope of creating a political movement in Oklahoma City sank amid the general collapse of the Oklahoma City building boom in 1911. The completion of two major packing plants in 1910 and 1911 and the generally slower growth of the city after 10 years of "new"

111

construction and feverish speculation meant less work all around. The nation-wide depression in 1912 and 1913 aggravated Oklahoma City's special difficulties.[42] The exodus of building tradesmen removed a group of workers who had been more eager than others to "organize" the city and to support Socialist efforts to replace the local labor leaders and change the goals and tactics of the movement. As a Socialist workingman looked wistfully back upon the decline of his movement, he estimated that in 1911 there had been nearly 1,200 dues-paying members of the Carpenters' Union, a "good percent" of whom were legal voters and Socialists. All the building trades were strong and the plumbers, gas-fitters, and steam-fitters all had separate locals. In mid-1913, the carpenters had barely 150 members and the trades, even when combined, had only a few members more than the minimum required to hold a charter. He claimed that the proportion of union to nonunion workers was nearly the same as in 1911, but that there were far fewer workers. He concluded that the "secret lies in the fact that there are now but few buildings being erected in the city. There is no work. The mechanic has to follow his job."[43]

The "mechanic" who followed his job was difficult to retain in any trade union, let alone politically-active trade unions associated with the Socialist party. The building tradesmen who came to Oklahoma City to work upon the packing plants did not enjoy the steady association of a neighborhood, a large factory, or even a company town—associations which could produce common social perceptions and economic demands.

In the printing trades, where employment and union membership remained fairly steady, the devotees of "bread and butter" unionism continued to prevail. They were a bulwark for the conservative approach to trade union affairs. As organized craft workers with privileges and employment to protect, the printers shunned and fought the Socialists in the Trades Council. When Socialist insurgents temporarily won control of the Trades Council in late 1911, disestablished the *Labor Unit* as the official paper of the Council, and mounted a campaign to make Oklahoma City a "closed shop" town, the conservative trade unionists raged at this foolish radicalism. As Mont R. Powell put it, "You cannot unionize this city by knocking it." He suggested that if employment opportunities were poor, advertisements should be placed in trade journals throughout the region to inform workers that the labor supply was adequate in Oklahoma City. "But," he said, "under no circumstance lambast and frighten capital away. It is capital that we want in Oklahoma City and unless we get it here, there will be a vaster number of idle walking the streets."[44] He complained that the demands of labor militants for a closed shop and the Socialists' uncompromising antagonism to businessmen would only insult and drive away numerous capitalists who allegedly lent labor sympathy and aid.

The reply of this craft unionist illustrates the sharp difference between the assumptions of "business" unionists concerned to protect the advantages of the already organized in a period of economic stringency and the assumptions of Socialists who would fight business power by trying to organize all workers and to convert them to socialism as a political solution. In the short run, the strategy of "business" unionists was probably more realistic in that it kept the full weight of the business community from being thrown down upon the existing unions. Nevertheless within two years both the Democratic city commissioners and the Democratic state administration had proven themselves consistently hostile to organized labor, much to the embarrassment of the trade unionists who had urged their fellows to vote Democratic.[45]

In the long run, neither the Socialists nor the conservative trade unionists had any future in Oklahoma City. In 1913 the owners of the city's major daily newspaper, the *Oklahoman,* ran the printers' union out of their shops. In 1921 the city's business community confidently launched a campaign for the "open shop" and dislodged the printers' union from the most important shops. When the businessmen decided to eliminate unionism, they were not impressed by the spirit of "cooperation" manifested by narrowly-organized, cautious, and weak trade unions. The labor and Socialist movements in Oklahoma City were never stronger than in 1911 when conservative unionists and militants (Socialist and non-Socialist) fought each other for the leadership of working men temporarily resident in the city and momentarily aroused by the arrogance of local businessmen.

NOTES

1. Oklahoma *Pioneer,* November 12, 1910.
2. For an excellent discussion of the social and economic development of Texas and Oklahoma in the 1890s and 1900s, see the Yale Ph.D. thesis of James R. Green. Mr. Green has been kind enough to let me read extensively in his manuscript chapters.
3. Ibid.
4. For a more complete discussion of the Socialist program and the response of poor farmers and town businessmen to it, see Garin Burbank "Agrarian Radicals and Their Opponents: Political Conflict in Southern Oklahoma, 1910–1924," *Journal of American History* 58:1 (June 1971), 5–23.
5. Oscar Ameringer, *If You Don't Weaken* (New York, 1940), pp. 3, 40, 193–223.
6. Oklahoma *Pioneer,* December 3, 1910.
7. Oklahoma *Pioneer,* April 13; October 1, 8, 15; December 3, 1910; March 4, 18, 1911 *et passim.*
8. Oklahoma *Pioneer,* May 11, 1910; January 28, February 18, 1911; for the businessmen's campaign against the allegedly "corrupt" and "inefficient" ward government, see the Oklahoma City *Times,* September 19, 26, October 3, November 4, 24, December 7, 1909; January 19–23, March 23, 29, May 6, 7, October 16, 1910; March 14, 16, 1911.

9. Melvyn Dubofsky, *We Shall be All: A History of the IWW* (Chicago, 1969), pp. 19–35.

10. Department of Commerce, Bureau of the Census, *Census Taken in the Year 1910*, Vol. I (Population), 94, 723, 729; Vol. 3 (Population), 480.

11. Department of Commerce, Bureau of the Census, *Census Taken in the Year 1910*, Vol. 9 (Manufactures), 1001, 1004, 1006, 1013.

12. Oklahoma Department of Labor, *Fourth Annual Report* (1910–1911), 134–47.

13. Department of Commerce, Bureau of the Census, *Census Taken in the Year 1910*, Vol. 3 (Population), 480.

14. See any issue of the Oklahoma *Labor Unit* during 1911.

15. Keith L. Bryant, Jr., "Labor in Politics: The Oklahoma State Federation of Labor in the Age of Reform" *Labor History*, 11:3 (Summer 1970), 268, 273–74.

16. Oklahoma *Labor Unit*, November 20, 1909.

17. For the events and results of the strike seen from three different points of view, see the Oklahoma City *Times*, March 6–13, 1911; Oklahoma *Labor Unit*, March 4, 11, 18, 1911; and the Oklahoma *Pioneer*, March 4, 11, 18, 1911.

18. Oklahoma *Labor Unit*, March 11, 18, 1911.

19. Oklahoma *Pioneer*, March 18, 1911; Oklahoma *Labor Unit*, March 25, 1911.

20. *Daily Oklahoman*, May 10, 1910; Oklahoma City *Times*, May 7, 1910. The *Daily Oklahoman's* "official" results listed the totals as 2259 "yes" and 2310 "no." By my own calculation, the total vote, obtained by adding the individual precinct votes, was 4394, not the 4569 published in the newspaper. The "yes" vote, based upon the precinct totals, was 2147, not 2259; the "no" vote was 2247, not 2310.

   Unfortunately the City Clerk's office has retained no records of precinct results and boundary lines for the 1910 and 1911 elections. Thus we must rely solely upon newspaper tabulations of voting results and the reporter's vague characterizations of wards as "silk stocking" (the seventh) or "working class" (the third, fourth, and eighth, all on the south side of the city). Such are the perils of doing political research in a city where the official records are not merely incomplete but positively scarce!

21. Oklahoma *Labor Unit*, April 30, 1910.

22. Oklahoma City *Times*, October 25. 1910.

23. Oklahoma City *Times*, November 6, 22, 1910.

24. Oklahoma *Pioneer*, January 28, February 18, 1911.

25. Oklahoma *Labor Unit*, March 4, 11, 1911.

26. Oklahoma City *Times*, March 8, 1911.

27. Voting results can be found in the *Daily Oklahoman*, May 10, 1910, and March 10, 1911.

28. Department of Commerce, Bureau of the Census, *Census Taken in the Year 1910*, Vol. 3 (Population), 450.

29. Oklahoma *Labor Unit*, April 8, 1911; Oklahoma *Pioneer*, April 8, 1911.

30. Ibid.

31. Oklahoma *Labor Unit*, May 6, 1911.

32. Oklahoma *Pioneer*, March 18, 25, 1911 through May 13, 1911.

33. Ibid., May 8, 1911.

34. *Daily Oklahoman*, May 8, 1911. Neither newspaper nor manuscript evidence reveals the ethnic background and social character of Socialist leaders and followers. Three of the five Socialist candidates in May, 1911, had German names. But on an earlier city ticket, only six of sixteen Socialist candidates had German names. Oklahoma City *Times*, March 10, 1911.

35. Oklahoma *Labor Unit*, May 6, 1911.

36. *Daily Oklahoman*, May 10, 1911.

37. The coefficient of correlation between the 1911 Socialist vote and the 1910 anti-commission government vote was .61; and between the Socialist vote and the

1911 anticommission government vote, .46.

38. Oklahoma *Labor Unit*, May 13, 1911.

39. Oklahoma *Labor Unit*, April 22, 1911. Under the heading, "Have put up strong ticket," the editors of the *Labor Unit* described the five Democratic candidates as successful businessmen and bankers connected with large business and property interests in the city.

40. Oklahoma *Labor Unit*, May 13, 1911.

41. Oklahoma *Pioneer*, May 20, 1911.

42. Oklahoma City *Times*, February 6, 1912, and April 27, 1914. The value of postal receipts was a favorite editorial device for measuring business activity. In 1914 the *Times* editor presented the following progression as a sign of "steady growth:" 1907—$180,153; 1908—$202,149; 1909—$261,191; 1910—$355,393; 1911—$370,232; 1912—$372,468; 1913—$377,570.

43. *Social Democrat* (Oklahoma City), July 9, 1913. The decline in the *number* of union members can be traced in the fourth and fifth annual reports of the Oklahoma Department of Labor.

44. Oklahoma *Labor Unit*, December 23, 1911. For the controversy over the "closed shop" campaign mounted by Socialists and other militants, see the Oklahoma *Labor Unit*, December 2, 9, 16, 23, 1911, and January 13, 1912. For the Socialist version of the insurgency, see the Oklahoma *Pioneer*, December 2, 23, 1911, and January 6, 27, 1912.

45. Oklahoma *Labor Unit*, August 5, December 23, 1911; March 1, April 12, May 17, 24, 31, June 14, 1913; February 14, 1914; Oklahoma *Pioneer*, July 1, November 4, December 23, 1911; *Daily Oklahoman*, December 17, 1911.

MICHAEL H. EBNER

5. SOCIALISM AND PROGRESSIVE POLITICAL REFORM: The 1911 Change-of-Government in Passaic

The reorganization of municipal governments, a central feature of urban progressivism, raises fundamental questions regarding political reform.[1] Samuel P. Hays, in a widely discussed study of the subject, has contended that despite the reformers' utilization of the ideology of democratized local government, in reality they aimed to limit rather than expand broad-based participation in the decision-making process. Labelling the proponents of this aspect of the movement "structural" (as contrasted with social") reformers, Melvin G. Holli believes that they represented ". . . the first wave of prescriptive municipal government which placed its faith in rule by educated, upper-class Americans and, later, by municipal experts rather than lower classes."[2]

Among the most articulate critics of the movement to restructure municipal governments were the spokesmen for the Socialist party. "Their fears and opposition," writes James Weinstein in *The Corporate Ideal in the Liberal State,* "came from the belief that [new] charters would, by design or not, eliminate workers or their representatives from active participation in the process of government."[3] Utilizing the setting of Passaic, New Jersey, where a successful campaign to change its government occurred in 1911, this study examines the role of the local Socialists in terms of the socio-political system there. Quite necessarily, attention will focus on the factors which differentiated socialism from progressivism.

In seeking to understand the failure of the Socialist party (SP) in the United States, its relationship to the new immigrants, who figured largely in Passaic's political system, has aroused considerable discussion. Gabriel Kolko once cited Trotsky's caustic quip to the effect that the SP was a party of dentists. Conversely, it has been argued by James Weinstein that Socialists of working-class and trade-union backgrounds played influential political roles at the municipal level, while party members drawn from the middle class possessed genuine empathy for those who toiled with their bodies.[4]

To be sure, as Paul Buhle observes in his reinterpretation of Debsian socialism, by 1910 the party confronted "certain fundamental choices" on how best to expand its base. Continued participation in political democracy was only one option, while the other was to eschew such involvements in order to concentrate primarily on organizing the industrial proletariat. Weinstein contends that the Socialist party's continuing devotion to the electoral process constituted its most likely strategy in its pursuit of American society's loyalties, whereas the alternative, as embodied in the activities of the Industrial Workers of the World, afforded too limited an approach. He writes, "While the romantic appeal of the Wobblies has triumphed in literature and history, as a social force the IWW did not approach the Socialist party in its impact on contemporary American life." Recent monographs by William M. Dick and Sally M. Miller reaffirm that the dilemma identified by Buhle stood central to the crisis of American socialism in the pre-World War era.[5]

Organized anticapitalistic politics dated back to 1879 in Passaic, when a branch of the Socialist Labor party (SLP) was formed. Throughout the eighties it remained all but invisible, although in the depression of the mid-nineties the party developed a small coterie of followers, corresponding with the efforts for its national revitalization undertaken by Daniel DeLeon. Locally its peak came in the gubernatorial contest of 1895, when the SLP candidate polled 2.9 percent of the city-wide vote, as contrasted with 2.3 percent in the congressional election of 1894 and .2 percent in the presidential canvass of 1892. Thereafter, as a result of a doctrinal schism in 1898, its fortunes diminished as they did elsewhere. Nevertheless, in the presidential election of 1900 the SLP outpolled its fledgling rival, the Social Democratic party, taking 1.1 percent of the local votes, as contrasted with .5 percent. By 1904, however, the newly formed Socialist Party of America, organized three years earlier, polled 3 percent more than the SLP in amassing 4.1 percent of the votes locally in that year's presidential election; in fact, even the remnant of the Populist party, fielding a national ticket for the last time, outdrew the SLP in the city by .3 percent. In the next nonlocal election for which data exists, the presidential race of 1912, the SP ticket of Eugene V. Debs, in winning 6.1 percent of the votes city-wide, increased its margin over the SLP slate of electors by 5.8 percent.[6]

Although the evidence is inconclusive, the Socialist Party of America apparently organized its Local Passaic in 1904 and the party sponsored

117

candidates in that year's municipal elections, as well as in succeeding contests. Its platforms went substantially beyond the political and social ideas expressed by progressives in Passaic, although certain issues converged with the most advanced reforms advocated nationally. The SP advocated the establishment of public parks and playgrounds, additional public baths in congested neighborhoods, upgraded surface transit, as well as "universal" transfers for passengers, intensified supervision of tenement dwellings, a hospital for tubercular patients, a dispensary to provide health-care services for the impoverished, and municipal ownership of public utilities. In the mayoralty contest of 1909 the party's candidate, David S. Webster, a trade unionist, scored his Republican and Democratic counterparts; both had supported "retrenchment" in municipal expenditures which occurred after Mayor Frederick R. Low, an avowed "New Idea" Republican Progressive, left office. Webster declared, "This means that the workers get nothing." In 1910, when the Socialist candidate for councilman-at-large was John Luthringer, Jr., also an active trade unionist, he alluded to the recent election of Emil Seidel as Socialist mayor of Milwaukee, and proclaimed that "In six short months Milwaukee has come to be known as the most efficiently governed city in the United States."[7]

One aspect of the Socialist platform of 1909 that deserves particular scrutiny is David Webster's call for concerted attention to the problems of *Dundee,* the immigrant and factory district in the First Ward of Passaic. Admitting that a "complete solution" of Dundee's problems would require "a complete reconstruction of society," he contended that "A Socialist council would reclaim land . . . tear down unsanitary tenements and in their place, build clean, sun-lighted model homes to be rented to the poor at or near the cost of maintenance." Tied to this program for renewal of housing, however, was Webster's statement on the saloon issue, which may very well have earned him more enmity than approbation from the predominantly eastern European population in Dundee. Scoring the existence of saloons there, he proposed that the "warmth, music, and companionship" provided by them be relocated in social centers, free from the "fearful price" patrons paid for beer and liquor. Notably, in Milwaukee the Socialist platform of 1910 opposed anti-liquor legislation, realizing its potency as a divisive factor.[8]

In order to fully comprehend the relationship of the Socialist party to the 1911 change-of-government process, it is essential to examine at least cursorily the socio-economic structure of Passaic. Into the 1850s it had been a sleepy, almost obsolete, village known as Acquakcanonk Landing. Not formally incorporated as a village until 1869, and achieving the status of a city four years later, it developed rapidly into a small industrial center that specialized in the manufacture of textile-related goods, espe-

118

cially woolen and worsted products. By 1900 it ranked fourth nationally in the value of its annual output of worsted. In 1912 almost one of every two of the nearly 22,000 industrial workers in Passaic and nearby Garfield were employed in the worsted mills, with an additional 22.5 percent in allied textile areas; the greatest nontextile employer was the rubber industry.[9]

Demographically the year 1910 constituted a benchmark in the city's growth. Its population had tripled in the decade from 1870 to 1880 to 6,532, and in each of three succeeding decadal periods it doubled, reaching 54,773 in 1910; thereafter the pace slowed markedly, with the city showing a small decrease in the 1920 to 1930 period. In 1910 only 13.8 percent of Passaic's residents were native-born whites of native parentage, while 33.2 percent were second generation Americans, and 52 percent were foreign-born; another 1 percent of the population was black. Immigrants from southern and eastern Europe, the so-called *new* immigration— from Russia, Austria-Hungary, and Italy—made up nearly four of every five among its foreign-born; the principal groups of *old* immigrants were the Irish, English, Scotch, German, and Dutch.

Physically a small city, Passaic covers only 3.25 square miles. At the time of its incorporation as a village it had been subdivided into three wards, and subsequently, as shown on the following map, a fourth was drawn in 1887. The First and Fourth Wards composed the eastside of the city, with the Second and Third Wards making up its westside. In 1910 the largest segment of foreign-born residents (53.3 percent of the city's 28,467) were in the First Ward, while the heaviest concentration of native-born whites of native parentage (33.5 percent of 7,536) were in the Third Ward. The other eastside ward, the Fourth, included the largest number of second generation Americans (39.1 percent of 18,209), making it a "zone of emergence" for the offsprings of the *old* immigrants.[10] The population of the Second Ward, which runs north-to-south through the center of the city, combined elements of Wards Three and Four in terms of its population composition, and also included 60.9 percent of the 535 black residents.

A mode of analysis for viewing the arrangement of Passaic's population in 1910 is the index of dissimilarity, which measures the extent to which a certain group is found in a particular ward in larger quantity than its proportion to the total population. An index of .000 signifies absolute integration of a given group throughout the four wards, and 1.00 denotes total segregation.[11]

Applying this method, several conclusions can be drawn. As Table 1 illustrates, the second generation ethnics had the lowest index, .071, meaning that they enjoyed the widest dispersion. Conversely, the Austrian-born

119

TABLE 6-1

Passaic's Population in 1910

Index of Dissimil- arity	Group	Percent of City's Tot. Pop.	Ward 1	Ward 2	Ward 3	Ward 4
.071	NBW/FoMP[a]	33.3%	8,739	2,748	1,609	7,113
.097	Italian	5.4	1,454	379	60	1,079
.157	French	.1	12	17	7	22
.187	Roumanian	.1	15	19	6	6
.205	misc. FB[b]	.4	47	45	52	88
.221	Irish	2.0	152	210	169	548
.222	Russian	7.2	1,551	124	65	2,202
.254	Hungarian	11.9	4,104	49	56	2,325
.314	Oriental	.1	5	8	0	13
.320	German	3.8	266	263	177	1,391
.338	Scotch	.8	30	154	69	168
.355	Swiss	.1	4	16	17	40
.380	English	1.3	57	252	193	221
.407	Swedish	.3	7	51	56	52
.434	Dutch	2.3	94	643	185	325
.470	NBW/NP[c]	13.8	245	2,337	2,523	2,431
.473	Black	1.0	91	326	48	70
.512	Canadian	.3	7	49	60	29
.520	Austrian	16.0	7,386	49	59	1,254

SOURCE: *Thirteenth Census of the United States, 1910,* Vol. 3, *Population,*
Washington: (G.P.O., 1913), 153.
a. Native-born white of foreign or mixed parentage
b. Miscellaneous foreign-born
c. Native-born white of native parentage

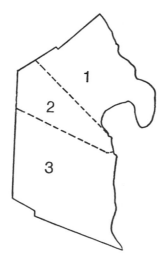

PASSAIC
1869 – 1887

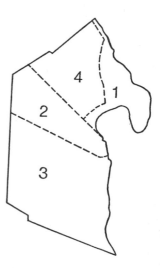

PASSAIC
1887 – 1967

(an ambiguous census category in 1910 that includes Poles, Slovaks, other Slavs, and Jews), constituting Passaic's largest bloc of immigrants, with 16 percent of the total population, were segregated to a greater degree than any other grouping, .520; the First Ward contained 84.4 percent of the 8,748 Austrian-born, with another 14.3 percent in the Fourth Ward, and the remaining 1.3 percent on the westside. The native-born whites of native parentage were also highly segregated, having an index of .470; two of every three in this group lived in either the Second or Third Ward, and in the latter they made up almost half of its population.[12]

The political system of Passaic reflected its socio-economic structure. The Republican party epitomized local progress and prosperity, as well as respectability and responsibility, extending back to the 1860s. As industrialization took hold by the early seventies, the pioneer mill owners quickly gained acceptance within its ranks. Beginning in the nineties, as the impact of the new immigration intensified, virtually every campaign included appeals to the residents of the First Ward to vote wisely and as Americans, which could be equated with the casting of Republican ballots. No opportunity was lost to remind ethnic voters that their continued employment in the textile mills depended upon a "sound," tariff-protected economy.[13]

The dominant role of the Republicans in Passaic is better understood when political behavior is placed within a geographical context. The bulwark of the party's strength was on the westside of the city, be it a race for the mayoralty, governorship, congress, or the presidency. Except for the mayoralty contest of 1885, when the Republicans abandoned their own nominee as a result of an intraparty division, neither the Second nor Third Wards ever voted Democratic majorities in forty-four contested elections between 1879 and 1912. What Democratic strength existed came from the eastside, particularly the First Ward. Only the allegiance of the Fourth Ward—the city's "zone of emergence"—reflected a more complex pattern. Its electorate started moving away from the Republican column in the congressional election of 1902, and by the period 1910 to 1912 voters there produced Democratic victories in the gubernatorial and presidential races as well as two congressional contests.[14]

By the close of the nineteenth century, therefore, Passaic's sociopolitical fabric had begun to endure stresses. Labor disorders became increasingly prevalent, with the *new* immigrants beginning to reveal their disgruntled feelings. The frequency of such unrest corresponded with the emergence of the Democratic party as a legitimate rival to the Republicans. In 1904 the Fourth Ward elected a Democratic councilman for only the second time since its organization in 1887; significantly, this newly elected official was Jewish, thereby becoming the first *new* ethnic to gain a seat on the city's governing body, and thus advancing the function of the ward as

121

the "zone of emergence." In 1906 another Democrat from that ward, William A. Reid, a second generation American of Irish Protestant parentage, was elected assessor in a city-wide contest, and his reelection three years later marked the first time that a candidate of his party won consecutive terms in an at-large contest; as will be discussed elsewhere in more detail, a partial explanation of his success was the fact that his Democratic affiliation was offset by his Protestantism. Still a further manifestation of the changing political locus appeared in 1910, when two Democratic councilmen of Slavic birth, Edward J. Levendusky and John L. Labash, were elected in the First Ward; importantly, those who had represented the ward heretofore were Democrats of *old* ethnic backgrounds.[15]

At the same time that Democrats in Passaic enjoyed an upsurge, throughout New Jersey the Republican party was experiencing an internal challenge akin to the nation-wide Progressive reform movement. Beginning in 1901 with the election of insurgent Mark Fagan as mayor of Jersey City, the so-called "New Idea" movement reached Passaic County in early 1906. Its objectives included political reforms, such as fair elections, the end of corruption, the elimination of boss control in the Republican party, and the direct election of United States Senators, as well as a host of economic proposals—most of them based on the lessons of Fagan's administration—such as equal taxation and the limitation of franchise grants.[16]

Although the "New Idea" ebbed statewide after 1906, in Passaic it continued to make inroads. Its candidate in the mayoralty primary of 1907, Frederick R. Low, successfully contested the nomination, defeating Bird W. Spencer, the city's foremost Republican politician and the mayor of Passaic for three consecutive terms from 1879 until 1885. For purposes of this analysis, it is especially important to understand the strengths and weaknesses of reform Republicans who sought nomination or election in Passaic between 1906 and 1909. As Table 2 reveals, the candidates of the "New Idea" movement failed to attract sustained support, particularly in First Ward. Even at the peak of Low's popularity, in the mayoralty primary of 1907, the "New Idea" cause did not win a majority of the Republican votes in that ward; likewise, citizens in the Fourth Ward began moving away from the reform camp after that primary. Moreover, as the 1908 data in the general election indicates, when eastside voters were confronted with a split Republican slate for the assembly—a reformer and four "regulars"—they rejected the "New Idea" candidate. Undeniably, the greatest appeal of the Republican reformers was on the westside.[17]

The electoral strength of the Socialist party was based in the Fourth Ward. Of the 3,859 votes cast in the mayoralty election of 1909, David Webster, the SP candidate, received 103, a mere 2.6 percent of the total. The successful Republican nominee, Spencer, won 63.4 percent city-wide,

122

TABLE 6-2
"New Idea" Support, 1906–1909

	Ward 1	Ward 2	Ward 3	Ward 4	CITY
1906 County Primary	24.6	66.6	72.5	50.6	55.7
1907 Mayoralty Primary	49.1	63.1	74.7	62.8	63.8
1907 Mayoralty*	48.2	68.8	80.4	49.4	59.6
1908 Assembly Primary	31.1	53.6	70.6	44.5	52.5
1908 Assembly*					
"New Idea" Republican	8.2	14.7	16.6	10.9	12.5
Regular Republicans[a]	9.65	14.65	15.85	11.3	12.7
Democratic[b]	12.9	5.95	4.45	9.4	8.2
1909 Mayoralty Primary	16.3	32.4	49.3	35.3	35.8

a. median vote for four "regular" Republicans
b. median vote for five Democrats
* All computations based upon two-party votes

TABLE 6-3
Socialist Parties Support, 1892-1912
(Percentage of Total Votes)

Election	Ward 1	Ward 2	Ward 3	Ward 4	CITY
1892 President SLP	.8	.1	.3	.5	.2
1894 Congress SLP	4.3	1.0	1.1	2.3	2.3
1895 Governor SLP	6.3	1.4	.5	2.4	2.9
1896 President SLP	1.5	.2	.0	1.0	.8
1900 PRESIDENT					
SLP	1.7	.7	.1	1.4	1.1
SDP	.6	.5	.1	.9	.5
1904 PRESIDENT					
SLP	1.8	.4	.4	1.5	1.1
SP	6.5	2.8	1.7	4.5	4.1
1909 Mayor SP	2.2	1.0	2.1	4.4	2.6
1912 PRESIDENT					
SLP	.4	.4	.1	.3	.3
SP	6.2	5.7	2.1	8.7	6.1

123

carrying all four wards. Importantly, 55.9 percent of the Socialist votes came from the Fourth Ward. Likewise, in 1910 the Fourth Ward provided John Luthringer with his strongest support in the race for councilman-at-large, and again in 1912 for Eugene Debs in the presidential contest. This pattern, as noted in Table 3, reflected a shift in the strength of the party, in that until 1904 the First Ward had been its greatest source of votes; surely this resulted from the exodus of *old* immigrants and their offsprings out of Dundee, and into the "zone of emergence." Local leaders recognized this, launching a literature distribution campaign in the Fourth Ward midway through 1910, akin to the so-called "bundle brigades" which canvassed key electoral districts in Milwaukee to deliver the message of its Social Democrats, hoping that their efforts would yield similar success in Passaic.[18]

By early 1911, throughout New Jersey attention focused on the question of wholesale reform of municipal government. Since 1869 Passaic's local government was decentralized and partisan, reflecting nineteenth-century misgivings over too broad an administrative authority being vested in a single executive or legislative body. Although the mayor was elected city-wide, he possessed limited powers; in addition, an assessor and tax collector were elected at-large, further diminishing the executive prerogatives of the chief executive. The council was elected by wards, although beginning in 1896 a single councilman-at-large was also elected to serve as the presiding officer of that branch. Until 1908 the board of education was elected in ward, partisan contests; then, as the result of a referendum supported by Mayor Low, the format was altered, with school trustees being appointed by the mayor in an effort to overcome localism and politics in educational affairs. Notably, the most significant opponent of this change was Edward J. Levendusky, the First Ward Democrat, whose election to the school board in 1906 had put the first Slavonic into a consequential public office. Although fradulent ballots had left the referendum in doubt for several months, the final count gave 53.3 percent of the vote to the proposition; only the First Ward electorate opposed the change, with a bare 19.9 percent supporting it.[19]

Some seventeen days prior to taking his fourth oath of office as mayor, on January 1, 1910, Bird Spencer established an informal charter revision committee. He authorized the body to prepare recommendations as to how municipal government could be refashioned so as to make it more responsive to the public. He had chosen an apt moment to take a reform stance. Like Frank Hague in 1913, who favored governmental reform in Jersey City two years after he had opposed the same proposal, Spencer seemingly recognized that Passaic would be affected by the state-wide campaign to modernize municipal administration. Rather than be controlled by circumstances, he set out to master them.[20]

The favorite alternative of the reformers was the commission form that first had gained notice when adopted in Galveston, Texas, in 1901, and then in Des Moines, Iowa, in 1907. "The most essential and fundamental features . . ." said an official from Des Moines in speaking to an audience in Passaic, "are the eliminating of ward and party lines, the concentration of power and responsibility in a single body of five officials elected by the people of a united city, and the introduction of direct legislation." Under the Walsh-Leavitt Act, passed by the New Jersey legislature in April 1911, municipal administration was divided among five *commissioners*, each of whom was to serve as a *director* of a specific department, such as revenue and finance, public affairs, public works, public safety, and parks and recreation. One of the five board members was designated by his fellow commissioners as mayor, although the office lacked any veto power. "From the standpoint of pure business administration," wrote Charles A. Beard in his *American City Government,* published in 1912, "the commission form of government has many features to commend it." As in Des Moines, elections under New Jersey's enabling legislation were to be conducted along nonpartisan, city-wide lines, but each municipality in the state was left to decide in a referendum whether or not to adopt the commission plan.[21]

Although Mayor Spencer had provided Passaic's change-of-government movement with its initial impetus, by early summer, 1911, he had lost control of the local situation. Rather, those in the forefront of the campaign to win the referendum scheduled for late July were associated with the local Board of Trade, which had organized its own charter review panel independent of Spencer's. The competing study groups divided over the mayor's insistence that the authority of the chief executive under the proposed format should exceed that of the other four commissioners. Over time this difference intensified. (This was inevitable, perhaps, given Spencer's past presidency of the State Board of Assessors, a regulatory agency that generally was acknowledged to be subservient to railroad interests seeking protection of their tax shelters, and his employment as a tax agent of the gas and electric utility conglomerate, the Public Service Corporation, both of which excited the ire of New Jersey reformers.) In fact, the day after New Jersey's Governor Woodrow Wilson, a strong (if belated) proponent of the Walsh-Leavitt Act, spoke to an audience of 1,200 in the city, Mayor Spencer openly disclaimed that he was covertly opposing approval of the commission government format.[22]

The most vocal and persistent opposition to the referendum question emanated from Local Passaic of the Socialist party. In mid-December 1910, as the Board of Trade made plans for a public lecture on commission

125

government, David Webster, by then the city's most active Socialist, unsuccessfully proposed, "In order to give the citizens of Passaic a fair opportunity to judge the desirability of such a change in government, I would . . . suggest that an opposition lecturer be allowed to present arguments at the same public meeting." As the referendum approached, Dr. Morris Korshet, a physician who was the party's leading theoretician, observed that "The same men that are now dominant in the old parties will, without doubt, be candidates for the commission government if installed." He also added, as Socialists would in Milwaukee when confronted by a similar situation in 1914, that since political awareness and party cohesion were in the best interests of the working classes, the introduction of nonpartisanship would have a dilatory effect on the future of political socialism in the community. Another party spokesman, Israel Mufson, added that "Under the commission plan one-third of the city will control the other two-thirds." What these critics did not raise, however, was the more conceptual issue of the actual operational deficiencies in the commission format.[23]

With the referendum on change-of-government going down to defeat elsewhere in New Jersey during the early summer of 1911, efforts to achieve passage in Passaic grew especially intense. As the balloting drew near, a publicity campaign was mounted to persuade the voters to support the change. To afford the movement a nonpartisan legitimacy, a Commission Government League was organized with bipartisan, city-wide backing. Importantly, its principal spokesman was a real estate agent, Charles F.H. Johnson, who also served as the secretary of the Passaic Board of Trade. (Johnson was on the brink of a dynamic career in the civic and industrial affairs of the city that would culminate with twenty-three years as the president of Botany Worsted Mills, the leading textile producer locally until its departure from the city after the Second World War.)[24]

The Commission Government League was sustained largely by the industrial community, although its leadership successfully projected it as a city-wide effort. Corporate donations came from several firms engaged in textile and rubber production, while additional funds were provided by individuals involved in the executive management of the industries; when a deficit existed at the end of the campaign it was cleared by Peter Reid, Passaic's pioneer industrialist and philanthropist. Beyond these major gifts the League made much of the single dollar contributions received from throughout the city, listing the names of small donors along with those of more prominent subscribers. Also, the League's ranks were ideologically inclusive enough to include persons who had been associated with the local "New Idea" Republicans. (No evidence has been found, however, on the stance of Frederick Low, the former "New Idea" mayor; his counterpart in Jersey City, Mark Fagan, subsequently gave reluctant support to

126

the adoption of commission government there, actually returning to the mayoralty—after a hiatus of six years—in 1913 under the new form.)[25]

On July 25 better than two of every three (67.6 percent) of those voting in the referendum cast "yes" ballots for the change-of-government. In the Third Ward the pro-change tally reached 86.4 percent, followed by 76.2 in the Second Ward, and 64.7 percent in the Fourth; only in the First Ward did the electorate oppose the question, with just 31.1 percent voting affirmatively. Notably, only 53.2 percent of Passaic's registered voters (as of October 30, 1910) participated in the special election, with the highest turnout in the Third Ward (57.8 percent) and the lowest in the Fourth (50.9 percent); by contrast, in the balloting for governor in 1910, 84.7 percent of the registered voters had cast either Republican or Democratic choices, and in the presidential election of 1912 the figure reached 86.3 percent for the combined Republican, Democratic, Progressive, and minor party slates. Still, to the reform-minded Jersey City editor and ardent proponent of the Walsh-Leavitt Act's implementation throughout the state, Joseph A. Dear, the successful campaign in Passaic appeared "hard and intelligent."[26]

Sixty-two candidates filed for election in the initial contest for Passaic's Board of Commissioners. First came a primary, and then the top ten vote-getters contested for the five positions in a runoff. Forty-one of the primary entries were registered Republicans, and twenty-seven of them resided in either the Second or Third Wards. An additional sixteen candidates were Democrats, nine of whom were from the west side. Five Socialists also filled positions, all of them Fourth Ward residents. In all, the Second Ward made the largest contribution of candidates, twenty-one, and the smallest number, six, hailed from First Ward. Officially, only the name of the candidate, listed alphabetically, appeared on the ballot, minus any partisan or residential identification.[27]

TABLE 6-4
1911 Commission Candidates by Party and Residence

	Ward 1	Ward 2	Ward 3	Ward 4	CITY
Republican	2	14	13	12	41
Democratic	4	7	2	3	16
Socialist	0	0	0	5	5
Totals	6	21	15	20	62

The five Socialist aspirants were David S. Webster, John Luthringer, Jr., Albert Weyse, Jacob Bromberg, and Solomon Menaker. Special efforts were made to push Webster's candidacy. As already noted, both Webster and Luthringer were active unionists, the former as a Linotype operator

127

and the latter as a machinist; indeed, when the Passaic Trades & Labor Council was founded in December 1910 by an alliance of ten local unions, nine of them affiliated with the American Federation of Labor, it was Luthringer who was elected as its first president, with Webster named a trustee.[28] Menaker was a "manufacturer," the nature of which is unclear; Bromberg was listed as a "secretary," and Weyse a painter. Both Webster and Luthringer were native-born, the former of Scottish ancestry and the latter of French and Swiss stocks; Weyse was a native of Germany. Information on Bromberg and Menaker is not available, but it appears likely that both were Jews of either Austrian or Russian backgrounds.

Social data on the other candidates also is revealing. Of thirty-nine Republicans for whom data exists, 33 percent were native born of native parentage, as contrasted with 28 percent among the fourteen Democrats. Another 35.7 percent of those Democrats were second generation, while in the Republican case the figure was 35.8 percent; in each instance these second generation Americans had parents of *old* ethnic stocks, although four of the five Democrats were Irish Catholics, the remaining one being Irish Protestant, while among fourteen Republicans there were four Irish Catholics and a like number of Germans, three Englishmen, two Hollanders, and one Irish Protestant. Of the five foreign-born Democrats, four of them were from lands associated with the *new* immigration; conversely, among the ten Republicans of foreign birth, only two were from southern or eastern Europe.

Occupationally, it was significant that of seven lawyers who sought election to the Board of Commissioners, six were Republicans. Likewise the lone physician in the race was Republican. In terms of commercial pursuits, distinctions between Republicans and Democrats, as well as the five Socialists, become less clear, although to some extent the fault lies in the nature of the available data. Republicans boasted three real estate agents, as contrasted to one Democrat. The Republicans included the lone "janitor" among the sixty-two candidates. Both Democrats and Republicans counted a single mill foreman, undertaker, and saloon keeper. One Democrat, Levendusky of the First Ward, was a civil engineer, but the Republicans included three engineers in their ranks. Three Republicans listed themselves as retired, but no Democrat was in that category. Both parties included manual tradesmen, i.e., plasterers, painters, masons, inkmakers.

The actual electioneering in the 1911 campaign focused on the integrity of the candidates and their reputations as public servants. The Socialists, however, propounded their ideas on the issues, placing special emphasis on Passaic's urban-ethnic composition. "Should the people of Passaic confer upon me the honor of electing me as commissioner," Solomon Menaker promised, "I would devote my utmost effort to make our city—for

128

the Poles, Hungarians, Italians, Germans, Jews and Irish—a place whose fame would resound in all the countries whence these people came. . . ." Speaking of "the great number of foreign workers . . . who fill our mills and factories" as "the great asset that Passaic possesses," Menaker added, "I would appropriate the greatest part of the city's budget for the improvement of the health and comfort of these people." Candidate Webster sounded a similar note, observing that, "If elected, I would consider that I represent the 30,000 working people of this city."[29]

The election results confirmed the misgivings of the commission government opponents. In the sixty-two candidate primary field the strongest race made by any of the five Socialists was Webster's thirteenth place finish, forty-one votes behind the tenth place, which disqualified him from the runoff; in fact, Webster was the only one to finish higher than twentieth, as Tables 5 and 9 indicate. Eight of the ten candidates in the runoff were Republicans; all but one of these eight, moreover, resided on Passaic's westside, with three from the Second Ward, four from the Third Ward, and the remaining Republican from the Fourth Ward. Importantly, the two Democratic finalists were from the First and Fourth Wards.

The fate of Councilman Levendusky in the primary and runoff is particularly instructive. The Slavonic Democrat was the only candidate residing in the First Ward to attain a runoff position, having placed seventh in the primary. In his own ward he led the primary field, while in the Fourth he finished sixth, in the Second he was nineteenth, and in the Third was twenty-ninth. Subsequently he placed sixth in the runoff, missing the fifth position by a margin of seventeen votes. Again, as Table 6 indicates, he had run first in his own ward, third in the Fourth, but in the Third Ward placed eighth and in the Second ninth. Of his total vote in the runoff, only 32.5 percent was drawn from the westside, the least of the ten candidates on the ballot; the five victors collected totals from the Second and Third Wards combined ranging between 37.9 and 57.3 percents.

The newly elected Board of Commissioners was made up of three men residing in the Third Ward—George N. Seger, J. Hosey Osborne, and Adrian D. Sullivan—and two from the Fourth—John Kehoe and William A. Reid. Only Reid was a Democrat by prior affiliation, the remaining four being Republicans. The board was Protestant except for Sullivan, an Irish Catholic. Levendusky had been the only new ethnic, as well as First Ward resident, to survive the primary. The leading Jewish candidate, Philip Richmond, finished twelfth, thirty-nine votes short of making the runoff, and the only Italian entry in the field of sixty-two, Dominick DeMuro, placed fifty-first. Thus, the Jewish and Slavic communities, each of which had gained direct representation in municipal government through participation

129

TABLE 6-5
1911 Commission Election Primary
(Top Twenty Candidates)

CANDIDATE RANK CITY-WIDE	RANKINGS BY WARDS			
	Ward 1	Ward 2	Ward 3	Ward 4
1. Kehoe R4	7	1	6	1
2. Seger R3	17	2	1	3
3. Reid D4	5	4	7	2
4. Spencer R3	9	3	2	5
5. Sullivan R3	4	8	11	4
6. Osborne R3	27	7	4	8
7. Levendusky D1	1	19	29	6
8. Wise R2	40	6	3	20
9. Bredin R2	10	5	28	10
10. Bowes R2	30	11	13	12
11. Boyle D2	31	12	10	21
12. Richmond R4	3	36	38	11
13. Webster S4	12	25	23	7
14. Swan R2	14	13	17	13
15. Matthews R3	24	16	5	38
16. Coman R2	38	9	9	30
17. Schleich R3	15	28	21	9
18. Rose R3	16	22	8	25
19. Rosenberg D4	8	38	48	14
20. Greely D2	18	14	32	22

TABLE 6-6
1911 Commission Election Runoff

CANDIDATE RANK CITY-WIDE	RANKINGS BY WARD			
	Ward 1	Ward 2	Ward 3	Ward 4
1. Kehoe R4	2	1	2	1
2. Reid D4	4	2	5	2
3. Seger R3	7	3	1	5
4. Osborne R3	6	4	4	6
5. Sullivan R3	3	6	7	4
6. Levendusky D1	1	9	8	3
7. Wise R2	10	5	3	8
8. Spencer R3	8	8	6	9
9. Bredin R2	5	7	10	7
10. Bowes R2	9	10	9	10

in Democratic politics, lost their positions.[30]

The new commissioners fell into the usual range of commercial, entrepreneurial, and professional pursuits. Sullivan was a lawyer, Seger a retired building contractor, Kehoe owned a livery and trucking concern, and Osborne and Reid were insurance and realty brokers, although the latter had been a clerk in a textile mill for many years. A perceptible contrast existed occupationally between the new Board of Commissioners and the outgoing city council. The latter had not included a single lawyer; its makeup included two engineers, two construction firm heads, two salesmen, two saloon keepers, an undertaker, a mill foreman, and a man whose occupation was listed as "superintendent." Interestingly, as well, only one of the five commissioners, Sullivan, had never held elective office before, although he had been appointed as city attorney in 1899, serving until 1910, when he declined reappointment by Mayor Spencer.

The advent of commission government ended forever the elective career of Bird Spencer, the city's most durable politician. In the primary he had finished fourth, but in the runoff only eighth, failing to place higher than sixth in any ward. Although endorsed editorially by the *Passaic Daily News* (which proclaimed, "He knows the city's business methods from A to Z . . . "), the four-time mayor's prospects were severely undermined by a concerted effort launched by the Board of Trade to insure his defeat at the polls. While the reason for this determined anti-Spencer thrust cannot be explained precisely, it would appear that his difficulties with the business and industrial community stemmed from the divergence of opinions earlier in 1911 in the change-of-government movement. Ironically, Spencer, like the *new* ethnic politicians, found himself victimized by those seeking to reform municipal administration by eliminating partisanship and decentralization of authority.[31]

The statutory abolition of partisanship and ward representation did not necessarily alter the voting behavior of Passaic's electorate instantaneously. In both the primary and runoff elections the established pattern of Republican dominance of municipal contests was abundantly clear; the party's majorities in the First Ward underscored its influential role in local politics, as Table 7 reveals. Also, it is important to note that the First Ward, which in 1910 was the most populous, exercised the least influence in terms of its contribution to the total vote, as seen in Table 8. Moreover, although the changes are not significant statistically, it should be at least noted that the eastside wards, the First and Fourth, decreased their participation in the runoff.[32]

In the final analysis, however, it was the ethno-religious factor which loomed above all other considerations in the municipal elections of 1911. Adrian Sullivan's case affords a clear illustration. As already noted, he was

131

TABLE 6-7
1911 Commission Elections: Party Strength

Candidate	Ward 1	Ward 2	Ward 3	Ward 4	Total
Republican	55.4	73.8	83.3	62.7	68.4
Democratic	38.5	22.3	14.0	27.9	25.5
Socialist	6.1	3.9	2.7	9.4	6.1
RUNOFF					
Republican	68.8	81.1	82.7	73.6	76.7
Democratic	31.2	18.9	17.3	26.4	23.3

TABLE 6-8
1911 Commission Elections: Ward Distribution of Votes Cast

Ward	Total Population (1910)	Ward's % of T.P.	Ward's % of Total Votes Cast Primary	Ward's % of Total Votes Cast Runoff
1	22,266	40.6	14.5	14.3
2	7,719	14.1	26.2	27.0
3	5,411	9.9	21.4	22.1
4	19,377	35.4	37.9	36.6
Totals	54,773	100.0	100.0	100.0

TABLE 6-9
1911 Commission Election Primary: Socialist Candidates

Candidates	RANKINGS BY WARDS Ward 1	Ward 2	Ward 3	Ward 4	CITY
Bromberg	26	48	49	31	42
Luthringer	20	42	46	15	31
Menaker	25	47	44	28	36
Webster	12	25	23	7	13
Weyse	47	49	45	27	40
MEDIAN	27.5	37	36	19	27.5

a Roman Catholic of Irish stock, third generation American, who resided in the Third Ward and was a registered Republican. He ran fifth in both the primary and runoff. It was Sullivan's ethnicity, rather than his partisan affiliation or residency, that seemingly accounts for the fact that he ran better in the First and Fourth Wards than he did on the westside, as Tables 5 and 6 demonstrate; in the First Ward he placed fourth in the primary and third in the runoff, leading all other Republicans from the Second and Third Wards, and also surpassing William Reid, the Fourth Ward Democrat who was an Irish Protestant. By contrast, Reid ran ahead of Sullivan on the westside, indicating that his Democratic affiliation prior to 1911 must have been less objectionable to voters than Sullivan's Catholicism. For yet another successful office-seeker, George Seger, a different set of circumstances existed. A Third Ward Republican of German Protestant heritage, he placed second in the primary and third in the runoff; although he ran no lower than third in Wards Two, Three, and Four, in the First Ward he placed seventeenth among the primary entries, and in the runoff he ranked seventh.[33]

The election further revealed that the pattern persisted in which the First and Third Wards constituted Passaic's most divergent voting districts. Strictly in terms of partisanship the First Ward's total Republican primary vote was 27.9 percent lower than the Third Ward's as seen in Table 7. In the field of sixty-two candidates the top five recipients of votes in the Third Ward were Republicans, four of whom resided there, while the other lived in the adjacent Second Ward. In the First Ward, none of the five who finished among the winners in the Third Ward balloting ran as well there; second behind the frontrunning Levendusky in the primary was Councilman Labash, the Slavonic Democrat who placed thirty-third in the city-wide tally; in fact, Labash was the lone primary candidate who finished out of the top twenty but achieved a winning position in any of the ward returns. Reid was the only Protestant to rank in the top five in the First Ward, his strong identity as an established Democratic vote-getter obviously compensating for his religion; we have already seen that Sullivan was the lone resident of the westside among the first five in the ward. Finally, Philip Richmond, the Fourth Ward Republican, ranked third among the primary candidates in the First Ward, as contrasted with twelfth city-wide, which can best be attributed to his visibility as the leading Jewish entry in the election; in the Third Ward he placed thirty-eighth, and in the Second he was thirty-sixth, suggesting that his religion offset his partisan affiliation on the traditionally Republican westside of the city.[34]

The Fourth Ward, whose voters accounted for nearly four of every ten votes cast in the primary and runoff, continued to fulfill its role as a "zone of emergence." In the primary the five leading candidates in that ward corresponded to those who finished in the winning positions city-wide, although their order of placement did not match precisely. This suggests a cosmopolitan, as opposed to parochial, perspective on the part of its electorate, especially in contrast to the voting behavior of the First Ward. Actually, the electoral behavior of the Fourth Ward demonstrated its socializing function as a bridge that connected the First Ward to the westside of Passaic. The strongest candidate in the Third Ward, both in the primary and runoff, Seger, placed third and fifth respectively in the Fourth Ward returns; similarly, the leading First Ward candidate, Levendusky, placed sixth among primary candidates in the Fourth Ward, and advanced to third in the runoff. Interestingly, the leading candidate in the Fourth Ward, Kehoe, ran only seventh in the First Ward and sixth in the Third in the primary, although city-wide he placed first in both elections. Finally, it should be observed that the patterns of voting in the Second and Fourth Wards had more similarities than differences, a fact that lends credence to the gross political disparity between the First and Third Wards.[35]

The Fourth Ward also figured importantly in terms of the electoral strength, albeit limited, of the Socialist party. Its five candidates amassed 1,249 votes in the primary, 51 percent of them being cast there; of the remainder, the Second and Third Wards each produced 17.2 percent and the First Ward another 14.6 percent. Table 9 shows that Webster, Luthringer, and Weyse achieved their highest positions in the Fourth, whereas Menaker and Bromberg made their strongest showings in the First Ward; seemingly, the concentration of Jewish voters in the First Ward aided the candidacies of Menaker and Bromberg, just as it did for Philip Richmond. City-wide the median rank of the five Socialists was 27.5, the lowest ward median being 37 in the Second, and the highest being 19 in the Fourth Ward; the forty-nine place finishes by Weyse in the Second and Bromberg in the Third constituted the weakest performances by individual candidates.

"There is still a Socialist local here that is not yet dead," wrote Israel Mufson in the aftermath of the party's defeat in the election. He added that his fellow Socialists were not "angry" with the electorate, suggesting that, "They realize that you need more of an education on Socialist philosophy. . . ." In October 1911, soon after the runoff contest had been completed, a monthly tabloid, *The Issue,* was launched as "the official organ of the Socialist Party of Passaic, N.J." Its first number heralded the local speaking engagement of Congressman Victor L. Berger, the Milwaukee Socialist, whose electoral success in 1910, coupled with the advent of a Socialist municipal administration in that city, symbolized the promise of political achievement for the party's membership throughout the nation.[36]

The editorial thrust of *The Issue* focused on the socialist interpretation of municipal affairs. Its editor was none other than David Webster, the recently vanquished candidate for the Board of Commissioners. *"The Issue* wishes to bring Socialism to Passaic . . . . It wants to talk to you about the common things that happen on Main Street, or in the new commissioners' offices, or down in the First Ward," its initial editorial commentary proclaimed. As for the recently concluded municipal election, it reported, "The great mass of the working class of this city have been neatly eliminated from politics; businessmen are now completely in the saddle, and we are to have a businessman's government, which has no place for the workers or working class demands." In analyzing the five members of the newly elected local government, the socialist organ concluded, "And the mountain labored and brought forth—the same bunch of politicians."[37]

Foremost among the questions that remain is why the Socialists were unable to muster greater electoral opposition to the referendum. While historians correctly contend that this particular *reform* belied the democratizing features attributed to it by proponents, the foregoing analysis of the campaign to change the format of government in Passaic uncovers the beguiling nature of the rationale propounded in its favor. Unlike the range of socio-cultural and economic reforms sponsored by Progressive mayors, such as Frederick Low and Jersey City's Mark Fagan, backers of the Walsh-Leavitt Act in the city had only to proselytize a single issue, devoid of its being associated with an individual politician; indeed, the one politician who sought to personalize Passaic's change-of-government process—Mayor Spencer—found himself excluded, first from the referendum campaign and ultimately from public office. A major factor in the success of the movement, of course, was the Commission Government League, whose sponsors convincingly forged a highly visible, broad-based coalition in order to advance the prospects of the new format's adoption by the voters. Finally, the commission concept, both locally and nationally, had developed into something of a panacea, portending a rapid solution of an assortment of urban social and economic problems. Given this optimistic tone, it was relatively easy to convince the public of its worth, especially with the commercial and industrial sectors of the community rendering financial support to underwrite the pursuits of the League. As Christopher Lasch has written in *The Agony of the American Left*, "Even when they originated in humanitarian impulses, progressive ideas led not to a policy of liberation but to a blueprint for control."[38]

Another area of concern involves the orientation of the Socialists within Passaic's socio-economic setting. The evidence already presented appears to establish that by 1911 its constituency, in terms of electoral support, emanated primarily from the Fourth Ward. Nevertheless, as early as 1909, when David Webster campaigned for the mayoralty, the party endeavored to achieve inroads into the Dundee district of the First Ward, the

135

heartland of the *new* ethnic population; to be sure, in 1910 the victory of Mayor Seidel in Milwaukee was aided considerably by his ability to attract traditionally Democratic votes in a ward that was populated largely by Poles. Unquestionably, the Socialists in Passaic should have been gratified in July 1911, when 68.9 percent of those participating in the change-of-government referendum cast "no" votes. Yet, the slate of five candidates entered by the party in the following municipal election lacked a single resident of that ward, much less a representative of its large Slavic Catholic community. Instead, as already seen, the two *new* ethnic candidates of the Socialists were both Jewish.[39]

An explanation as to why this occurred remains largely inferential. Perhaps the Socialists did attempt to include a Slav on its slate in 1911, only to find their intentions thwarted. Certainly the success achieved by the Social-Democratic party of Milwaukee in 1910 had been preceded by nearly a decade of failures to gain substantial Polish electoral backing. Another dimension of the problem, aside from the fundamental, and often cited, cultural reasons which underscore this overall problem, has to do with the diminishing participation of the First Ward's residents in the political process. Although 40.7 percent of Passaic's population lived there in 1910, it contributed only 15.1 percent (754) of the 4,980 registered voters in the city, whereas the Third Ward, with just 9.9 percent of the total population residing there, accounted for 21.5 percent (1,072) of all voters; by contrast, in 1900, when 45.6 percent of the population resided in First Ward, it included 26.1 percent (1,252) of the 4,796 registered voters, while the Third Ward, with 12.4 percent of the city's population, provided 17.6 percent (845) of all voters. This appreciable decline in the electoral influence of the First Ward was caused, at least partially it would appear, by the changing nature of its population in terms of its social function as the inner urban core.[40]

The change-of-government campaign, and subsequent municipal election, illustrate the inherent limitations of socialism in Passaic. Although voters in the First and Fourth Wards, particularly the former, had opposed the candidates and ideas of "New Idea" Republicanism, it also remained difficult to harness convincing electoral support for the Socialist party, a movement which overtly appealed to class consciousness. Gabriel Kolko borrows from Thorstein Veblen to account for socialism's deficiency in its effort to alter American society, adducing "a class structure without decisive class conflict, a society that had conflict limited to smaller issues that were not critical to the existing order, and on which the price of satisfying opposition was relatively modest from the viewpoint of the continuation of the social system."[41]

In the end it seems logical to conclude, no less, that the critique offered by Socialists of the commission government concept afforded succor for the campaign to carry through that particular reform. Whereas the Commission Government League proffered a seemingly viable alternative to the existing form of municipal government, the Socialists offered nothing so concrete. Rather they simply resorted to the contention that the mayor-council plan better served the interests of the working class.

NOTES

1. Samuel P. Hays, "The Changing Political Structure of the City in Industrial America," *Journal of Urban History*, 1:1, (November, 1974), 6–38.
2. Samuel P. Hays, "The Politics of Reform in Municipal Government in the Progressive Era," *Pacific Northwest Quarterly* 55 (October 1964), 160; and Melvin G. Holli, *Reform in Detroit, Hazen S. Pingree and Urban Politics* (New York, 1969), p. 163. For a study of a similar effort to alter municipal governance, some forty years earlier, consult Douglas V. Shaw, "The Making of an Immigrant City: Ethnic and Cultural Conflict in Jersey City, New Jersey, 1850–1877," (unpublished doctoral dissertation, University of Rochester, 1973).
3. James Weinstein, *The Corporate Ideal in the Liberal State, 1900–1918*, (Boston, 1968), p. 107; also refer to idem., *The Decline of Socialism in America, 1912–1925*, (New York, 1967), pp. 107–18.
4. Gabriel Kolko, "The Decline of American Radicalism in the Twentieth-Century," *Studies on the Left*, 6:5, (September-October, 1966), 15; and James Weinstein, "Socialism's Hidden Heritage: Scholarship Reinforces Political Mythology," *Studies on the Left*, 3:4, (Fall, 1963), 93f. Also illuminating is Staughton Lynd, "Why Is There No Socialist Movement in the United States?" *Reviews in American History*, 2:1, (March, 1974), 115–20, as well as Gerald Rosenblum, *Immigrant Workers, Their Impact on American Labor Radicalism*, (New York, 1973).
5. Paul Buhle, "Intellectuals in the Debsian Socialist Party," *Radical America* 4:3 (April 1970), 44; idem., "Debsian Socialism and The 'New' Immigrant Worker," in *Insights and Parallels, Problems and Issues of American Social History*, ed., William L. O'Neill, (Minneapolis, 1973), 249–77; James Weinstein, "The IWW and American Socialism," *Socialist Revolution*, No. 5, (September-October, 1970), 40f.; and idem., *The Decline of Socialism in America*, 1. Also consult Michael H. Ebner, "The Passaic Strike of 1912 and The Two IWW's," *Labor History* 11:4 (Fall 1970), 452–66, on the radical union's role at Passaic. The two recent studies alluded to are William M. Dick, *Labor and Socialism in America, The Gompers Era*, (Port Washington, 1972), esp. 107, and Sally M. Miller, *Victor Berger and The Promise of Constructive Socialism, 1910–1920*. (Westport, 1973), pp. 17–116.
6. D.H. Leon, "Whatever Happened to an American Socialist Party? A Critical Survey of the Spectrum of Interpretations," *American Quarterly* 23 (May 1971), 236–58, provides an up-to-date review of secondary scholarship. For local background see *Weekly Item*, November 15, 1879; *Passaic Daily News*, November 3, 1879, October 27, 1893, September 17 & October 9, 1894, November 2, 1895, September 1, 1900, June 19, August 21 & September 9, 1901, and August 15, 1904; and *Passaic City Herald*, October 5, 1894.
7. *Passaic Daily News*, September 18, 1905, October 2, 1908, October 9, 1909 and October 9, 1910; *Passaic Daily Herald*, October 3, 1908, October 11 & 30, 1909, and October 2, 1910. Also consult Frederick I. Olson "Milwaukee's First Socialist Administration, 1910–1912: A Political Evaluation," *Mid-America* 43:3 (July 1961), 197–207.
8. Marvin Wachman, *History of the Social-Democratic Party of Milwaukee, 1897–*

1910, (Urbana, 1945), p. 80, quotes the platform of 1910 there as proclaiming that, "The saloon is the proletarian's clubhouse." Also consult on this point, Jon M. Kingsdale, "The 'Poor Man's Club:' Social Functions of the Urban Working-Class Saloon," *American Quarterly* 25:4 (October 1973), 472—92.

9. Michael H. Ebner, "Passaic, New Jersey, 1855-1912: City-Building in Post Civil War America," (unpublished doctoral dissertation, University of Virginia, 1974), 1-123 provides a more complete analysis of socio-economic structure.

10. For political manifestations within the "zone of emergence" see Zane L. Miller, "Boss Cox's Cincinnati: A Study in Urbanization and Politics," *Journal of American History*, 54:4 (March 1968), 823—38; Richard C. Wade, "Urbanization," in *The Comparative Approach to American History*, ed; C. Vann Woodward, (New York, 1968), pp. 191—95; and Robert R. Dykstra, "Stratification and Community Political Systems: Historians' Models," *American Behavioral Scientist* 16:5 (May—June, 1973), 707—12.

11. Sam Bass Warner, Jr., and Colin Burke, "Cultural Change and the Ghetto," *Journal of Contemporary History* 4:4 (October 1969), 173—87, and Howard P. Chudacoff, "A New Look at Ethnic Neighborhoods: Residential Dispersion and the Concept of Visibility in a Medium-Sized City," *Journal of American History* 60:1 (June 1973), 76—93.

12. The 1910 federal enumeration category "Austria" actually included all nationals in the Austro-Hungarian Empire. By 1920, in the aftermath of post-World War political realignments in eastern Europe, the classifications Poland, Yugoslavia, and Czechoslovakia were added. According to the federal census that year Passaic had 8,324 Polish-born residents, constituting 13 percent of its total population, thus making up the largest ethnic group there; at that point 68.8 percent of these Polish-born lived in the First Ward, and another 27.4 percent in the Fourth. Importantly, only 1,462 persons were listed in 1920 as Austrian-born, as contrasted with 8,748 in 1910.

13. Ebner, "Passaic, New Jersey, 1855-1912," pp. 162-174.

14. Ward election data is not available before 1879. All data discussed herein, and subsequently, has been culled from the daily press and the annual manuals issued by the state legislature. In instances where nonlocal newspapers provide the voting data they are cited specifically.

15. Ebner, "Passaic, New Jersey, 1855-1912," pp. 216-223.

16. Ransom E. Noble, Jr., *New Jersey Progressivism before Wilson*, (Princeton, 1946), pp. 43—64; Eugene M. Tobin, "The Progressive as Politician: Jersey City, 1896—1917," *New Jersey History* 91:1 (Spring 1973), 5—23; and John D. Buenker, *Urban Liberalism and Progressive Reform* (New York, 1973), p. 31.

17. Mansel G. Blackford, "Reform Politics in Seattle During the Progressive Era, 1902—1916," *Pacific Northwest Quarterly* 59 (October 1968), 177—85, although not providing systematically analyzed voting data, does make the important distinction as to the electoral behavior of different types of working class districts, noting a pattern of divergence akin to that in Passaic's First and Fourth Wards. On the state-wide demise of the "New Idea" movement refer to Noble, *New Jersey Progressivism before Wilson*, 65—99, and Arthur S. Link, *The Higher Realism of Woodrow Wilson and Other Essays*, (Nashville, 1971), p. 49.

18. Miller, *Victor Berger and the Promise of Constructive Socialism*, p. 38; *Passaic Daily News*, June 13, 1910; and *Passaic Daily Herald*, October 21, 1910. Complete data on the municipal contest of 1910 are not available, but fragmentary evidence does point to the strength of Luthringer in Fourth Ward.

19. Seymour J. Mandelbaum, *Boss Tweed's New York*, (New York, 1965), pp. 46—58; Michael H. Frisch, *Town into City, Springfield, Massachusetts, and the Meaning of Community, 1840—1880*, (Cambridge, Mass., 1972), pp. 213—17; William J. Pape, in collaboration with William W. Scott, *The News' History of Passaic, From Earliest Settlement to the Present Day*, (Passaic, 1899), pp. 71—89; David B. Tyack, "City Schools: Centralization of Control at the Turn of the Century," in *Building an Organizational Society, Essays on Associational Activities in Modern America*, ed; Jerry Israel, (New York, 1972), pp. 57—72; and *Passaic Daily*

News, February 8, 1901, May 20, 1903, October 31, 1908, and March 8, 1911.
20. George Montgomery Hartt, "Biography of Bird W. Spencer," in *Passaic Daily News,* July 29, 1931; Arthur S. Link, *Wilson, The Road to the White House,* (Princeton, 1947), p. 265f.; Mark S. Foster, "Frank Hague of Jersey City: The Boss as Reformer," *New Jersey History* 86:2 (Summer 1968), 106–77; and *Passaic Daily News,* December 13, 1909.
21. *Passaic Daily News,* January 20, 1911; John M. Matthews, "The Commission Statute in New Jersey," *The Annals* 38:4 (December 1911), 104–07; and Charles A. Beard, *American City Government, A Survey of Newer Tendencies,* (New York, 1912), p. 96.
22. Charles J. Beirne, S.J., "Jersey City's Commission Government," *Proceedings,* New Jersey Historical Society, 82:2, (April 1964), 109–13, is essential on the writing and passage of the Walsh-Leavitt Act; also see Hartt, "Biography of Bird W. Spencer" and *Passaic Daily News,* November 18, and December 30, 1910, and January 25, February 1, and July 21–22, 1911. It should be added that over time the failure to provide the mayor with additional authority became widely recognized as an essential defect of commission government.
23. *Passaic Daily Herald,* December 15, 1910, and July 1 and 17, 1911; Frederick I. Olson, "Victor Berger: Socialist Congressman," *Transactions, Wisconsin Academy of Sciences, Arts & Letters* 58 (1970), 30f., and idem., "Milwaukee's First Socialist Administration," 206. For the defects of the commission plan see Weinstein, *The Corporate Ideal in the Liberal State,* 97ff.
24. Lloyd Sponholtz, "The Initiative and Referendum: Direct Democracy in Perspective, 1898–1920," *American Studies* 14:2 (Fall 1973), 43–64, is instructive as to how such devices were applied to manipulate the electorate. Consult the daily press for July, 1911, on the activities of the League; on Johnson see the obituary in *Passaic Herald-News,* May 10, 1952, although it neglects his instrumental role in the change-of-government.
25. Roy Lubove, *Twentieth-Century Pittsburgh, Government, Business, and Environmental Change,* (New York, 1969) 20ff., and Weinstein, *The Corporate Ideal in the Liberal State,* pp. 92–116, are important on the role of organizations such as the Board of Trade; for an instance of corporate and commercial opposition to a similar change-of-government see J. Paul Mitchell, "Boss Speer and the City Functional, Boosters and Businessmen versus Commission Government in Denver," *Pacific Northwest Quarterly* 63 (October 1972), 155–64. On local detail refer to *Passaic Daily News,* July 8–12, September 30, and October 11, 1911.
26. Joseph A. Dear, "Adoptions and Rejections Under the Commission Statute of New Jersey," *The Annals* 38:4 (December 1911), 108; Richard J. Connors, A *Cycle of Power, The Career of Jersey City Mayor Frank Hague,* (Metuchen, 1971), 17 and 29ff.; and Roger Durand, "Ethnicity, 'Public-Regardingness,' and Referenda Voting," *Midwest Journal of Political Science* 16:2 (May 1972), 259–68. On registered voters, since 1910, see *Passaic Daily News,* October 24, 1912.
27. Social and political data in this and succeeding paragraphs are culled from the daily press, city directories, and the state census manuscripts for 1905 and 1915.
28. John H. M. Laslett, *Labor and the Left, A Study of Socialist and Radical Influences in the American Labor Movement, 1881–1924,* (New York, 1970), passim. Illuminates the link between the SP and the AFL.
29. *Passaic Daily Herald,* August 10, 21, 1911.
30. Levendusky ran again in 1915, also losing by a close margin. In 1919 a Jewish candidate was victorious, thus becoming the first *new* ethnic to gain election under the commission format; the same year Passaic also selected its first Irish Catholic as mayor. In 1931 the Jewish candidate who first had been elected in 1919 ran at the head of the field of entries, but declined to accept the mayoralty for reasons altogether removed from his ethnicity. In 1935 a candidate of Italian background was elected to the board, and in 1943 he became Passaic's first *new* ethnic stock mayor. Not until 1947 was a candidate of Slavic heritage successful in winning a seat; in fact, that year all five board members were of *new* immigrant extraction. In 1967 the voters abandoned commission government, replacing it with the council-manager format; in 1973 the voters opted for yet another change-of-government, choosing the mayor-council ("strong" mayor) plan.

31. Hartt, "Biography of Bird W. Spencer;" *Passaic Daily News,* July 31 and August 1 and 18, 1911. Suggestive on politicians such as Spencer is Monte A. Calvert, "The Manifest Functions of the Machine," in *Urban Bosses, Machines, and Progressive Reformers,* ed; Bruce M. Stave, (Lexington, Mass., 1972), pp. 45—55.

32. Lloyd Sponholtz, "The 1912 Constitutional Convention in Ohio: The Call-Up and Nonpartisan Selection of Delegates," *Ohio History* 79:3-4 (Summer-Autumn, 1970), 209—18, provides an excellent case study of the vagaries of nonpartisanship; also consult Erich C. Stern, "The Non-Partisan Election Law: Reform or Anti-Socialism," *Historical Messenger* (Milwaukee County Historical Society), 16:9, (1960), 8—11, and Phillips Cutright, "Nonpartisan Electoral Systems in American Cities," *Comparative Studies in Society & History* 5 (1962—1963), 212—26.

33. Daniel N. Gordon, "Immigrants and Municipal Voting Turnout: Implications for the Changing Ethnic Impact on Urban Politics," *American Sociological Review* 35:4 (August 1970), 665—81, illustrates the behavioral alterations which nonpartisanship often forces on an urban polity. For detail on Sullivan, Reid, and Seger refer to the respective biographical sketches provided in William W. Scott, *History of Passaic and Its Environs,* 3 vols., (New York & Chicago, 1922).

34. n.a., *Jewish Roots, A History of the Jewish Community of Passaic and Environs,* (Passaic, 1959), 81, as well as *Passaic Daily News,* October 31, 1900, and Scott, *History of Passaic and Its Environs,* Vol. 3, 536f., on Richmond. On the function of ward representation see Roger B. Kasperson, "Ward Systems and Urban Politics," *Southeastern Geographer* 9:2 (November 1969), 17—25.

35. Warren E. Stickle III, "The Applejack Campaign of 1919: 'As Wet as the Atlantic Ocean,' " *New Jersey History* 89:1 (Spring 1971), 18, categorizes the Second Ward, in addition to the First and Fourth, as being composed of "Newer Americans" by that point in time.

36. *Passaic Daily News,* September 18 and 30, 1911, and *The Issue* (Passaic), October 1911. Except for this one number, I have been unable to find copies of the Socialist monthly, despite carefully searching locally and nationally; a photocopy of the October 1911 number is available in the Passaic Historical Collection, Forstmann Public Library. Weinstein, *The Decline of Socialism in America,* pp. 84—93, is essential on the Socialist local press.

37. *The Issue* (Passaic), October 1911.

38. Christopher Lasch, *The Agony of the American Left,* (New York, 1969), p. 10, and *cfn.*, 2. Also illuminating is Milton Kotler, "The Disappearance of Municipal Liberty," *Politics & Society* 3:1 (Fall 1972), 83—116.

39. *Passaic Daily News,* May 2, 1907, May 3, 1909, and May 2, 1910, as well as *Passaic Daily Herald,* July 18, 1908, all provide evidence of Socialist party activity in the Polish community; also consult Wachman, *History of the Social-Democratic Party of Milwaukee,* p. 70, and Edward Kantowicz, "The Emergence of the Polish Democratic Vote in Chicago," *Polish-American Studies* 29 (Spring-Fall, 1972), 78.

40. Victor R. Greene, "For God and Country: The Origins of Slavic Catholic Self-Consciousness in America," *Church History* 35:4 (December 1966), 446—60, and Richard S. Sorrell, "Life, Work and Acculturation Patterns of Eastern European Immigrants in Lackawanna, New York, 1900—1922," *Polish Review* 14 (Autumn 1969), 76, are illuminating in explaining the socio-economic milieu of first generation eastern Europeans; also consult Wachman, *History of the Social-Democratic Party of Milwaukee,* 42f., 53, 64f., 70 & 76. Henry F. Bedford, *Socialism and the Workers in Massachusetts, 1886—1912,* (Amherst, 1966), p. 264, is suggestive on voting; for local data refer to *Passaic Daily Herald,* October 31, 1900 and *Passaic Daily News,* October 24, 1912.

41. Kolko, "The Decline of American Radicalism in the Twentieth Century," 17f., as well as Buhle, "Intellectuals in the Debsian Socialist Party," p. 57, idem., "Debsian Socialism and the 'New Immigrant' Worker," 276f., and Lasch, *The Agony of the American Left,* 28ff.

WILLIAM C. PRATT

6. "JIMMIE HIGGINS" AND THE READING SOCIALIST COMMUNITY:
An Exploration of the Socialist Rank and File

Over the past twenty years, a considerable amount of scholarship has been
devoted to the American Socialist movement. We now have useful book-
length treatments that examine the movement's origins, its heyday and decline, and its connection with organized labor, as well as biographies of its
most prominent figures, Eugene Debs and Norman Thomas. Dozens of articles and papers presented at professional meetings also have added to our
understanding of American socialism.[1] But very little of this scholarship
concerns itself with the rank and file party members or the mythical "Jimmie Higginses" who did the day-to-day work required to build and sustain
a successful political movement.[2] Since both the limited success and the
ultimate failure of American socialism were in part due to the accomplishments and shortcomings of the "Jimmie Higginses," more scholarly attention to the rank and file should contribute to our overall understanding of
the movement.

   This essay is a beginning effort to examine the rank and file in one
locale—Reading, Pennsylvania—in the 1930s. Its findings are drawn from a
larger study of the Reading Socialist experience in which I am now engaged.
The time period covered in this particular study is the decade of the 1930s,
when the Reading movement enjoyed its greatest strength. The fact that
the Reading comrades achieved their success much later than the alleged
"golden age" of American socialism does not necessarily make their case
substantially different from earlier Socialist efforts.[3] But for those historians who may differ on this point, the current study should be useful for
comparisons with Socialist movements such as those of Bridgeport, Connecticut, and Milwaukee, Wisconsin, which also were enclaves of municipal

socialism in the 1930s.

The setting of the study—Reading, Pennsylvania—is approximately fifty miles northwest of Philadelphia in the middle of the "Pennsylvania Dutch country." (The Pennsylvania Dutch are actually descendents of German immigrants who settled in Pennsylvania before the nineteenth century.) From its early days in the mid-eighteenth century, this city had a marked German influence which persisted into the twentieth century. Although immigration from Eastern and Southern Europe added to Reading's population in more recent times, it was not "in sufficient [enough] numbers to overbalance the weight and mass of generations of Germans." In 1920, for example, when the city's population approached 108,000, less than 9 percent of that total was foreign-born. One student observes: "The city of Reading . . . occupies in this century a unique position among industrial centers of its size and type in that it lacks their usual degree of ethnic and religious heterogeneity."[4]

Reading's population peaked in 1930, reaching 111,000, and has steadily declined ever since. During the 1920s, the city and the surrounding area became an important textile center and were considered as the "center of gravity" of the hosiery industry. The city's work force was of a "predominant 'working class' character," as manual laborers accounted for 72.7 percent of it in 1930. At the same time, however, a higher percentage of Reading's families owned their own homes than almost any other city of its size in the country. In 1920, 46 percent of the homes were owned by their occupants, and, ten years later, that figure climbed to 59.5 percent.[5] On the surface, considering the notoriously conservative reputation of the Pennsylvania Dutch, along with this unusually high percentage of home-ownership, the city may seem an unlikely setting for a vigorous Socialist movement. And one observer notes: "The power and prestige of the Socialist Party in staid, conservative old Reading presented one of the most unusual paradoxes in the city's history."[6]

Yet Reading was long an outpost of American socialism. Its socialist past is traced back to the summer of 1896, when a handful of disgruntled local Populists organized a section of Daniel DeLeon's Socialist Labor party. This group later affiliated with the Socialist Party of America (SP) in 1902 and eventually elected several local candidates between 1910 and 1916. The Reading comrades survived World War I and the Red Scare and continued to be a relevant force in city politics for the next several decades.

Reading socialism is particularly interesting to students of American radicalism because its greatest successes came *after* World War I. The Reading movement did not make its first political breakthrough until 1927 when it captured city hall and two seats on the school board. During that campaign, the key issue proved to be an unpopular assessment of the in-

142

cumbent Democratic administration and the Socialists skillfully exploited it in this city of home owners. In 1931 and again in 1933, the Reading SP suffered temporary setbacks due to fusion campaigns of the Democrats and Republicans. The Socialists regrouped and, in the most vigorous campaign effort in their history, retook city hall in the 1935 election. That year, the SP also won three county offices for the first time, giving "the older parties the worst election shock in Berks County history."[7] In 1930, 1932, and 1934, the Socialists also elected the city's two state legislators.[8] During the 1927–1935 period, the SP was *the* major party in *city* politics. After 1935, the socialist political machine faltered, but it remained a political contender until the late 1940s.

TABLE 7-1
Successful Socialist Candidates, 1927-1943[9]

Election Year	Office	Percentage of Vote
1927	Mayor	49.9
	Two city councilmen	48.8, 47.9
	City Controller	38
	Two school directors	49.5, 42.5
1929	Two city councilmen	43, 41.6
	Two school directors	39, 38.9
1930	Two state legislators	38.4, 37
1932	Two state legislators	38.7, 37.2
1934	Two state legislators	51.4, 49
1935	Mayor	49.6
	Three city councilmen	46.3, 45.5, 45.8
	City controller	46.1
	City treasurer	45.7
	Three school directors	51.2, 50, 48
	County commissioner	46
	Two county prison inspectors	45.9, 45.6
1943	Mayor	39.2

Reading socialism's atypical success story was due to several factors. David Shannon, in his *The Socialist Party of America,* lists several internal shortcomings of the Socialist movement that contributed to its failure. When comparing the record of the Reading Socialists with Shannon's checklist of the SP's internal weaknesses, the vast differences between the Reading experience and that of the national movement are apparent. In Reading, the Socialists built a strong political machine; concerned themselves with local issues in local politics (while, at the same time, not forgetting that they really were Socialists); ran a full slate of local and state candidates; attracted organized labor to their cause; and spoke in "common sense" language to the general public of the city.[10] (That the ranks of the Reading SP membership, including many of their prominent spokesmen, were heavily weighted with Pennsylvania Dutch names also proved to be a valuable asset in this predominantly Pennsylvania Dutch community.)[11] For several decades, then, Reading socialism avoided the traditional shortcomings that characterized so much of political socialism elsewhere in American society.

Both among the leadership and the rank and file were a hard core of "true believers" that was not only convinced of the desirability of socialism, but that also believed in its inevitability. For example, one Reading Socialist who was his party's mayoralty candidate twice in the 1950s, told a magazine writer in 1957: "I joined the Socialist Party in 1907. We thought we saw a Socialist society coming then."[12] Such faith had been common among many American Socialists early in the movement's history, David Shannon observing: "This faith in the party's success, the buoyant, optimistic view that Socialism was inevitable and probably fairly close, is one of the keys to understanding the Socialist Party before the 1920s." He also points out that this faith is helpful in explaining

the dedication many people gave the movement, sacrificing what little comfort they might have been able to have to work anonymously and unceasingly for the Cause. The 'Jimmie Higginses' . . . had to have a faith that their work was for the benefit of mankind and that it would be successful.[13]

In Reading, the "Jimmie Higginses" sustained such faith long after the decline of the Socialist movement nationally, and, as a result of that faith, eventually were able to construct a successful Socialist political machine.

They were able to sustain that faith because Reading socialism was more than a political movement. In fact, to many of its hard core, it was almost a complete way of life. Socialist ideology played a role here, explaining the world in which the Reading Socialists lived, as well as promising a better one in the Cooperative Commonwealth. But even more important in sustaining this faith were the party institutions which both buffered the active membership from a hostile environment and provided for their social needs. In addition to annual election campaigns, the SP had frequent educational meetings, picnics, and women and youth groups, all of which called upon widespread participation from members and served to keep the local movement intact.[14] By 1920, the Reading comrades also owned and operated several economic enterprises. These included a publishing company, which published the weekly party paper, the *Reading Labor Advocate*, a small cigar factory which produced several brands of cigars, such as the "Karl Marx," and a cooperative store. The party also owned the Labor Lyceum, a three-story building in downtown Reading, which housed the party headquarters, the cigar factory, and a hall which was used by both the party and some local unions.[15] Henry Stetler, an earlier student of Reading socialism, concluded that the Reading movement

functioned not merely as a political party but as a many-sided association which reached out and encompassed within its scope a wide variety of social and economic activities not ordinarily engaged in by the traditionally American political parties. In other words, socialism in Reading has a social structure much broader in scope than its political structure.[16]

The existence of this "social structure" characterized Reading socialism by World War I, and it played a substantial role in enabling the local organization to survive despite repeated defeat in the pre-1927 era. With the 1927 victory, however, the SP no longer had to assume a defensive posture. The party's nonpolitical institutions were revitalized and expanded, absorbing many of the new recruits of the movement. Political success was due in large part to the party's "social structure," but that structure in turn was reinforced as a result of the political victory.[17] An examination of the Reading Socialist "community" in the 1930s, the era of its greatest strength, should help us better understand how the party's "social structure" contributed to its political operations, as well as revealing the particular role of the "Jimmie Higginses."

The individual party branch was a basic component of the party "social structure."[18] Its weekly meetings provided the "Jimmie Higginses" with frequent opportunity not only to do the leg work for the movement, but also to participate in the formulation of party policy. Local Berks County was the overall party organization in the Reading area, and this body, along with the county or executive committee, made policy and directed the Reading movement. But it was in the individual branch that many of the policy recommendations originated that later were introduced and adopted at the monthly Local meeting. A sampling of the city branch minute books reveals wide participation in party affairs by the rank and file. The "Jimmie Higginses" held the elected offices within the branch, including the post of branch organizer. In addition to these permanent positions, the branch delegated a considerable number of tasks to special committees and they too almost always were staffed with the rank and file. Sometimes the inclination to delegate responsibilities to special committees approached the absurd, as the following example from a minute book demonstrates: "Moved by Comrade Cramp seconded by Eugene Shaffer that a committee of three be appointed to see that there was a fire started and building heated for Monday night meeting." After the women's group requested the same service, the original motion was ruled out of order.[19]

Although it would be an exaggeration to claim that branch meetings were purely rank and file affairs, the minute books do reveal a relative lack of involvement by the more prominent members of the Reading movement. Party leaders, of course, participated in such meetings, reporting and frequently lecturing on a variety of topics, but they seem to have been preoccupied with their other responsibilities and did not dominate affairs at the branch level. Since the Reading SP organization had a large number of tasks to be performed, they were distributed widely out of necessity, and that increased the sense of participation.

The branch meeting was the recruiting ground for campaign workers "in each precinct to distribute literature, get voters registered, get voters to the polls, watch the count of the vote, and all the other routine tasks of political party workers."[20] For some time, the Reading comrades had prided themselves in the "Flying Squadron," their efficient campaign literature distribution team. The "Flying Squadron" was made up of "Jimmie Higginses" from each city branch and boasted of being able to cover every block within the entire city of 110,000 inhabitants in one half hour. Probably the most impressive "Flying Squadron" performance was in the 1935 campaign. That year, Reading's "Jimmie Higginses" distributed a total of 626,165 pieces of literature, including nine different issues of the *Pioneer*, a four-page socialist propaganda sheet that was always distributed during a Reading campaign.[21]

Other campaign tasks were also divided among branch volunteers, and care was taken to see that each ward had enough workers, including watchers and pollmen. The individual branches were responsible for arranging street meetings for the wards within their jurisdiction and the minutes of one branch in 1934 reveal that its organizer "urged all members to attend all meetings to swell the crowds."[22]

Old party fusion had defeated the SP in 1931 and again in 1933, since the Socialists had been unable to obtain a majority of the vote in either contest. After the 1933 setback, the local party underwent considerable self-appraisal. A voter survey was conducted in every precinct of the city, and concluded that the lowest registration was in working class neighborhoods. To increase the SP vote, the party established a "block system," in which "Jimmie Higginses" conducted a door-to-door registration campaign.

146

An effort was made, according to the local organizer's report to the national office, "to check on every person over 21 in every household." Lists of such persons were prepared and delivered to the appropriate ward clubs, which had been organized and controlled by the local party branch. The organizer's report noted that the "Block workers are selected from their own voting districts," and "are familiar with their neighbors and generally know how they vote. All those who are unsympathetic to our Party are stricken from the lists, and are not visited on Registration and Election Day."[23]

Socialists gave considerable credit to their "block system" for the increased SP vote in 1934 and 1935. In 1934, for the first time in local party history, a Socialist candidate attracted over 50 percent of the total vote. Darlington Hoopes, an incumbent Socialist legislator, garnered 15,029 votes, almost 4,000 more than his 1932 showing. Despite the fact that several thousand fewer people participated in this contest than the 1931 municipal election, Hoopes's vote surpassed that of the party's previous high that year. (The incumbent Socialist mayor had received 14,395 votes in his losing effort in 1931.) Hoopes's running mate in 1934, Lilith Wilson, also won reelection to the legislature due to a partial failure in the fusion ranks. The following year the "block system" contributed to the local Socialists' greatest success. The 1935 election was marked by the greatest voter turnout in the city's history. In contrast, the 1936 presidential election, despite the appeal of FDR, drew over 3,700 fewer voters.[24]

The individual branch also provided for the educational and social needs of its membership all year round. Branch meetings often were forums for lectures and discussions on socialism and other topics of current interest. Frequently, members of the party, both from the ranks of leadership and of the "Jimmie Higginses," would speak at meetings. While local AFL leader George Rhodes spoke on the "Power of the Press," rank and filer William Schweren talked about "Revolution and Evolution" to the branches in 1933.[25] Debates between various branches were also held from time to time, and the following note was found in the pages of one branch minute book: "Comrades—The Southern Branch of Local Berks County Challenges you to a debate [sic]. The Subject, and the place as the branches see fit."[26]

During the week, branch headquarters were utilized as recreation centers for the membership. Card parties and other social gatherings were constantly announced in the *Labor Advocate*.

CARD PARTY TONIGHT AT GIBRALTAR

All card players are invited to attend a hassenpeffer party tonight (Friday) at 8 o'clock in the Gibraltar Fire Co. hall, under the auspices of the

Gibraltar branch. Valuable prizes and good lunch will be there to make the event enjoyable. In connection with the party will be an address by Stewart Tomlinson.

. . .

TWO BIG CARD PARTIES SATURDAY NIGHT

If you are looking for a good time on Saturday night, here are two offerings for your selection:

Labor Lyceum: Card party under the auspices of the women of the Central branch. Good food, fine prizes and a happy crowd.

Northeast Women: Card party at 1311 North Ninth street with good lunch and valuable prizes.[27]

Much of the work for these affairs, as one might suspect, was performed by the women of the various branches. Getting women involved in the Socialist movement had been a problem for the party nationally, and although the Reading Socialists met with more success in this area, they too felt that a disproportionately small percentage of women participated. Many branches had their own separate women's groups and representatives of those bodies made up the county-wide "Women's Committee." Women provided much of the labor needed to make party social and fundraising projects a success, and these projects in turn served to partially fulfill a needed social function for them.[28] But Socialist women in Reading were not limited to a purely "women's auxiliary role." Among the ranks of the party workers were "Jennie Higginses," who played an important role in the Reading Socialist political machine as well. And a few Socialist women were elected to prominent local offices, including the state legislature and the Reading school board. Overall, however, women in the Reading Socialist movement were clearly in a subordinate position.[29]

The Reading comrades also tried to build a Socialist youth movement in the 1930s. The youth group of the national SP was the Young Peoples Socialist League (YPSL), and its members were called "Yipsels." Although Reading had had a "Yipsel" organization earlier, it faded away in the 1920s. Following the 1929 election, however, the local "Yipsels" were reorganized and given a meeting place in the Labor Lyceum. This group, like the women Socialists, came to play an active, if secondary role in the Reading SP movement. Many of them entered the ranks of the "Jimmie" and "Jennie Higginses," and provided much assistance during election campaigns. "Yipsel" meetings featured speeches and debates, but the real "Yipsel" drawing card was its program of social activities. Planned functions such as singing, dramatics and sports, were supplemented by informal affairs, such as swimming parties and doggie roasts in the country.[30]

One of the most important economic and social institutions of the Reading movement was Socialist Park, the party's picnic grove. Purchased in 1929, this facility provided the party with thousands of dollars in income, as well as serving as a recreation center for the membership. Operation of the park demanded a lot of man-hours from the "Jimmie Higginses." During the summer season, the party conducted several of its own picnics. These featured concerts by the Socialist orchestra, planned recreation for the children, baseball games between the branches, dances, supper, and finally prominent Socialist speakers. Socialist mayor, J. Henry Stump, Norman Thomas and Milwaukee's Socialist mayor, Daniel Hoan, were frequent picnic orators, and addressed crowds that numbered over 15,000 people. On occasion, Amos Lesher, who would be elected a Socialist county commissioner in 1935, spoke to picnic crowds in Pennsylvania Dutch.[31]

Since Socialist Park provided excellent facilities and a wide range of entertainment, thousands of non-Socialists from the area also attended Socialist picnics. As the picnic committee chairman pointed out, these picnics performed a valuable educational role. Non-Socialists were introduced rather painlessly to Socialist propaganda and also saw that the Reading comrades didn't have horns.[32] Socialist Park, efficiently operated by the party in the early and mid-thirties, may have been the best propaganda device that the Socialists had at their disposal.

This brief discussion of the party's "social structure" suggests how the Reading Socialist movement offered its membership almost a complete way of life. Numerous social activities served to create a sense of community among the "Jimmie Higginses." Smoking a Socialist-made cigar, listening to the Socialist orchestra and chorus, working the concession stand at Socialist Park—all of these things tended to hold the party together between elections and after defeats.

In 1936, however, the Reading Socialist community was disrupted and subsequently torn apart by a fratricidal split. Reading factionalism had surfaced in late 1935 and, although it had local causes, merged with the Militant-Old Guard controversy that divided the party on the national level. Since the early 1930s, the national organization had been seriously split between a militant coalition nominally headed by Norman Thomas and the Old Guard, led by old-time Socialists. Generational, tactical, and ideological differences all played a role in this controversy, but the elements of a power struggle for control of the Socialist movement were also present. Finally in May of 1936, the SP split and most of the Old Guard left the Militant-controlled organization soon afterwards. Several SP state organizations, including the Jasper McLevy-controlled Connecticut party and the Pennsylvania party, were dominated by the Old Guard and they too left during the summer of 1936.[33]

Throughout the early 1930s, the Reading comrades generally had managed to avoid involvement in the national controversy, but, in late

149

1935 and early 1936, local developments drew them into it. The Reading leadership and its following, gradually identified as the Old Guard, found themselves struggling with an almost purely rank and file group for control of the Reading movement. This group felt that its members had not been given sufficient recognition for their contributions to the movement and may have felt that prominent local Socialists like James Maurer and Mayor J. Henry Stump had received too much credit for what the "Jimmie Higginses" had done. In some cases, especially among a few "Yipsels," there was also a strong feeling that the existing leadership was too conservative and should be replaced by a more dynamic group.[34] Although it would be an oversimplification to explain this factionalism and the subsequent split solely in terms of a power struggle between the local party elite and a group of dissident "Jimmie Higginses," that was an important part of the controversy.

Reading factionalism was further complicated by the growing number of new party members. Since the Reading Socialists first gained control of city hall, their membership had grown by leaps and bounds. Local party records show that the combined city-county membership went from 570 in April of 1928 to 2,350 in July of 1936. By August of that year, the *Labor Advocate* claimed that the local organization was the largest in the SP and accounted for one-sixth of the entire national membership.[35] Obviously, a large percentage of this new membership was not made up of dedicated "Jimmie Higginses." In fact, many of the newcomers are best described as "patronage Socialists," who apparently had joined the SP with the hope of landing a city job when the Socialists gained power. After the 1935 victory, the SP was flooded with job applications. Since there were only 400 patronage jobs available, a substantial number of applicants were bound to be disappointed. Open factionalism broke out soon after the SP election triumph, and job-hungry Socialists often proved to be likely recruits for the dissidents.[36]

Throughout the spring and summer of 1936, the Reading comrades were preoccupied with fighting among themselves. Then, in mid-August, the Reading Socialists split into two separate organizations, each claiming a majority of the local membership and its considerable property holdings. The Reading Old Guard had helped take the state SP out of the national organization, while the Militant or "leftist" faction maintained its loyalty to the Norman Thomas group. Throughout August, the daily press reported the day-to-day developments of the local split in great detail.[37] Gradually, it became clear that the Old Guard had not only maintained the support of almost all local SP public officials and a majority of the membership, but it also retained control of the major party institutions and possessions. The Old Guard did complain, however, that their socialist opposition had strip-

150

ped the kitchen at Socialist Park of all its equipment and that it "had been canvassing the paper's [*Labor Advocate's*] advertisers in an effort to injure the paper."[38]

The Reading Old Guard organization also maintained the SP line on the November ballot. In this election campaign, however, the Old Guard "Jimmie Higginses" found themselves opposed not only by the Democratic and Republican machines, but also by a bitter group of their own former comrades, the leftist "Jimmie Higginses." In November, the once efficient SP vote-getting machine was swamped in a Democratic tidal wave, and the SP candidates finished third in every contest.[39]

The 1936 split marked the end of Reading Socialism as a viable political alternative in municipal politics. Every branch and almost every party institution had been weakened by the split, and several county branches quickly disappeared. Publicity of the controversy alone may have been enough to insure the defeat of the Old Guard slate in the 1936 contest, but the effects of the split upon the ranks of the "Jimmie Higginses" were of a more serious consequence.[40] A substantial number of rank and file activists no longer worked for the old socialist organization, but now were among its political enemies. In fact, the chief object of most leftists after 1936 seemed to be the destruction of the other socialist organization. Although the leftist group gradually faded into irrelevance, most of its members never were reconciled with their old comrades and became Democrats instead.[41]

The split also took its toll among the "Jimmie Higginses" who had not sided with the leftists. Their ranks had been disrupted and they never again were able to bring out the full Socialist vote. Roosevelt, of course, received the vote of thousands that had voted for Socialist candidates the year before.[42] But to discuss the 1936 election in Reading solely in terms of a Socialist voter bolt to FDR is an oversimplification. In 1936, despite the drawing power of FDR, 3,710 fewer people voted than had in the 1935 municipal election. Roosevelt certainly was able to attract a very sizeable percentage of recent SP voters, but the total vote in every ward in the city declined between 1935 and 1936. This decline probably can be best explained by the split that crippled the Reading Socialist community. Of the five wards with the smallest percentage of decline, two of them never had been carried by the SP in the 1930s, while two more of them were carried for the first time in 1935. On the other hand, three of the six wards with the greatest percentage of decline almost always had been in the Socialist column in the 1930 to 1935 period. Apparently, many former Socialist voters stayed home in 1936, some because they were disgusted with the fight, others because the "Jimmie Higginses" did not get them to the polls like they had the year before.

After 1936, many Reading Socialists lost their "buoyant optimistic view that Socialism was inevitable . . . ." A considerable number of them quickly became Democrats, while many others drifted into that camp over the next several years. A 1940 report on the Reading situation stated that the Reading Socialists were "badly discouraged and demoralized," and the developments of the next several years, with few exceptions, gave them little reason to change their attitude. Party membership continued to decline, dropping from 670 in 1939 to 370 in 1943.[44] More ominous, however, may have been the steady increase in the average age of the membership. By early 1944, it had climbed to fifty or more. The "Yipsel" movement had disappeared in the late 1930s, and, despite several attempts, never was successfully reorganized.[45] In 1939, the SP had been turned out of city hall in what was described as "one of the dullest election campaigns in recent years . . . ." The SP press continued to report a great amount of voter apathy in municipal elections, and this was reflected in the poor voter turnout. Following the 1943 election, the *Labor Advocate* commented:

TABLE 7-2
Decline in SP Vote[43]

Lowest percentages		Highest percentages	
Ward 14	2%	Ward 6	14.9%
3	2.8	11	14.2
8	6.3	1	13.9
7	6.5	4	13.7
15	6.7	13	12.5
		5	12.4

"As in the case of every election since 1935, the number staying away from the polls was greater than those who voted."[46] Had the Socialists possessed a larger number of younger "Jimmie Higginses," perhaps they would have been once again capable of conducting exciting and vigorous campaigns as they had done in the 1927--1935 era. But even when political opportunities occasionally presented themselves to the SP in the 1940s, it no longer had the manpower to take advantage of them. In 1943, Stump managed to unseat an unpopular incumbent and win his third term as mayor. This time, however, his coattails were not long enough to carry any other SP candidates with him to city hall.[47] Four years later, he was turned out of office by 214 votes. Both elections had been close enough that had the party still had a cadre of "Jimmie Higginses" it would have regained control of city hall. But by 1947, party activists were not numerous enough even to provide poll workers for every precinct. This election was the last one in which the SP was a serious factor.[48] The atypical success story of Reading socialism had finally ended.

Further research on the Socialist rank and file, both in Reading and other locales, should enhance our understanding of how the SP functioned in its day-to-day activities. This approach also suggests new possibilities for a history of the American Socialist movement "from the bottom up." Socialist spokesmen and the party press long acknowledged the important role played by the "Jimmie Higginses," and perhaps it is time for historians to do the same.

NOTES

1. Recent published works include Howard H. Quint, *The Forging of American Socialism: Origins of the Modern Movement* (Indianapolis: Bobbs-Merrill Company, 1964); Ira Kipnis, *The American Socialist Movement, 1897–1912* (New York: Columbia University Press, 1952); David A. Shannon, *The Socialist Party of America: A Political History* (Chicago: Quadrangle Books, 1967); Daniel Bell, *Marxian Socialism in the United States* (Princeton: Princeton University Press, 1967); James Weinstein, *The Decline of Socialism in America, 1912–1925* (New York: Monthly Review Press, 1967); John Laslett, *Labor and The Left: A Study of Socialist and Radical Influences in the American Labor Movement, 1881–1924* (New York: Basic Books, 1970); William M. Dick, *Labor and Socialism in America: The Gompers Era* (Port Washington, N.Y., Kennikat Press, 1972); Ray Ginger, *Eugene V. Debs: A Biography* (New York: Collier Books, 1970); Wayne Morgan, *Eugene V. Debs: Socialist for President* (Syracuse: Syracuse University Press, 1962); Murray B. Seidler, *Norman Thomas: Respectable Rebel*, Second Edition (Syracuse: Syracuse University Press, 1967); Bernard K. Johnpoll, *Pacifist's Progress: Norman Thomas and the Decline of American Socialism* (Chicago: Quadrangle Books, 1970). Some recent articles are cited in D.H. Leon, "Whatever Happened to the American Socialist Party: A Critical Survey of the Spectrum of Interpretations," *American Quarterly* 23 (May 1971), 236–58.
2. The name "Jimmie Higgins" was coined by Ben Hanford, the SP's 1904 vice-presidential candidate. Ginger: *Eugene V. Debs*, p. 246, "What did Jimmie Higgins do? He did everything. Whatever the Party wanted to be done, THAT was Jimmie's job." Ben Hanford, "Jimmie Higgins," reprinted in *Reading Labor Advocate*, September 5, 1930, p. 8. See also David A. Shannon, "Introduction," in Upton Sinclair, *Jimmie Higgins* (Lexington: University of Kentucky, 1971), p. xi.
3. Daniel Bell has designated the 1902–1912 period as "the 'golden age' of American Socialism." Bell, *Marxian Socialism*, p. 55. Most historians, at least until very recently, agree that 1912 was the "peak" year of the movement. For *contra* view, see Weinstein, *Decline of Socialism.*
4. Raymond Ford, "Germans and Other Foreign Stock: Their Part in the Evolution of Reading, Pennsylvania" (Unpublished Ph.D. dissertation, University of Pennsylvania, 1963), p. 194; Henry G. Stetler, *The Socialist Movement in Reading, Pennsylvania, 1896–1936: A Study in Social Change* (Storrs: The Author, 1943), pp. 15–16.
5. Ibid., p. 10; Kenneth E. Hendrickson, Jr., "The Great Berks County Hosiery Strike: A Critique of the Constructive Disorder Thesis" (unpublished paper read at the Missouri Valley History Conference in Omaha, March 10, 1972), p. 2; Stetler, *Socialist Movement in Reading*, 12, 14; U.S. Bureau of the Census, *Abstract of the Fifteenth Census, 1930,* 436.
6. John Peter Lozo, *School and Society in the City of Reading Relative to Recreation, 1900–1935* (Philadelphia: The Author, 1938), p. 60.
7. Stetler, *Socialist Movement in Reading*, pp. 31–40. For Reading socialism's wartime and Red Scare experience, see Kenneth E. Hendrickson, Jr., "The Socialists of Reading, Pennsylvania and World War I–A Question of Loyalty,"

Pennsylvania History 36 (October 1969), 430—50.

8. Quoted in *New York Times,* November 7, 1935, p. 3. For a detailed account of this period in the Reading SP's history, see William C. Pratt, "The Reading Socialist Experience: A Study in Working Class Politics" (unpublished Ph.D. dissertation, Emory University, 1969), pp. 67—229.

9. Computations from Stetler table, *Socialist Movement in Reading,* pp.169—70, and unofficial returns, *Reading Eagle,* November 5, 1943, p. 1.

10. Shannon, *Socialist Party,* pp. 258—62.

11. Stetler writes: "The leaders of the Reading Socialist party were not only native American but also largely of Pennsylvania-German descent. Since the latter group is ethnically dominant in the community, the hazard of having 'outsiders' attempt to superimpose an alien 'ism' upon them was avoided." Stetler, *Socialist Movement in Reading,* p. 143.

12. Dan Wakefield, "The Socialist Survivors," *The Nation,* 184 (February 2, 1957), 98. See also Stetler, *Socialist Movement in Reading,* p. 33.

13. Shannon, *Socialist Party,* p. 8.

14. Personal interview with Mark L. Brown, December 23, 1967. For a sample of SP social activities in the pre-1920 period, see Reading *Labor Advocate,* June 5, 1915; July 10, 1915; March 4, 1916.

15. See Raymond S. Hofses, "Why Reading?" in William M. Feigenbaum, ed., *Socialism Today* (New York: Socialist Party, [1928], p. 31, Socialist Party Collection, Duke University, hereafter cited as SPC (Duke).

16. Stetler, *Socialist Movement in Reading,* p. 64. Stetler's conclusion is based on his discussion, pp. 53—64. See also pp. 151—53. My own treatment here is indebted considerably to Stetler. In his work, however, he did not make any special effort to treat the rank and file, nor did he utilize some of the sources cited in this article. (Many of them were not available to him when he did his research in the late 1930s and early 1940s). Frederick I. Olson found that the Socialist movement in Milwaukee also functioned "as a many-sided association." See Olson, "The Milwaukee Socialist Party, 1897—1941" (unpublished Ph.D. dissertation, Harvard University, 1952), pp. 82—83.

17. Raymond Hofses, editor of the *Labor Advocate* from 1918 until 1951, actually credits the Socialist management of the party's economic enterprises with a role in the 1927 victory. "Through the success of their economic organizations the Socialists of Reading demonstrated their fitness to administer public affairs. When the people turned away from the old party politicians in 1927, they turned to the Socialists because the latter had a background of achievement which proved them capable and trustworthy." "Why Reading?" p. 31.

18. By the early 1930s, there were five city branches (a sixth was added in 1936), and the county or rural branches ranged in number from four in mid-1931 to nineteen in late 1934. Reading *Labor Advocate*, June 12, 1931, p. 5; February 14, 1936, p. 1; October 5, 1934, p. 6. The city branches, however, contained the majority of the membership and almost all the prominent members of the local movement.

19. "Minute Book of Northeast Branch," January 2, 1934, p. 268. Branch and local minute books cited in this study are part of Darlington Hoopes' papers which are available on microfilm at the Pennsylvania State University and from Rhistoric Publications.

20. Shannon, *Socialist Party,* pp. 258—259.

21. Personal interview with L. Birch Wilson, late December, 1967; personal interview with Darlington Hoopes, April 15, 1968; James Hudson Maurer, *It Can Be Done* (New York: Rand School, 1938), p. 147; "Address of Mayor Henry J. [sic] Stump of Reading, Pennsylvania, opening 1930 Convention of the Socialist Party of Pennsylvania," SPC (Duke). Hoopes said that the efficient distribution of literature was the primary factor in winning elections. For the 1935 campaign, see Ralph O. Bigony, "Report to National Office," [c. January 1936], SPC (Duke).

22. See "Central Branch Minute Book," June 12, 1933, p. 38; October 2, 1933, p. 52; October 30, 1933, p. 56; October 8, 1934, p. 109 (source of quotation).

23. Personal interview with Brown, December 23, 1967; Bigony, "Structure and Function . . . " [1936] SPC (Duke).

24. Personal interview with Brown, December 23, 1967; Reading *Labor Advocate,* November 9, 1934, pp. 1, 2; November 16, 1934, p. 3; Clara Mosteller, to Birdsboro Branch, March 5, 1936, Hoopes Papers. For vote totals, see Stetler tables, *Socialist Movement in Reading,* pp. 169, 174, 177. Recent political research stresses the importance of grass roots contacts on the precinct level. See Phillips Cutright and Peter Rossi, "Grass Roots Politicians and the Vote," *American Sociological Review* 23 (April 1958), 171—79; Cutright, "Activities of Precinct Committeemen in Partisan and Nonpartisan Communities," *Western Political Quarterly* 17 (March 1964), 93—108.

25. Reading *Labor Advocate,* January 13, 1933, p. 3.

26. Alvin Stone to Northeast Branch, August 22, 1930, "Minute Book of Northeast Branch."

27. Reading *Labor Advocate,* January 13, 1933, p. 3.

28. Lilith Wilson to Comrade, mimeographed, May 23, 1928, SPC (Duke). Ms. Wilson, a Reading legislator in the 1930s, had chaired the National Women's Committee of the SP, 1928—1929. Shannon, *Socialist Party,* p. 193. See also Emma M. Sands, "Report of the Women's Committee of the Socialist Party of Local Berks—Reading, Penna., Year of 1933—34," SPC (Duke); Stetler, *Socialist Movement in Reading,* pp. 152—53.

29. Wilson to Comrade, May 23, 1928, SPC (Duke). See also Clara Mosteller to Birdsboro Branch, March 5, 1936. Hoopes Papers. A Reading newspaper recently commented that "each woman who won or held a top elective office in Reading or Berks County was associated with the Socialist Party", "Free Elections Guaranteed by William Penn," in Supplement, Section I of Reading *Eagle,* January 28, 1968, p. 11. One Socialist woman was appointed city treasurer to complete the term of her deceased father.

30. Reading *Labor Advocate,* October 9, 1915; "Minute Book of Local Berks," December 5, 1929, p. 197; personal interview with Clayton and Myrtle Mengel, March 31, 1968.

31. See George M. Rhodes, "A Brief History of the Socialist Park, Reading *Labor Advocate,* November 18, 1932, p. 7; November 25, 1932, p. 7; December 2, 1932, p. 7. In 1932, an *Advocate* headline claimed that 30,000 heard Thomas and Reading's J. Henry Stump at one picnic. The same story, however, reported that Reading's daily papers estimated the turnout at 20,000 and 8,000 respectively. Ibid., August 5, 1931, p. 1. For Lesher speech announcement, see ibid., August 14, 1931, p. 1.

32. Rhodes, ibid., December 2, 1932, p. 7.

33. For the discussion on the national split, see Shannon, *Socialist Party,* pp. 211—17, 235—44; Bell, *Marxian Socialism,* pp. 157—60, 162—69; Johnpoll, *Pacifist's Progress,* pp. 77—177.

34. Brown, "Flood Tide to Suicide: An Account of the 1936 split in the Socialist party of Berks County" (unpublished manuscript in Brown's possession, Reading, Pennsylvania); personal interview with Brown, December 23, 1967; personal interview with Brown and Clayton Mengel, March 31, 1968.

35. "Minute Book of Local Berks," April 5, 1928, p. 132; "Minute Book of the County Committee," July 16, 1936, p. 2; Reading *Labor Advocate,* August 21, 1936, p. 1. The membership had dipped to less than 100 prior to the 1927 election. Reading *Eagle,* November 21, 1927, p. 1; personal interview with Wilson, late December, 1967.

36. Sarah Limbach to Sonia Teitelman, June 18, 1936; James Maurer, "Why I resigned from the Socialist Party," *Pennsylvania Bulletin* (July 1936), 3, SPC (Duke); personal interview with Brown and Clayton Mengel, March 31, 1968; personal interview with George M. Rhodes, April 6, 1968; personal interview with Max Putney, June 8, 1968. Hoopes referred to the Militant leader as a "patronage Socialist." Personal interview with Hoopes, April 15, 1968.

37. Brown, "Flood Tide to Suicide." See Reading *Eagle,* August 15, 1936 to September 1, 1936, for a front page story on the split every day.

38. Reading *Labor Advocate*, October 16, 1936, p. 3; "Minute Book of the Reading Publishers Cooperative Association," September 19, 1936, p. 171.
39. Reading *Eagle*, November 4, 1936, p. 1. The "leftists" conducted a "sticker" campaign in the 1936 election with very poor results.
40. Darlington Hoopes feels that the publicity given the split was the best weapon the old parties had. Personal interview with Hoopes, April 15, 1968. See also Reading *Labor Advocate*, November 6, 1936, p. 1; Bigony, "Supplement to the Berks County, Pennsylvania Situation" [November 1936], Norman Thomas Papers, New York Public Library.
41. Personal interview with Brown, December 23, 1967. Several former leftists received city jobs in the Democratic administration that succeeded the SP in 1940. See Reading *Labor Advocate*, January 19, 1940, p. 1; February 2, 1940, p. 1.
42. Organized labor in Reading began to defect to the Democrats in 1936 and the AFL central body, the Federated Trades Council, endorsed FDR that year. See Pratt, "The 'Nationalization' of the Reading, Pennsylvania, Labor Movement, 1936 to 1948" (unpublished paper read at the Missouri Valley History Conference, in Omaha, March 12, 1970).
43. Total vote decline computation based on Stetler tables, *Socialist Movement in Reading*, pp. 173, 177. Ward vote decline computation based on unofficial returns, Reading *Eagle*, November 5, 1935, p. 6; November 4, 1936, p. 9. Wards Seven and Eight were the only two that Stump, the SP mayoralty candidate, did not carry in 1935. Perhaps it is significant that these two wards had the highest mean housing and rental value in the city in 1930. Stetler table, *Socialist Movement in Reading*, p. 187. The remaining low decline wards cited in the chart, Wards Fourteen, Three and Fifteen were carried by an SP legislative candidate for the first time in 1934. On the other hand, of the six wards with the greatest decline in the vote, Wards Six and Thirteen were Socialists strongholds, even providing Norman Thomas, the SP presidential candidate, with pluralities in 1932, and Ward Eleven had been carried by the SP legislative candidates, 1930-1934. Computations based on unofficial returns, Reading *Eagle*, November 5, 1930, p. 4; November 4, 1931, p. 5; November 9, 1932, p. 3; November 7, 1934, p. 8. In each of the eleven precincts in which Stump had attracted 400 or more votes in 1935, the 1936 vote declined.
44. "Minutes of State Executive Committee," November 24, 1940, SPC (Duke); February 16, 1940; January 20, 1943, Hoopes Papers.
45. Darlington Hoopes's estimate, Darlington Hoopes to August Claessens, January 19, 1944, Hoopes Papers. See also Bob and Bea Miller to Virginia or Irwin, July 28, 1944; Bob and Bea Miller to Bill Becker, September 9, 1944, SPC (Duke). For efforts to reorganize the Yipsels, see Reading *Labor Advocate*, December 22, 1939, p. 4; May 19, 1944, p. 3; "Minute Book of Executive Committee of Local Berks," November 20, 1946, p. 13; Reading *Labor Advocate*, August 22, 1947, p. 5; September 5, 1947, p. 5; "Minute Book of Executive Committee of Local Berks," June 15, 1949, p. 63.
46. Reading *Times*, November 6, 1939, p. 1 (source of first quotation). Stump was defeated by 688 votes. Stetler table, *Socialist Movement in Reading*, p. 173. For reports of voter apathy, see Reading *Labor Advocate*, November 7, 1941, p. 1; October 30, 1942, p. 1; November 5, 1943, p. 1 (source of second quotation).
47. Reading *Eagle*, November 3, 1943, p. 1; November 17, 1943, p. 16. Stump was the only Reading mayor in the twentieth century to be elected to more than one term until 1971.
48. Ibid., November 5, 1947, p. 1. Howard Penley to Bill [Becker] or Harry [Fleischman], November 10, 1947, SPC (Duke).

BRUCE M. STAVE

7. THE GREAT DEPRESSION AND URBAN POLITICAL CONTINUITY: Bridgeport Chooses Socialism

For two and a half decades spanning the Great Depression, World War II, and the post-war years, the city of Bridgeport, Connecticut was governed by members of the Socialist party. However, with Jasper McLevy and his fellow Socialists in City Hall from 1933 through 1957, Bridgeport underwent no great substantive transformation. If anything, that city's socialism brought with it government business as usual, although sometimes more efficient and economically sound than that practiced by the Socialists' predecessors and successors. When the voters cast their ballots in 1933, they elected officials who bore the party label "Socialist," but who would perform as good-government reformers. In this respect, they mirrored the general experience of municipal socialism in the United States. By 1957, when the Socialists were voted out of office, their brand of government had lost appeal to a new generation of voters and newcomers to the city, who felt few ties to the twelve-term mayor. Moreover, McLevy's business supporters called for new departures, which the Mayor refused to pursue. Municipal socialism in Bridgeport reflected the politics of urban continuity.

The election that catapulted Jasper McLevy and his followers to power occurred simultaneously with the period of urban political realignment that first brought Franklin D. Roosevelt to the presidency. That realignment, which developed into the New Deal coalition, has received a great deal of attention in recent years from historians interested in twentieth-century American political behavior. The majority of studies have employed local voting data to explain a national phenomenon; they have accepted as their model the nationalization of American politics. While often realiz-

157

ing that political life at the local level is of an entirely different order from that at the national, relatively few scholars have considered the vitality and variety of local politics during the Great Depression.[1]

Even historians such as Jerome M. Clubb and Howard W. Allen, who have advocated the study of voting patterns for lesser offices rather than the presidency, have based their own work on voting in national rather than local elections. Analyzing off-year congressional voting, they claim, "these elections are apparently less subject to short-term and essentially evanescent forces and more clearly reflect underlying partisan divisions and patterns of political participation within the electorate." While this may be the case, congressional contests often relate more to national issues, even in off-years, and are not necessarily precise indicators of local partisanship, interests, and cultural divisions.[2]

The choice of a city's mayor serves as a more reliable index of local politics; grass roots issues, alliances, and ethno-cultural attractions are more salient at the city hall level.[3] Shifts in partisan control at the local level can be at least as revealing with respect to political realignment as can change in national politics. This is illustrated by a study of the political affiliations between 1929 and 1942 of mayors of the 92 largest cities in the country in 1930. (See Table 1.) In 1929, Republicans, in most instances elected prior to that year, controlled 48.9 percent of the city halls in urban America; by 1935 Democratic control equalled that proportion, with Republican strength sliding to 18.4 percent, a figure significantly below the Democrats' in 1929.[4] The major shift in partisan control of these 92 city halls had occurred before 1932, lending support to the belief that the Roosevelt presidential election was part of a long-term "critical period" rather than a "critical election" in itself.[5]

A year after FDR's first presidential victory, the 1933 mayoralty elections in these cities continued the aggregate shift to the Democrats. However, indicative of the tenacity of localism in the face of national trends, not all municipal elections moved in that direction. A bastion of Republicanism such as Pittsburgh swung to the Democrats in 1933. Cleveland shifted from Democratic control to Republican. New York City toppled Tammany in favor of the Fusion ticket headed by Progressive Republican, Fiorello LaGuardia. To some, fearful of Depression induced radicalism, the results in Bridgeport when McLevy ousted the Democratic incumbent might have appeared as the biggest political change of all. While by no means contending that corruption is the only variable, or even the key one, it is suggestive that in these cities, scandal and charges of municipal corruption preceded the shifts; in turn, this suggests that what might have been acceptable practice in times of prosperity grew too costly for local constituencies with the coming of economic hard times and the bankruptcy of

158

TABLE 8-1
Party of Mayors in Selected Years, 1929–1942, for the
92 Cities over 100,000 Population, 1930*

	1929		1932		1935		1938		1942	
	N	%	N	%	N	%	N	%	N	%
Republican	45	48.9	21	22.8	17	18.4	14	15.2	16	17.4
Democratic	28	30.4	43	46.7	45	48.9	42	45.7	41	44.5
Third	2	2.2	1	1.1	4	4.4	3	3.3	2	2.2
Non-partisan & City Manager	14	15.2	23	25.0	23	25.0	33	35.8	30	32.6
No Information	3	3.3	4	4.4	3	3.3	0	0	3	3.3
TOTAL	92	100	92	100	92	100	92	100	92	100

*In 1930, 93 cities had populations of over 100,000. However, because of its unique governmental arrangement, Washington, D.C. has been omitted from these calculations. The list of cities was obtained from Table 3- Directory and Governmental data for the 1,809 Cities over 5,000 Population: 1938 in Clarence E. Ridley and Orin F. Nolting, eds., *The Municipal Year Book* 5 (Chicago, 1938), pp. 248-50, and is based on federal census population statistics for 1930. Information concerning the partisan affiliations of the 92 mayors was gathered from the lists of mayors published in the *World Almanac, 1929,* pp. 206-07; *1932,* 176-77; *1935,* 855–56; *1938,* 947-48; *1942,* 761 62. Since these lists were often incomplete regarding partisan affiliation, a *letter of inquiry* was sent to the mayor's office in 45 cities for which information was lacking; this represented a total of 65 of the 460 mayoral years being considered (92 cities multiplied by the 5 years for which information was gathered). These letters inquired about each city's mayor and his partisan affiliation during the years for which there was no data. Thirty-seven replies were received supplying information about fifty-five additional mayoral years. In this manner, the data base for the table above was increased and the number of cities for which no information existed was minimized. I would like to thank the many mayors, city clerks, councilmen, and publicists who cooperated with this study.

many municipal governments. As a contemporary observer pointed out, "In the cases where notoriously corrupt political machines were spanked, it is doubtful whether the zeal for honesty was as important as the feeling that in these hard times, no city can afford the wastefulness which goes with a graft ridden administration."[6]

In New York, the Seabury investigations of city corruption helped pave the way for the flight from the country and resignation of Tammany's dapper Mayor Jimmy "Beau James" Walker and the replacement of his temporary successor by Fusion candidate, La Guardia. In Pittsburgh, the shift took the form of a scandal-plagued Republican administration being replaced by a Democratic mayor, William Nisley McNair; McNair temporarily won for the Democrats the votes of a large proportion of the city's native white, upper-class population, who were disenchanted with the tarnished Steel City GOP. Cleveland Republican, Harry L. Davis, defeated the Democratic incumbent in a campaign which highlighted grand jury charges alleging that vice and crime were prevalent in the party. In Bridgeport, a series of bridge contracting scandals affecting both major parties encouraged the transfer of office from the incumbent Democrats to the Socialists led by Jasper McLevy.[7]

Despite this seemingly fundamental change in the city's voting behavior and political philosophy, the advent of socialism in the Park City actually marked the continuance of business as usual and ultimately led to Bridgeport's urban deterioration in the post-World War II years. The Italian-American newspaper *L'Aurora* warned that with the election of McLevy and his Socialist followers "the fair name of the City of Bridgeport, as the industrial capital of Connecticut, [was] seriously menaced by the Red Peril." But, *The New Republic* came closer to the mark when it commented in November, 1933, that "The Socialist administration in Bridgeport is another interesting sign of the restlessness of the voters, but we do not believe that it is anything more fundamental. Neither in Reading, Pennsylvania, in Milwaukee, nor any other town which has elected Socialist officials, has much been done which is anymore far reaching and effective than could have been done by an intelligent group of Goo-goos!" Political continuity, not change, would be the chief characteristic of Bridgeport in twenty-four years of Socialist rule.[8]

Bridgeport, which appeared to some as in the vanguard of Depression-induced radical socialism, and to others as simply on the verge of efficient reform government, did not come into existence as a corporate unit until 1836, almost two hundred years after it had been settled by the English. Construction of the Housatonic railroad encouraged the settlement of approximately 3,000 people to incorporate into a city. By the time of the Civil War, the population had more than quadrupled to over 13,000 with

160

Bridgeport rapidly being transformed into a manufacturing center speciali-
zing in the production of sewing machines, carriages, and the making of
shirts. The city's proximity to New York, about sixty miles away, spurred
its growth by providing both a labor supply and a ready market for manufactured goods. With a good harbor and excellent rail connections, and the
coming of the brass and weapons industries after the war, Bridgeport's
growth was assured during the late nineteenth century.[9]

By the turn of the century, after population rate increases of nearly
77 percent during the 1880—1890 decade and 45 percent during 1890—
1900, Bridgeport housed 71,000 people, almost one-third of whom were
foreign born. The last great burst of population growth for the city came
during the World War I decade, which saw a 40 percent rate of increase;
Bridgeport's population was approximately 143,500 in 1920. For Bridgeport, with its armaments industry, World War I meant jobs which served to
attract thousands of workers to the city. During the latter part of 1915
and the early part of 1916, the Remington Company, one of the nation's
leading weapon producers which had located in the city, hired a new employee every twenty minutes. Its January 1915 work force of 1,500
rose to 3,000 by November and skyrocketed to 16,000 by April of the following year. Estimates hold that by 1916 about 170,000 people resided in
Bridgeport and the labor turnover rate reached as high as 300 percent.
Thus, many more individuals passed through Bridgeport during the decade
than had settled there in 1920; it was a city in flux, beset by housing, traffic, and other problems created by the wartime in-migration. Bridgeport's
decennial growth rate, however, never again approached that of the 1910—
1920 decade, being little over 2 percent during the 1920s, 3 percent during
the Depression decade, and about 8 percent during the 1940s. During the
1950s and 1960s, as was the case with many central cities, the population
actually declined by 1.2 percent and 0.1 percent. However, the total emigration from the city, which was primarily white, was much larger than aggregate figures show because of large Black and Puerto Rican in-migration.[10]

Thus, the population of the industrial city which Jasper McLevy and
his Socialists administered from 1933 through 1957 grew little; but, by the
end of the era, a significant demographic change with equally important political consequences had developed. When McLevy first took office, he governed a city of 147,000, almost three-quarters of which was foreign stock.
One estimate of the city's ethnic groups during the late 1930s had Italian
and Irish each comprising approximately 20 percent of the population,
British-Americans 13 percent, Slovaks 10 percent, Hungarians 9 percent,
Jews 6.5 percent, and Germans and Austrians together an equal proportion
to the Jews; they were followed in descending order of size by Poles,
Swedes, French-Canadians, Lithuanians, and Russians. A majority of the

161

city's church members were Catholic. Negroes made up only 2 percent of the population. The large mass base of German ethnics common to the other two major socialist cities of the Depression decade, Milwaukee and Reading, Pennsylvania, was not present in McLevy's Bridgeport.[11]

Coming to power in an ethnic city, the Socialists also assumed control of an industrial city beset by the Great Depression. Although the crash of 1929 affected Bridgeport during the fall of that year, its full effect was not felt until two years later. A moderate amount of unemployment had existed throughout the 1920s in the city, but it never totaled more than 5 percent of the adult working population and was always considered temporary. Even immediately after the crash, the development of a permanent unemployment problem seemed remote to most Bridgeporters. Companies like General Electric, which had moved to the city in 1920, proceeded to add to their physical plants or planned to build new ones. However, by February 1930, the mood began to change. A Republican member of the Common Council introduced a resolution urging the city to provide emergency relief work for the unemployed; by April, local public works projects supported 300 men and their families. The inadequacy of such assistance rapidly became apparent when authorities reported that almost 12,000 persons had applied for relief to private charities since the first of the year.[12]

Weekly payrolls plummeted to the point that by the summer of 1931 fewer workers were employed in Bridgeport than in 1914. The thirty largest factories reported that their employees had worked 493,176 man-hours in 1931 compared to 912,381 in 1923. The average monthly case load of the City Welfare Department increased from 1,809 in 1930 to 2,942 in 1931; by the end of the year, welfare needs had forced the city into an estimated deficit of over $1,000,000, and the worst was yet to come. Estimates of unemployment in the spring of 1932 ran as high as 25 percent of Bridgeport's labor force, and the city's added borrowing to meet the welfare crisis pushed it perilously close to the statutory limitations on municipal debt. At the beginning of 1933, all municipal employees received a 20 percent cut in wages; and the Democratic mayor, Edward T. Buckingham, sought assistance from private sources.[13]

In 1932, Buckingham had asked local public utilities for a $500,000 loan. Although the loan was refused, the utilities agreed to pay their taxes a year in advance, which made $340,000 available for the municipal payroll. This amount helped, but fell far short of the total needed. Bridgeport tapped private sources again in 1933, when it conducted an "Industrial Rehabilitation Drive" to remodel and repair plant structures within the city; Bridgeport industrialists pledged more than $1,000,000 to help themselves while simultaneously aiding the city's unemployed by creating jobs. The

162

plight of the unemployed, however, already had reached a danger point. During the spring of 1933, the Bridgeport Medical Society appointed a committee to investigate the many cases of malnutrition and scurvy reported among those living on direct relief. It labeled as "dangerous" their diet which consisted largely of fat salt pork, onions, beans, and potatoes.[14]

Shortly thereafter, in April 1933, the municipal Welfare Department received a larger number of applications for relief than ever before in its history. The total had risen from 44,161 to more than 80,000 within a twelve-month period. Private charitable agencies, hampered by lack of resources, were also unable to help much because of the strict rule by the Welfare Department that it would drop any family from its rolls if the private agencies gave them additional assistance. Impoverished Jews, who observed religious dietary laws, were especially affected because they could not eat meals served by the Welfare Department's commissary; Jewish relief agencies had to bootleg kosher food to these victims of both the Depression and the welfare bureaucracy.[15]

Bridgeport's destitute single and homeless men were placed in a camp near Redding, Connecticut, where they received food, clothing, lodging, and $1 a week in return for five and a half days of work. For those who did have work, conditions deteriorated. From about 1930 on, for example, many small garment factories—often "fly by night" concerns which found existence difficult in New York and New Jersey—moved into Bridgeport. Paying extremely low wages, and characterized by unsanitary conditions, the "sweatshop," by 1933, emerged as a local problem. Thus, even with the advent of federal programs such as the NRA and PWA prior to the November municipal elections, the Socialists inherited from their Democratic predecessors a city immersed in economic despair.[16]

The Socialist victory had not come entirely by surprise. As early as the spring of 1930, Minnie Cederholm, the party's state Treasurer-Secretary, informed national headquarters that there appeared to be a good deal of competition for nomination to state offices "which shows that Connecticut is quite active." Seven months later, she reported that there was an increase of almost 50 percent in the vote for the Socialists in 1930 over their 1928 total. The party's vote gained in almost every town in the state. Moreover, party membership in Connecticut had increased and locals that had not functioned since the Progressive era came alive. Mrs. Cederholm enthusiastically pointed out that "There are no special problems in our state as to organizing, it is just that for the past few years the comrades had lost heart but I am sure we have all found ourselves and are going out to win the next city elections, the state is just seeping with enthusiasm and rearing to go [sic]. The prospects were never any brighter than this time for party building, no deficits facing the state organization with everything

163

looking favorable we are bound to build up and keep going up."[17]

Her enthusiasm was not unwarranted. The Connecticut Socialist party annual membership jumped from 109 in 1928 to 743 by October 1936; a high of 939 was reached in 1935. The greatest gains accrued between 1932 and 1933, the year Jasper McLevy was elected mayor. Although the numbers are small in comparison to Connecticut's total 1930 population of 1,600,000, the 1933 Connecticut party total comprised approximately 4 percent of the SP's national membership of 18,548. In that year, the small New England state held the ninth largest membership behind New York, Wisconsin, Pennsylvania, Massachusetts, California, Illinois, New Jersey, and Ohio; by 1935, it placed sixth following New York, Pennsylvania, Wisconsin, Massachusetts, and Illinois. The city of Bridgeport housed a large proportion of the state total.[18]

From the Bridgeport Socialists' perspective, however, Jasper McLevy's near victory in the 1931 mayoralty election appeared more important than the increase in state party membership. In that year, the Socialist candidate won 36 percent of the vote, with 15,054 Bridgeporters casting their ballots in his behalf; only 3,000 votes separated McLevy from the triumphant Democrat, while the Republican candidate ran a poor third. One Socialist alderman, Fred Schwarzkopf, several Socialist selectmen, and other minor officers were elected. Schwarzkopf later served as city clerk and as the mayor's political alter ego in City Hall.[19]

McLevy, the Socialist standardbearer and perennial candidate, was born in Bridgeport to two Scotch immigrants, Hugh and Mary Stewart McLevy, on March 27, 1878, the oldest of nine children. After an elementary education, he went to work at age fourteen, first in local factories and then as an apprentice in the roofing trade, which had been a family occupation for generations; he worked with his uncle for several years and ultimately started his own roofing business. As a skilled craftsman, McLevy worked actively in the labor movement; he joined the AFL in 1900 and was vice president of the Connecticut Federation of Labor, organizer of the Central Labor Union of Bridgeport and also of the city's Building Trade Council. He served several times as international president of the Slate and Tile Roofers' Union.[20]

On October 11 of the same year that he joined the AFL, McLevy became a member of the Socialist party, Branch 10, Local Bridgeport along with four others. For several years, he had been participating in discussions and arguments about socialism at Charles Porzenheim's tobacco shop in the heart of the city. Although initially opposed to the socialist philosophy, Edward Bellamy's *Looking Backward* impressed McLevy greatly and won him as a convert to the cause. He stood for minor municipal office the year that he joined the party. By 1911, McLevy ran as the party's top

164

candidate, winning 24 percent of the vote cast for mayor. From then on, he ran in every election for that office until the late 1950s.[21]

Although McLevy's proportion of the vote in 1911 was less than that of the Socialist candidate for mayor in Reading during the same year or Milwaukee a year earlier—the two major cities that would have strong Socialist movements when McLevy was finally elected in 1933—the Bridgeport Socialists did elect one alderman during the Progressive years. Hopelessly outnumbered 23 to 1, the alderman, Fred Cederholm, could do little but unsuccessfully introduce resolutions into the Common Council and oppose "anti-working class legislation." The program that the Bridgeport Socialists presented resembled those of Socialists in other cities at the time: a public bathing house for the people of Bridgeport's east side, a municipal market place, public comfort stations, a municipal light and power plant, reduced trolley fares, and civil service covering firemen, policemen, and other important city employees. Limited by charter restrictions, the fear of driving industry from their cities, and the knowledge that a socialist municipality in a capitalist country was restricted in its activity, the Progressive-era municipal Socialists, just as would be the case for their counterparts during the New Deal and after, proposed little more than many non-Socialist reformers.[22]

In the intervening years between the Progressive era and the coming of the Great Depression, McLevy actively served the Socialist party; he not only stood for mayor in every contest, but ran for governor several times, acted as a party organizer, and served on the state and national executive committees of the Socialist party. Years later, a former Socialist party member reminisced that it was McLevy's coming to speak in Springfield, Massachusetts in 1931 that won her over to joining the party. Thus, by the time of the Depression and his 1931 near victory, McLevy had a state and national, as well as local, reputation. Between 1931 and his triumph in 1933, the veteran Socialist campaigner and his followers organized for victory and paid more attention to political manuevering than socialist ideology. Some Socialist dissidents opposed to McLevy's leadership contended he was degrading "the Socialist Party into a vote catching political organization."[23]

His detractors also claimed that McLevy, against socialist principles, supported evictions of the poor by recently elected Socialist sheriffs. When the national party leader, Morris Hillquit, visited Bridgeport, he tempered his enthusiasm for the 1931 mayoralty vote and minor office victories by noting that the election of Socialist sheriffs was a mistake. He informed the Bridgeporters that good Socialists do not throw people out on the street; they should either find them another place to live or pay their rent at the house from which they were being evicted. Although the disgruntled

165

Socialists agreed, McLevy did not take well to this suggestion. The dissidents, who enrolled themselves in correspondence courses in the meaning of socialism and who sponsored a lecture series in their clubhouse, saw the Socialists' first role as educating the public and not winning elections. Their complaints about McLevy to the national office, however, fell upon deaf ears. As one of the dissidents remarked, "They just didn't want to believe that anything like that was really going on in Bridgeport. They were counting on the McLevy name to bring them quite a few votes from this section of the country and they didn't want anything to spoil it."[24]

During this period, the McLevy Socialists were accused of being "100 percent American" as well as untrue to socialist principles. After the 1931 election, some German-American singers volunteered their services for a celebration honoring McLevy and the triumphant candidates. Two days before the affair, they received word that they were not wanted because "it was desired to give an American character to the affair and 'foreign offerings were not acceptable.' " By 1933, however, the Bridgeport Socialists changed their strategy in preparation for the coming election. Before the official opening of the mayoralty campaign, the Party sponsored an early summer picnic. Over 1,000 people packed a local park to pitch horseshoes, view a baby contest, dance to the music of the Four Aces, and listen to Fred Schwarzkopf make a stump speech which stressed that the foreign element in Bridgeport had been fooled too long by the false leaders among the old party politicians. The Socialists appealed directly to the city's ethnic groups to join them in a November victory.[25]

As the Bridgeporters girded for political battle—training sessions were held every Tuesday evening for campaign orators—the National Executive Committee (NEC) of the party met at Reading to discuss, among other points, municipal campaigns. It pointed out that the Socialist local planning a municipal campaign faced two possibilities: first, campaign to win office; second, convert the people to socialism. The Committee went on to remark that the strategy of soft-pedalling radical intentions in the hope of converting the public to socialism by actions once in office was doomed to failure because "an administration and officials elected by nonsocialists do not represent Socialism." Moreover, in time of depression when there was little money for constructive public works and services, the socialist administration in power, "without a clear mandate from the people for vigorous class action, is a pathetic figure and may be a dangerous obstacle to party growth and health." Hence, the ideal campaign was the "campaign to make Socialists, to explain the class struggle to workers, fought in part against the background of a city election but fought with equal vigor between elections, on the street corner, in the headquarters and in the classroom, in the party press, on the billboards."[26]

166

After pointing out that charter and other restrictions prevented the establishment of even modified municipal socialism, the NEC added,

and after all municipal Socialism is not what we want. Without the state and national government, we can never really have Socialism; with the state and national governments, we can have it without bothering with any of the makeshifts and half-measures we must put [up] with today. *Municipal office and the pursuit of it, are primarily useful to us in attaining a strong organization with which to build the workers commonwealth. It is not, and must never be, an end in itself. . . . The socialist who campaigns for municipal office should be a socialist first and a candidate second; he should never for one moment forget that socialism will not be attained through city hall.* (Italics added.)[27]

At its July 16 State Convention in West Haven, the Connecticut Socialist party convention chaired by Jasper McLevy reiterated this statement by urging members and locals who participated in municipal campaigns that "while promising good government, at the same time to keep uppermost the demands for a thorough going socialistic reconstruction of society." Shortly afterwards, however, as the Bridgeport campaign got underway, Darlington Hoopes wrote to Norman Thomas, "Apparently Jasper is set on getting elected and doesn't want to alienate any possible votes, even from anti-Socialists. That, in my mind, is very bad policy and the Party will pay dearly for it."[28]

Indeed, McLevy and his followers were determined to get elected. The large Socialist vote for mayor two years earlier brought forth unusual interest in the election; the series of bridge contracting scandals which affected both the Democratic and Republican parties and the general downturn of the economy all made the pot of gold at the end of the electoral rainbow seem within reach. The Socialist party represented a fresh answer to what were becoming old and increasingly irritating problems. Moreover, McLevy, having run in every mayoralty election since 1911, had, in contemporary political terms, "a high recognition factor."[29]

The long-time candidate for mayor won the unanimous backing of the delegates to Bridgeport's Socialist nominating convention. More than 150 people crowded into the city's Workmen's Circle Hall to witness the nomination and to adopt a platform, which McLevy helped to draft, pledging the Socialist party to work for:

a) A Reorganization of the Municipal Government to eliminate waste, inefficiency and corruption;
b) Municipal ownership of public utilities;
c) Introduction of the Merit System and Civil Service;
d) Itemized accounts of all city expenditures;

167

e) Strict Adherence to the City Charter;
f) Return of Home Rule for Bridgeport;
g) Opportunity for Expression of public opinion at Common Council
   meetings;
h) Discontinuance of Secret Board meetings;
i) Planned government in order to build for the future as well as to meet
   the needs of the present."[30]

In his acceptance speech McLevy charged that "those now in power
in the city [the Democrats] are more interested in spoils than in administering affairs of the city." He said that if he thought the Socialist party
would follow the other two parties in the spoils system, he would refuse
to be a candidate. He promised to fight any Socialist candidate who, if
elected, adopted the spoils system, and invited the party to force him out
of office if he followed the system in the event of election. He proclaimed
that the legislature had taken one office after another out of the hands of
the people and outlined the history of the "ripper" legislation affecting
the city down to the last session. He said Bridgeport was in such a
financial muddle that even the Democratic administration's own senators
and representatives were forced to vote to have financial control of the
city taken from the mayor and placed by the state legislature in the hands
of the Board of Apportionment and Taxation, whose members had their
terms extended. In 1933 the NEC had suggested that municipal platforms
advocate such reformist planks as: 1) slum clearance and rehousing; 2) adequate unemployment relief and public works; 3) a definite stand against
wage cuts to municipal employees and reduction in social services; 4) the
establishment of better clinics "not as charities but as preventives which
will in the long run save the city and the people"; 5) increased recreational
and educational facilities; and 6) advocacy of civil liberties and the rights
of organized labor. But, the stated purpose of the Bridgeport Socialist platform was merely to discover the answer to the question "How to achieve
honest, efficient and serviceable municipal government?" It had come little way from its forebears of the Progressive era.[31]

When a Citizens' Fusion group, with a clean government platform
very much like the Socialists', endorsed McLevy to head a ticket composed
of Republicans and Democrats, McLevy refused to join them. He shrewdly
pointed out that an individual elected as mayor without a board of supporting aldermen would simply be a figurehead in the municipal government.
He attacked the proposers of the suggestion as mere politicians; a local col-
umnist noted, "That's just the strategy of the fellow who is a very clever
politician himself. He has been playing the game for a good many years
and knows the strategy thoroughly."[32]

The Fusion group, which had the Citizens and Taxpayers Voters

League as a base, pledged to prevent business and industry from being tax-
ed out of the city. Under ordinary circumstances, it might appear strange
that a group with such a goal would support a Socialist. McLevy, however,
was no enemy of business. Some businessmen, hoping for a more efficiently run municipal government and a way out of the city's financial collapse,
actually helped to finance McLevy's 1933 campaign. They apparently did
not fear any "Red Peril" emanating from the practical Scotsman. Their
trust was not betrayed. Sixteen years after McLevy was first elected may-
or, Herman H. Steinkraus, then president of the United States Chamber of
Commerce and also head of Bridgeport Brass, appeared on "America's
Town Meeting of the Air." He told the radio audience, "We have a Socialist Mayor; he has been there for 16 years, but he never was elected because
he was a Socialist. He's a good, honest Scotsman who has handled our
money carefully, and we Republicans have put him in office." McLevy
would often reciprocate by telling friends, "You can trust the Republicans
more than the Democrats." As a consequence, throughout his political career, accusations persisted that the GOP financed McLevy's campaigns. If
he trusted the Republicans more, the Democrats at least thought they understood the man who governed Bridgeport. After McLevy's 1933 victory,
Connecticut's Democratic National Committeeman, Archibald McNeil, reported, "McLevy, in spite of his Socialist background, is a reasonable conservative, level-headed American citizen and an admirer of the President."[33]

The new mayor's vote in 1933 totaled 22,445, or 49 percent in a
three-way race, which gave the Democrats 35 percent and the Republicans
a mere 15 percent. Moreover, Socialists won twelve of the sixteen seats up
for election on the city's Common Council. Like their leader, the majority
of these officeholders were skilled workers, who demonstrated little desire
to bring about a workingman's revolution. Their effect on the city, would,
in John Dos Passos's phrase of a year earlier, be "about the same . . . as
drinking a bottle of near-beer." Despite the tepid quality of Bridgeport socialism, on the first May Day following the McLevy Administration's coming to power, pranksters surprised the entire city, including the Socialists,
by hoisting a red flag with hammer and sickle atop City Hall. The practice
of reformism would, however, temper the expectation of radicalism.[34]

Much of what the Bridgeport Socialists pointed to as the major accomplishments of McLevy's first two-year administration resulted from success in the 1934 state elections. The city elected three state senators and
two state representatives with the result that the state senate was composed
of seventeen Democrats, fifteen Republicans, and three Socialists. Wilbur
Cross, the Democratic governor, recognized the implications of the Socialist position of balance of power, and called a special meeting with party
leader McLevy shortly after the election. Ultimately, the Socialist legisla-

169

tors supported a wide array of reform legislation, such as an old age pension act, a child labor act, an act that reduced the maximum work week for women in industry to forty-eight hours, and several other social reforms that passed at the state level. More important for the city, however, the senators worked for a series of "Bridgeport bills" which allowed the Socialists to implement their local reform program.[35]

These included a civil service law setting up the merit system for municipal employees; an act which repealed state control over the city Board of Apportionment and Taxation, thereby giving exclusive control over municipal finances back to Bridgeport; an act which revised the pension system for the city's police and fireman in an attempt to end abuses in the methods of obtaining pension pay; and an act which amended the city charter to create a central maintenance bureau for the more efficient upkeep of all city buildings and property under the Director of Public Works. While these extended power to the city, another important measure transferred responsibility to the state for maintenance of a trunkline highway that extended from the towns of Fairfield to Stratford through Bridgeport. City maintenance of the through route led to the bridge scandals which preceded the Socialist victory in the Park City. As the Bridgeport situation illustrated, with the city dependent upon the state for its governmental authority, the success of municipal socialism was often a function of state politics. In Connecticut, in 1935, good fortune smiled upon the McLevyites.[36]

Thus, after their first two years in office, the Bridgeport Socialists pointed to the preceding measures along with the following as their chief accomplishments. They took pride in the fact that all city business was conducted in open rather than the closed meetings common to their predecessors and that all city purchases were being made on the basis of competitive bids. Moreover, they emphasized fiscal responsibility and rationalization. No new bonds had been issued since they took office; city departments and the general running of municipal affairs had been reorganized on business lines which resulted in increased economies and efficiency. They delighted in noting that when the Socialists came to power in 1933 the tax rate for Bridgeport was 32 mills, the bonded indebtedness $16,000,000, and the immediate deficit in the city treasury close to $1,000,000. The McLevy Socialists considered among their greatest accomplishments the reduction of the city's debt, the reduction of its tax rate, a restoration of Bridgeport's credit rating, and the maintaining of business and industry in the city. As one Bridgeport manufacturer remarked, "To McLevy this city is *his* business, just as much as my factory is my business."[37]

Thus, in the 1935 municipal campaign, it was not difficult for the Socialists, as McLevy contended, "to drive home into the minds of the people that we Socialists are essentially a constructive factor . . . ." Unlike his first victory, the election yielded the Socialist mayor 56 percent of the vote, a clear majority in a three-way race, which saw the Republicans second and the Democrats a poor third. Moreover, the Socialists elected every one of their candidates to office in an overwhelming victory. This included the first woman in the city's history to be elected to the Board of Aldermen. Sadie K. Griffin, of the city's second district, assured her colleagues that she could easily accustom herself to responding to the appellation Alderman, since some were puzzled at first whether the more proper form of address might be Alderwoman. Otherwise, the Bridgeport Socialists found themselves in the enviable position of outmoding the city charter, which provided that certain boards and commissions be divided evenly between members of the two largest parties in the Board of Aldermen. With only one party in that body, they were in full control of the city's politics.[38]

However, while holding local power, the Socialists, at the state level, could not withstand the 1936 Roosevelt landslide and the growing rift within the Party nationally. As a consequence of the 1936 elections, they lost all of their legislative seats, but defeat was short-lived. After another municipal victory in 1937, McLevy, to the chagrin of the Democrats, polled over 166,000 votes in the 1938 gubernatorial election. Capitalizing on scandals concerning the Merritt Parkway and the city of Waterbury, which tainted both major parties, the Socialists' image of honesty and efficiency attracted enough votes from the Democratic incumbent to swing the election to Republican Raymond Baldwin. As one observer wrote to James A. Farley after the election. ". . . the Democrats should, if possible, win McLevy over to their side as the Socialists vote Democratic except for McLevy."[39]

If some within the party of Roosevelt appeared concerned with wooing the popular Socialist mayor over to their side, McLevy's reputation was equally enhanced within his own party as with the opposition. On the national level during the 1930s when the Socialist party split between the Old Guard and the Militant factions over the Socialist attitude towards war, democracy and cooperation with the Communists, McLevy emerged as a leader of the former group. August Claessens wrote to the Bridgeport mayor, "You are now the biggest man in the American Socialist movement in the estimation of our comrades." Norman Thomas might have disagreed, but he did respect McLevy enough to remark that although he could not support him, McLevy was one of the two other possible Socialist Presidential candidates besides himself who "could get any sort of hearing for Socialism" in 1936; Dan Hoan of Milwaukee was the other. McLevy went on to lead the conservative wing of the party when he served as the first head of the Social Democratic Federation. Throughout most of his tenure in office, he would command the Bridgeport and Connecticut Socialists in their battles with the national party; it ultimately censured McLevy in 1950 for accepting the electoral support of conservative businesswoman Vivien Kellems and running for governor on a ticket that offered Miss Kellems as senator. She had noted that the McLevy controlled Connecticut Socialist party was "far to the right of either the Republican or Democratic parties. The Democratic Party has adopted all of the Socialist Platform. I am no Socialist, I am an American. Jasper McLevy is also an American, a truly great one. He and I stand for the same things. . . ." She listed as the issues of agreement direct primaries, economy in government, lower taxes and an active political role for women.[40]

If the national party found it increasingly difficult to accept McLevy's brand of socialism, what of the public? Obviously, electing him as many times as they did [see Table 2], the voters approved of the honest, efficient, frugal government that he offered; they did not expect, nor did they desire socialism in its purest form. Who supported the Bridgeport Socialist mayor? Did his electoral base shift from the time of his initial victory in 1933 to his defeat in 1957?

As Table 3 indicates, McLevy, in his first election to the Park City mayoralty, found his support in ethnic (foreign stock), low rent districts. While he did poorly in expensive home-owning areas,[41] he appealed to those owning homes in the $5,000–$7,500 bracket, a middle-cost level according to the census of 1930. By the time of his "Last Hurrah" in 1957, McLevy, while still maintaining his popularity in white ethnic areas, was drawing on upper income voters for electoral support. By this date, his brand of socialism no longer attracted the new urban lower class. In fact, he did poorly in areas where Bridgeport's growing black and Puerto Rican population resided.[42] On the other hand, the Democrats, who finally unseated McLevy in 1957, had been weaker with ethnics and stronger in higher rental and expensive home owning areas when the mayor first won election; by the time of his defeat, they drew their strength from low income areas and districts into which blacks and Puerto Ricans had moved. Unlike the usual New Deal coalition in which urban foreign stock was supposed to be aligned with the Democratic party, in Bridgeport this group tended to vote Socialist in mayoralty elections.

What appears to have happened is that groups which supported McLevy when he came to office for the first time continued to support him at the end of his political career; newcomers to Bridgeport's electorate felt less allegiance to the Socialist mayor. Most interestingly, multiple regression analysis indicates that age was often the most significant variable in determining the Socialist vote for control of City Hall.

TABLE 8-2

Mayoralty Vote in Bridgeport, 1931–1959

Year	1931	1933	1935	1937	1939	1941	1943	1945
				Percent				
Democratic	42	35+	20	21+	27+	22+	19+	21+
Republican	22	15+	24	9+	14+	10+	15+	14+
Socialist	36	49	56	68+	58	67	65	63

Year	1947	1949	1951	1953	1955	1957	1959	
				Percent				
Democratic	23	25	21	23+	34+	45.3	57+	
Republican	20	21	26	23+	19+	9.6	15+	
Socialist	57	54	53	53	45	45.1	27+	

Voting statistics were compiled from the Bridgeport *Municipal Register* for the year following the election except for 1941 when the *Bridgeport Post,* November 5, 1941, p. 15 served as the source.

TABLE 8-3

Socialist and Democratic Mayoralty Votes in Bridgeport, 1933 and 1957, and Relationship to Economic and Ethnic Variables, 1930 and 1960, for Voting Districts*

1930	Socialist 1933	Democratic 1933	1960	Socialist 1957	Democratic 1957
Rent	−.53	.35	Low income	−.71	.75
Homes, $5,000-$7,499	.62	−.46	High income	.55	−.65
Homes, Greater than $10,000	−.53	.34	Foreign stock	.56	−.65
Native White	−.31	.16	Black	−.49	.54
Foreign Stock	.54	−.39	Puerto Rican stock	−.75	.79

*I would like to thank Bruce Clouette and Edmond J. True, University of Connecticut doctoral students in history and political science, respectively, for their much appreciated assistance in making my language and data understandable to the computer and its reply intelligible to me. Voting return analysis for this study was performed on the IBM 360 Computer System at The University of Connecticut Computer Center under NSF Grant GJ-9. Statistics relating to the economic and ethnic variables above were compiled from the appropriate tables in the Fifteenth and Eighteenth (1930 and 1960) Census of the United States. In 1930, data were listed by voting district for each of the city's districts. In 1960, data were listed by census tract so that the tract information had to be transposed to political district boundries. For source of voting returns, see Table 2. The numbers above represent the Pearson's r (Pearson product moment correlation coefficient) and measure the strength of association or "correlation" between the voting and demographic data. For an explanation of "measurement of association," see Charles M. Dollar and Richard J. Jensen, *Historians' Guide to Statistics* (New York, 1971), Chapter 3. For the hazards of the ecological fallacy presented by this type of analysis, see footnote 43.

TABLE 8-4
Socialist and Democratic Mayoralty Votes in Bridgeport, 1933
and 1957, and Relationship to Age of Voters, 1930 and 1960,
for Voting Districts

Age Cohorts* (Youngest to Oldest)	Socialist		Democratic	
	1933	1957	1933	1957
1	.57	−.60	−.49	.66
2	.29	−.12	−.17	.14
3	−.56	.60	.46	−.68
4	−.58	.50	.43	−.55
5	−	.17	−	−.17

See Table 2 for references.
*1930 U.S. Census age cohorts were: 1 (21–34)years old), 2 (35–44 years old),
3 (45–64 years old), 4 (65 plus years old);
1960 U.S. Census age cohorts were: 1 (20–34 years old; the nature of the data
did not permit separation of 20 year old non-voters from other potential voters
in this age group), 2 (35–44 years old), 3 (45–54 years old), 4 (55–64 years old),
5 (65 plus years old).

TABLE 8-5
Relationship of Age Cohorts, 1930 and 1960, and Ethnic, Racial, and
Economic Variables, 1930 and 1960, for Bridgeport Voting Districts

	Age 1	Age 2	Age 3	Age 4	Age 5*
Foreign Stock, 1930	.48	.68	−.63	−.74	−
Native White, 1930	−.08	−.60	.39	.51	−
Rent, 1930	−.37	−.77	.69	.77	−
Homes, Greater Than $10,000, 1930	−.70	−.55	.78	.78	−
Foreign Stock, 1960	−.76	−.21	.47	.61	.46
Black, 1960	.64	.04	−.43	−.42	−.27
Puerto Rican Stock, 1960	.62	−.02	−.61	−.46	−.02
Low Income, 1960	.49	−.33	−.70	−.19	.24
High Income, 1960	−.69	.03	.67	.46	.13

*See Table 2 for references.
See Table 3 for 1930 and 1960 age groupings. 1930 age groupings for voting
districts correlated with 1930 demographic data; 1960 age groupings for voting
districts correlated with 1960 demographic data.

TABLE 8-6
Relationship of Ethnic to Economic Variables, 1930 and 1960,
for Bridgeport Voting Districts

Foreign Stock 1930		Foreign Stock 1960	
Rent, 1930	−.85	Low Income, 1960	−.47
Homes, $5000–$7,499, 1930	.84	High Income, 1960	.53
Homes, Greater Than $10,000, 1930	−.63		

See Table 2 for references.

An analysis of Table 4 indicates that when McLevy came to power in 1933, he did best in areas having the highest proportion of young voters, especially those in the twenty-one to thirty-four age group. By the time of his defeat in 1957, he had little support in this age cohort but did well in districts where older voters, forty-five to sixty-five years old, resided in large proportions. The situation for the Democrats was exactly the opposite. The data suggests that new and young voters, probably as a result of the Depression, made their allegiance to McLevy early in their voting cycle and maintained it as they moved into middle and older age. At the beginning of the Depression decade, as Table 5 demonstrates, the youngest age groups in Bridgeport's population were those related to foreign stock and lower income areas; by 1960 these age cohorts were negatively related to foreign stock, strongly related to blacks and Puerto Ricans, and still associated with low-income districts; however, the older groups, which had been negatively related to foreign stock at the beginning of the Depression decade, were now positively related. While the older Bridgeporters were among the more affluent segments of the population in both periods, as time passed and the population changed, Table 6 suggests the foreign stock improved economically with age. These were the voters who apparently supported McLevy at the beginning and conclusion of his administration; they grew old and middle class with him. Many might have known no other mayor but the Scot Socialist, who had led them and the city out of Depression.[43]

The longer he served, the more McLevy represented middle-class virtue to many of the Bridgeport citizens who had fought their way out of the Depression under his leadership. He had tailored a political organization and philosophy to meet the needs and desires of the industrial city. In the words of Norman Thomas, McLevy's administration "was an example of city good government rather than of applied socialism on a municipal scale. I have not always thought his conventional and doubtless sincere socialist speeches (in national campaigns) were matched by performance . . . . Jasper for many years has managed to rule the Connecticut party with an iron hand, although I think he has done this mostly by his own force of character, which was scarcely matched by other members of the party. In fact it has been his asset and as you know, he has been repeatedly elected as Mayor of Bridgeport on the basis of character and performance rather than socialism."[44]

It is perhaps not surprising that a pamphlet called "Bridgeport Underground, 1934--1951" informed the people of the city that they possessed a sewage treatment system far surpassing that of any other Connecticut municipality. "Instituted by the present administration in the '30s, complex engineering, legal and financial problems were met and overcome.

175

Handicapped by labor and material shortages during war emergencies, Mayor McLevy's unswerving determination had brought this program to a successful conclusion despite all obstacles. Much of this vast municipal enterprise is underground, unseen by the public it benefits." At its least, McLevy's rule in Bridgeport was the classic example of "sewer socialism."[45]

At most, Bridgeport's Socialist mayor aimed to make his city a "City Beautiful." And, for this goal, as early as 1935, the Fairfield County Planning Association awarded McLevy a citation for playing a leading role in developing the physical appearance of the county. The Socialists had displayed a great deal of enthusiasm for improving Bridgeport's recreational facilities and shore resorts, curbing pollution, constructing parks, building miles of esplanades through the streets of the city, and establishing playgrounds; McLevy reactivated Bridgeport's moribund City Planning Commission. During the Great Depression, he vigorously supported slum clearance and Bridgeport was the first city in Connecticut to comply with the federal government's regulations for the building of housing projects. Discussing his plans for Bridgeport's future, as the Depression waned in 1940, McLevy wrote, "I feel that the American City can be just as much a pleasing picture as the small town. Careful and constructive planning in my opinion will work this result."[46]

Ironically, by 1957, when McLevy was defeated in his attempt to obtain his thirteenth term in office, Bridgeporters demonstrated growing concern at the deterioration in the city's physical features, particularly in the downtown area. Businessmen, especially, awakened to the realization of the consequences—loss of trade, decline in industrial opportunities, and a white exodus to the suburbs.

Redevelopment emerged as a major issue in the campaign after New Haven's Mayor Richard C. Lee, who had undertaken a huge urban renewal program in the neighboring city, hailed McLevy's Democratic opponent as the man who could lead Bridgeport in a similar project. As the campaign unfolded, both the Democratic and Republican candidates urged immediate steps toward redevelopment and criticized the Socialists for being too slow in moving toward urban renewal and in keeping old and attracting new industry. McLevy, on the other hand, pointed with pride to achievements in slum clearance, public housing, and sewer extension, but advocated a cautious approach to redevelopment, stressing the tight fiscal outlook. He reminded the public that urban renewal was "not a give-away," and that the city had to acquire the areas for clearance with its own funds; in the same vein, McLevy contended that "the fundamental issue" was a sound fiscal policy and a municipal budget based on reality. He claimed that his administration had accomplished that goal and told voters, "No political party pays the debts. It is the people and the business houses who

176

pay. The money comes out of your pocket."[47]

Thus, in adhering to his first principles of frugality and efficiency, the Socialist who so often espoused these finally stood opposed to the aspirations of the business community that had once so vigorously supported him. Bridgeport's Socialist "businessman" was unwilling to take entrepreneurial risks and stood for continuity at a time when the city's industrialists, businessmen, and merchants sensed the need for urban change. For them, as for their counterparts across the nation, this change meant the narrowly focused physical redevelopment of the city's central business district, which often omitted a social component and served as a catalyst for urban unrest during the 1960s.[48] McLevy would not even agree to such limited reform. Moreover, a new generation, and especially new ethnic and racial groups that came to Bridgeport during the 1950s, felt less of an attachment to the seventy-nine-year-old mayor than those who had known him and followed his political career for decades. In 1957, Bridgeport's socialism was looking to the past while clumsily coping with the present and turning away from the future. Twenty-four years after they had first assumed power, Bridgeport's Socialists offered little different to a constituency looking for new approaches and new priorities in the management of urban government. McLevy's fiscally conservative socialism had grown too frugal for the needs of a modern community caught up in the politics of urban continuity.

NOTES

1. For the best compilation of essays on this realignment, which includes the work of political scientists and historians such as Samuel Lubell, V.O. Key, Jr., Angus Campbell, Carl N. Degler, John L. Shover, and others, see Jerome M. Clubb and Howard W. Allen, eds., *Electoral Change and Stability in American Political History* (New York, 1971); also of importance are John M. Allswang, *A House for All Peoples: Ethnic Politics in Chicago 1890–1936* (Lexington, Kentucky, 1971); Michael Paul Rogin and John L. Shover, *Political Change in California: Critical Elections and Social Movements, 1890–1966* (Westport, Connecticut, 1970); John L. Shover, "The Emergence of a Two-Party System in Republican Philadelphia, 1924–1936," *The Journal of American History* 60 (March 1974), 985–1002; John L. Shover, "Ethnicity and Religion in Philadelphia Politics, 1924–40," *American Quarterly* 25 (December 1973), 499–515; David Burner, *The Politics of Provincialism: The Democratic Party in Transition, 1918–1932* (New York, 1968); Bruce M. Stave, *The New Deal and the Last Hurrah: Pittsburgh Machine Politics* (Pittsburgh, 1970); J. Joseph Huthmacher, *Massachusetts People and Politics, 1919–1933* (Cambridge, Massachusetts, 1959); Joel H. Silbey and Samuel T. McSeveney, *Voters, Parties and Elections: Quantitative Essays in the History of American Popular Voting Behavior* (Lexington, Massachusetts, 1972); James L. Sundquist, *Dynamics of the Party System: Alignment and Realignment of Political Parties in the United States* (Washington, D.C., 1973); Walter Dean Burnham, *Critical Elections and the Mainsprings of American Politics* (New York, 1970); Everett Carll Ladd, Jr., *American Political Parties: Social*

Change and Political Response (New York, 1970); the local impact of the Great Depression generally is treated in Bernard Sternsher, ed., *Hitting Home: The Great Depression in Town and Country* (Chicago, 1970); the New Deal at the state and local level will be the subject of the fifth volume of the *Modern America* series, edited by John Braeman, Robert Bremner, and David Brody for Ohio State University Press and has received attention in James T. Patterson, *The New Deal and the States: Federalism in Transition* (Princeton, New Jersey, 1969); Samuel P. Hays has pointed out the difference between political life at the local and national levels, noting that "historians have erroneously assumed a uniform perspective in local and national political history, emphasizing that national history is either local and state history writ large or that local and state history is national history writ small. But political life at one level is of an entirely different order from that at another. They are linked not by logical similarity but by human interaction." Samuel P. Hays, "Political Parties and the Community-Society Continuum," in William Nisbet Chambers and Walter Dean Burnham, eds., *The American Party Systems: Stages of Political Development* (New York, 1967), p. 153.

2. Jerome M. Clubb and Howard W. Allen, "The Cities and the Election of 1928: Partisan Realignment?" in Clubb and Allen, *Electoral Change and Stability in American Political History*, pp. 241–242, originally printed in *The American Historical Review*, 79 (April 1969), 1205–20; voting for local offices is given attention in the works by Allswang, Shover, and Stave.

3. One need not fully agree with David P. Thelen's interpretation of progressivism to see the wisdom of his assertion that "The central fact about the progressive movement from its birth in the mid–1890s until its death in World War I was that it derived its greatest vitality from action at the *local* level." This was so because of the immediacy of local problems and the need to solve these problems. If this applies to the period following the depression of 1893, it might likewise apply to the years immediately following the Crash of 1929 before the advent of the New Deal and be true to a greater extent than believed even after FDR took office. In a general sense, local elections are often seen as the primary vehicles for solving local problems. I might add that their consequences are often later seen by the public as the primary causes for such local problems. For Thelen's interpretation of progressivism, see David P. Thelen, *The New Citizenship: Origins of Progressivism in Wisconsin, 1885–1900* (Columbia, Missouri, 1972); the quote is from Thelen, "Progressivism as a Radical Movement," in Howard H. Quint et al., *Main Problems in American History*, Vol. 2, 3rd edition (Homewood, Illinois, 1972), p. 154.

4. These percentages do not measure how many elections were won in the years listed by each party, but represent the party affiliation of the mayor in that year. In many instances, the mayors would have been elected in an earlier year, e.g., the 1932 figure might reflect elections in the years 1931 or 1929 depending upon length of term in office; the Democratic proportion declined slightly after 1935 while the Republican proportion fell throughout the Depression decade and picked up only slightly in 1942. In none of the sampled years did either of the two major parties have a decisive majority in their control of city hall in the nation's metropolises. This can be accounted for by the growth of nonpartisan or city manager government during the 1930s; furthermore, the mounting nonpartisanship may actually be the local Republican response to increased Democratic strength. One must be cautious in considering the significance of the nonpartisan label, which can sometimes be misleading. A highly Democratic city like Boston operated under nonpartisan elections so that its mayor would be classified "nonpartisan," even if he might have been such a Democratic wheelhorse as James Michael Curley. As the City Secretary of Fort Worth, Texas wrote to me (August 10, 1973), "Since the City of Fort Worth was first chartered in 1873, all of our elections have been nonpartisan. As you probably know, this area, until recent years, has been predominantly Democratic. Though they are elected in elections that are strictly nonpartisan, the mayors of the City of Fort Worth during 1932, 1935, and 1938 were Democrats." For the purpose of this study, Fort Worth, however, was classified as nonpartisan. I would contend, even with the above qualification in mind, that the percentages evidenced in Table 1

reflect the trend that occurred in control of America's city halls between 1929 and 1942.

5. A "critical election" has been identified as one in which there is a high degree of electoral involvement and a sharp alteration of pre-existing electoral patterns which persists through several succeeding elections. See: V.O. Key, Jr., "A Theory of Critical Elections," *The Journal of Politics* 17 (February 1955), 3—18, reprinted in Clubb and Allen, *Electoral Change and Stability in American Political History,* 27—44; the "critical period" concept contends that realignment occurs over a period of several elections and that no one specific election is the "critical" one for realignment. See: Duncan MacRae, Jr. and James A. Meldrum, "Critical Elections in Illinois: 1888—1958," *The American Political Science Review* 54 (September 1960), 669—83 reprinted in Clubb and Allen, 46—74. Much of the debate over the New Deal realignment revolves around the question of whether the realignment occurred over several elections. The debate stems from Samuel Lubell's assertion that "the Republican hold on the cities was broken not by Roosevelt but by Alfred E. Smith. Before the Roosevelt Revolution there was an Al Smith Revolution." See: Samuel Lubell, *The Future of American Politics*, 3rd ed. (New York, 1965); the key segment of Lubell's chapter, "Revolt of the City," is reprinted in Clubb and Allen, pp. 3—25.

6. Accounts of the outcomes of the municipal elections can be found in: *New York Times,* November 9, 1933; Charles Willis Thompson, "Meaning of the Elections," *The Commonweal* 19 (December 1, 1933), pp. 124—26; and "Turning Out the Ins," *The New Republic* 77 (November 22, 1933), 33—34 from which the quote is taken. One historian concerned with machine politics in the nineteenth century has suggested "that with WASP American culture the permissible level [of graft] tolerated stands at about 10 to 15 percent. When the graft level rose above this figure, a reform movement was bound to appear." See: Monte A. Calvert, "The Manifest Functions of the Machine" in Bruce M. Stave, ed., *Urban Bosses, Machines, and Progressive Reformers* (Lexington, Massachusetts, 1972), 48; during the Great Depression anything approaching the 10 percent graft level probably appeared unacceptable. Another historian, Melvin G. Holli, asserts that high governmental costs often triggered urban reform movements, but that boss politics was "far less the cause of burgeoning city expenses than good government reformers popularly believed." See: Melvin G. Holli, "Urban Reform in the Progressive Era," in Lewis L. Gould, ed., *The Progressive Era* (Syracuse, New York, 1974), pp. 133—51, quote from page 150.

7. For the New York City situation, see: Arthur Mann, *LaGuardia Comes to Power: 1933* (Philadelphia, 1965) and Herbert Mitgang, *The Man Who Rode the Tiger: The Life of Judge Samuel Seabury and the Story of the Greatest Investigation of City Corruption in This Century* (New York, 1963, 1970); for Pittsburgh, see: Stave, *The New Deal and the Last Hurrah;* for Cleveland, see: The *Cleveland Plain Dealer,* November 1—9, 1933, which carried front page stories concerning the grand jury allegations; an undated, but probably 1935, Socialist campaign brochure in the Socialist Party State and Local Organization (SPSLO-Conn-Duke hereafter)—Connecticut, file of the Socialist Party of America Papers (SPAP hereafter), Duke University, Durham, North Carolina, details the Bridgeport bridge contracting scandals.

8. *L'Aurora,* November 2, 1933 in McLevy Papers, University of Bridgeport, Bridgeport, Connecticut (hereafter McLPUB); "Turning Out the Ins," *The New Republic* 77 (November 22, 1933), 34. These papers, as well as the University of Bridgeport's Schwarzkopf Collection, have been recently recatalogued. The citations in this essay refer to the original files.

9. Information regarding Bridgeport's growth is from "Bridgeport, Connecticut: The Story of its Economic and Social Growth" (unpublished ms., 1941, p. 1 in Box 32 of W.P.A. Ethnic Groups Survey in the Records of the Work Projects Administration, Connecticut, 1935—44 (hereafter WPAEGS), Connecticut State Library, Hartford, Connecticut. This study was prepared by the workers of the Writer's Program of the W.P.A. in Connecticut; the population figure of 3,000 in 1836 is from the *Centennial Illustrated History of Bridgeport, Connecticut and the Central Labor Union of Bridgeport and Vicinity and its Organization* (Bridgeport, 1900, p. 44.

179

10. U.S. Census Office, *Abstract of the 12th Census of the U.S.*, 1900 (Washington, 1902), pp. 100, 103; in 1900, Bridgeport was the third largest city in Connecticut and the 54th largest in the United States. Slightly more than one quarter of Connecticut's population and 13.6 percent of the United States' population was foreign born in 1900 so that Bridgeport's foreign population was higher than both state, nation, and the two larger Connecticut cities, New Haven and Hartford, *Abstract*, pp. 42, 7; growth rates can be found in Table 2, Greater Bridgeport Regional Planning Agency, "Population Report Number 2" (Bridgeport, December, 1961); for the 1970 figure see: State of Connecticut, Department of Finance and Control, *Census 70: An Abstract* (Hartford, 1972), p. 20; for Bridgeport during WWI, see: "Bridgeport Connecticut," WPAEGS, pp. 29–30, 37–38; for the deceptiveness of decennial census figures, such as those for 1920, to measure how many individuals pass through a city, see: Stephan Thernstrom and Peter R. Knights, "Men in Motion: Some Data and Speculations about Urban Population Mobility in Nineteenth-Century America," in Tamara K. Hareven, ed., *Anonymous Americans: Explorations in Nineteenth-Century Social History* (Englewood Cliffs, N.J., 1971), pp. 17–47; The population of the city of Bridgeport declined by about 2,000 during the 1950–1960 census period. This was the result of losing 15,300 whites and gaining 8,700 nonwhites and 4,700 Puerto Ricans. See: Greater Bridgeport Regional Planning Agency, *Profile of Six Neighborhoods in the City of Bridgeport* (Trumbull, Connecticut, 1965), p. 10; by 1970, the black and Spanish speaking (Puerto Rican) population in Bridgeport was 25,546 and 14,103 respectively; in 1950, nonwhites numbered 6,856 and Puerto Ricans an estimated 1,168, see: *Profile of Six Neighborhoods*, pp. 10 and 32 and *Census 70*, p..20, and U.S., Bureau of the Census, Nineteenth Census of the United States: 1970, I, Part 8, Connecticut.

11. U.S., Bureau of the Census, *Fifteenth Census of the United States: 1930. Population*, III, Part I, 366 lists Bridgeport's population of 146,716 to include 40,759 foreign born and 64,979 native white of foreign or mixed parentage. Taken together, this amounts to 71.6 percent of the city being composed of foreign stock; in 1930, the state of Connecticut was 54.9 percent foreign stock. See: Nathan L. Whetten and Henry W. Riecken, Jr., *The Foreign Born Population of Connecticut, 1940* (Storrs: Agricultural Experiment Station. Bulletin 246. September 1943), pp. 12–14; ethnic group estimates are from Samuel Koenig and David Rodnick, *Ethnic Factors in Connecticut Life: A Survey of Social, Economic and Cultural Characteristics of the Connecticut Population* (New Haven, 1940), Table 2, Chapter VI, between pp. 3–4; 62 percent of Bridgeport's church members were Catholics compared to 53 percent in Milwaukee and 30 percent in Reading, the other two major Socialist cities during the Depression. This religious estimate is from Henry G. Stetler, *The Socialist Movement in Reading, Pennsylvania: A Study in Social Change* (Storrs, Connecticut, 1943), p. 50. For McLevy's popularity among foreign stock voters, see Table 3 of this essay.

12. "Bridgeport, Connecticut," WPAEGS, pp. 77–80.

13. Ibid. pp. 81–85; Albert E. VanDusen, *Connecticut* (New York, 1961), p. 298.

14. "Bridgeport, Connecticut," WPAEGS, pp. 84–86.

15. Ibid., p. 86; Robert Washman to Harry Hopkins, December 2, 1934, Group 24, Hopkins Papers, FERA-APA Narrative Field Reports, Franklin D. Roosevelt Library (hereafter FDRL), Hyde Park, New York.

16. "Bridgeport, Connecticut," WPAEGS, pp. 86–91.

17. Minnie Cederholm to Socialist National Headquarters (Press News), April 3, 1930, SPSLO-Conn.-Duke; Minnie Cederholm report, November 16, 1930, Schwarzkopf Collection, University of Bridgeport, Bridgeport, Connecticut (hereafter SchkfUB), Filebox No. 1.

18. Three hundred and twenty-nine new members joined the Party between 1932 and 1933 as it increased its membership from 411 to 740; membership reports by state, 1928–1935 and "Comparative Gain or Loss for first 10 months of 1932–1936," SPSLO-Conn-Duke; Greater Bridgeport Regional Planning Agency, "Population Report No. 2, December, 1961, Table I; George H. Goebel to Fred Schwarzkopf, August 23, 1934, SchkfUB; in August, 1934, Goebel stated that there were over 300 Socialist party members in Bridgeport.

19. City of Bridgeport, *Municipal Register*, 1932, p. 443; City of Bridgeport, *Manual*, 1936, p. 9.

20. City of Bridgeport, *Manual*, 1936, pp. 1—9; Campaign reprint of Webb Waldron, "Jasper Goes to Town," *The American Magazine*, April 1938, Tamiment Institute Library, New York City.

21. Minute Book, The Socialist Party, Branch 10, Local Bridgeport, October 11, 1900, SchkfUB; Waldron, "Jasper Goes to Town"; Stetler, *Socialist Movement in Reading*, pp. 48—49.

22. In 1910 Emil Seidel was elected the first Socialist mayor of Milwaukee with 46 percent of the vote while in 1911 Edward Leffler polled 30 percent for mayor in Reading, Pa., Stetler, *Socialist Movement in Reading*, pp. 48—49; Report of Legislative Committee of Local Bridgeport, Socialist Party, February 9, 1913, SPSLO-Conn-Duke; Report of Elected Officials, May 10, 1913, SPSLO-Conn-Duke; James Weinstein, *The Decline of Socialism in America, 1912-1935* (New York, 1969), pp. 108—09.

23. Oral History Interview with Mr. & Mrs. Alfred Baker Lewis, p. 12, University of Bridgeport Oral History Project (hereafter UBOHP) and Oral History Interview with George and Al Ribak, p. 15, UBOHP.

24. Oral History Interview with George and Al Ribak, pp. 11—16, UBOHP.

25. Julius Gerber to Minnie Cederhom, January 4, 1932, Filebox No. 1, SchzkfUB; *Commonwealth*, July, 1933, SPSLO-Conn-Duke. While the Bridgeport Socialists had no large German-American mass base such as those in Milwaukee and Reading, there were some German and Austrian Socialist activists such as Fred Schwarzkopf. Moreover, the *New Leader*, May 26, 1934 reported that McLevy had married Vida Stearns, whose "father, Edwin Stearns, is believed to be the oldest Socialist in America, having joined the movement in Germany around 1870."

26. *Commonwealth*, July 1933, SPSLO-Conn-Duke; "Municipal Problems," Statement adopted by Socialist Party National Executive Committee, July 4, 1933, pp. 1—2, SPAP-Duke; see Appendix of this book for Walter Lippmann's analysis of the Socialist role in municipal elections.

27. 'Municipal Problems," pp. 3, 5, SPAP-Duke.

28. *Commonwealth*, July 1933, SPSLO-Conn-Duke; Darlington Hoopes to Norman Thomas, September 27, 1933, Hoopes Papers. The author wishes to thank Professor William C. Pratt of the University of Nebraska at Omaha, and a contributor to this volume, for bringing this quote to my attention.

29. Clipping, *Bridgeport Times-Star*, August 30, 1933, Jack Bergen Scrapbook (hereafter JBSBK) loaned by Mr. Bergen to the author; campaign brochure concerning bridge scandals, 1935, SPSLO-Conn-Duke; Stetler, *Socialist Movement in Reading*, p. 131; In the two other cities where the Socialists were strong, Milwaukee and Reading, the same man ran for mayor over a large number of elections covering many years.

30. Bridgeport Socialist Party Platform and Bridgeport *Post*, August 31, 1933, clipping, JBSBK.

31. Ibid.; "Municipal Problems," p. 3; Unemployment relief is mentioned at the extreme end of the Bridgeport Platform statement, but is not listed among the major points of the platform; McLevy's disdain for "spoils" may have been based on a fear that emphasis on patronage would have had a disabling effect on the Party. This occurred in Reading during the 1930s when "patronage socialists" joined the party for jobs only. See: William C. Pratt, "The Reading Socialist Experience: A Study of Working Class Politics" (unpublished Ph.D. dissertation, Emory University, 1969), pp. 514—18; for the "ripper legislation" regarding the Board of Apportionment and Taxation, see: *New Leader*, June 22, 1935, 3, in which the Bridgeport correspondent, Abraham Knepler, contends that the legislature extended the board's term because it feared the Socialists assuming office and wished to dilute Socialist control.

32. Bridgeport *Post*, September 7, 1933, clipping, Bridgeport *Times-Star*, "The Wailing Wall," September 8, 1933, JBSBK.

33. Bridgeport *Post*, September 8, 1933, clipping JBSBK; Interview with John P. Shenton and Interview with George and Al Ribak, UBOHP; While Ribak opposed

McLevy and Shenton was a close and friendly associate of the Mayor, both interviews corroborated the connection of Bridgeport business with McLevy's 1933
campaign; for an example of an accusation that Republicans financed McLevy's
campaigns, see: Joseph H. Bates, Democratic Town Chairman, Pomfret, Connecticut to James A. Farley, December 19, 1938, OF 300 Election Forecasts Analyses, and Results, 1938, Arkansas -Iowa, Connecticut Folder, Box 89, FDRL;
Weekly People, editorial, Saturday, December 8, 1962; Interview with Abraham
Knepler. In his *Decline of Socialism,* James Weinstein points out that during the
Progressive era, "On a municipal level, Socialist administrations often met with
the approval, implicit if not explicit, of the large and more sophisticated business
interests," (p. 109); Archibald McNeil to Marvin H. McIntyre, November 15,
1933, McLevy File, FDRL.

34. City of Bridgeport, *Municipal Register,* 1934, p. 308, votes percentaged by the
author; *New Leader,* November 11, 1933, 1; listing of aldermen from City of
Bridgeport, *Municipal Register,* 1935, p. 31 were compared to occupations listed
in the Bridgeport City Directory, 1932 and 1934; Twelve of the aldermen serving during McLevy's first term were Socialists. The large majority were skilled
workmen: a steamfitter; two carpenters; a toolmaker; one roller and one machinist at Bridgeport Brass; a gas, oil and automobile repairman; a foreman in a city
department; a foreman for a manufacturing company; one night manager who
became an FERA foreman; one "manager"—company type unknown. The four
Democrats elected consisted of a lawyer, a bookkeeper, a shipping clerk and an
electrician. Of the twenty-four Common Council members who served during
the prior Democratic administration of Edward T. Buckingham, a lawyer, nine or
37.5 percent could be classified as white-collar workers or proprietors. Although
the Socialists elected twelve aldermen and the Democrats four in 1933, there
were three Republicans and ten Democratic holdovers in McLevy's first Common
Council. The holdovers were to serve for one year when the number of aldermen
would be reduced to a total of the sixteen elected in 1933. *(New Leader,* December 9, 1933), 1. The three Republicans and one of the Democratic holdovers combined with the Socialists to elect a Socialist president of the Board of Aldermen;
the full quote from John Dos Passos is "Becoming a Socialist right now would
have just about the same effect on anybody as drinking a bottle of near-beer."
It appeared in his "Whither the American Writer," *Modern Quarterly* 6 (Summer
1932), 11–12 and is cited from John P. Diggins, *The American Left in the 20th
Century* (New York, 1973), p. 122, *New Leader,* May 12, 1934, p. 12.

35. *New Leader,* November 10, 1934, p. 1, November 17, 1934, p. 1, December 15,
1934, p. 3, June 15, 1935, p. 1.

36. *New Leader,* June 1, 1935, p. 6, June 8, 1935, p. 2, June 15, 1935, p. 1, June 22,
p. 3.

37. 1935 campaign flier comparing Bridgeport in 1933 and 1935, SPSLO-Conn-Duke;
Fred Schwarzkopf to Raymond S. Hofses, February 23, 1937, SchkfUB; Waldron, "Jasper Goes to Town."

38. *New Leader,* June 22, 1935, p. 5, November 9, 1935, p. 1, November 16, 1935,
p. 2, December 7, 1935, p. 6; John P. Driscoll, "Growth of Bridgeport: City Election of 1937" undated in Miscellaneous Folder, Box 15, WPAEGS, Bridgeport
and New Haven; McLevy would appoint non-Socialists to commissions. These
would be chosen from Republican or Democratic primary lists and the two other
parties had less input into the selections than if they had been represented on the
Board of Aldermen; *New Leader,* December 28, 1935, p. 1.

39. *New Leader,* November 7, 1936, p. 2; for the national schism in the Socialist par-
ty, see: Bernard K. Johnpoll, *Pacifist's Progress: Norman Thomas and the Dream
of American Socialism* (Chicago, 1970), especially Chapter V; Paul Tison to
James A. Farley, December 16, 1938, Governor Wilbur Cross to James A. Farley,
December 5, 1938. (Quote from William F. Lahey, Democratic Town Chairman,
New Canaan, Connecticut to James A. Farley, November 14, 1938). OF 300,
Election Forecasts, Analyses and Results, 1938, Arkansas-Iowa, Connecticut
folder, Box 89, FDRL.

40. David A. Shannon, *The Socialist Party of America* (Chicago, 1967), pp. 244–45;
Johnpoll, *Pacifist's Progress,* Chapter V; August Claessens to McLevy, June 5,
1936, SchkfUB; Norman Thomas to Andrew Biemiller, May 8, 1936, SPAP;

Daniel Bell, *Marxian Socialism* (Princeton, N.J., 1967), p. 190; Note in SPSLO-Conn-Duke, dated August 27, without the year discusses the Kellems incident. The writer noted, "Shows practical problems throw you in with undesirable characters. What is more reactionary?"

41. Rental and housing data serves as a surrogate for income in the 1930 analysis; both are economic indicators.

42. See footnote 10 for black and Puerto Rican populations.

43. While the voting analysis is suggestive, one should be aware that it is based on aggregate data for Bridgeport's voting districts and is subject to the ecological fallacy. No claim can be made that certain specific individuals voted for the Socialists; however, it can be maintained with exactness that voting districts in which certain groups resided, along with others not in the group, voted in specific ways. The problem, unsolved for Bridgeport because of the nature of the available data, is to determine whether the group or nongroup members voted the way the majority of the district cast its ballots. For more on the ecological fallacy, see: Dollar & Jensen, *Historian's Guide to Statistics*, pp. 97—103, and the research notes in the *Journal of Interdisciplinary History* 4 (Autumn 1973), 237—62, 4 (Winter 1974), 417—33, and 4 (Spring 1974), 593—96.

44. Norman Thomas to T. Paul Tremont, August 15, 1955 (copy in possession of author).

45. "Bridgeport Underground, 1934—1951," SPSLO-Conn-Duke.

46. *New Leader,* August 1936, 1; William J. Burke, "History of Bridgeport," May 7, 1940, Emil A. Napolitano, "Growth of Bridgeport: History of Esplanades," Statement of McLevy with covering letter of William J. Becker to Dr. Rodnick, Connecticut Writers Project, New Haven, June 5, 1940, Miscellaneous Bridgeport Folder in Box No. 15, WPAEGS; the quotation is from McLevy's statement; for information about slum clearance, see: *New Leader,* June 21, 1934, p. 3, April 13, 1935, p. 3, July 27, 1935, p. 7, December 19, 1936, p. 1 and material in II-9500 Bridgeport, Connecticut (Project) in Record Group 196, National Archives, Suitland, Maryland. The confidential memo of Marvin H. McIntyre to Nathan Straus, October 25, 1937, OF300, Democratic National Committee Box 20, Connecticut A-Z folder, 1933—1937, FDRL, indicates that politics entered into the Bridgeport slum clearance situation. A Connecticut Congressman, A. C. Phillips, Jr., requested that no projects be assigned to Bridgeport until after the election.

47. Bridgeport *Post,* November 6, 1957, p. 36, November 3, 1957, p. 2; Bridgeport *Telegram,* November 1, 1957, p. 31. During the Great Depression, McLevy recognized the public works projects for what they were—work relief programs. His support for work relief with their small demand for local funding made the depression projects more acceptable to him than were the postwar programs.

48. For the consequences of postwar central business district urban renewal, see: Roy Lubove, *Twentieth Century Pittsburgh: Government, Business and Environmental Change* (New York, 1969), especially chapters six and seven; Kenneth J. Neubeck, *Corporate Response to Urban Crisis* (Lexington, Massachusetts, 1974); Raymond E. Wolfinger, *The Politics of Progress* (Englewood Cliffs, N.J., 1974); these discuss Pittsburgh, St. Louis, and New Haven, respectively.

WALTER LIPPMANN

ON MUNICIPAL SOCIALISM, 1913:
An Analysis of Problems and Strategies

Carl D. Thompson
Manager Information Department
The Socialist Party
National Office
Chicago, Illinois

Dear Comrade:-

It is a privilege to reply to your letter. You have opened a discussion
which neither of us is in any position to conclude. For it leads to the center of those difficulties which perplex every Socialist who has survived his
first period of omniscience. One thing your letter makes perfectly clear,
that however inevitable the road to Socialism may be in our theoretical
text-books, there is nothing inevitable about the tactics of today and to-
morrow. You have to meet these problems in your official position, and
you are puzzled. The comrades who write to you for help are puzzled. The
immense discussion in our press shows that the movement as a whole is
puzzled. If all of us could admit this frankly we should have made the first
great step toward a solution, for that is the only atmosphere in which complicated problems are ever solved. With that in mind I have held back my
reply to your letter until after the November elections. There is no use trying
to precipitate an open discussion at a time when everybody has to pretend
that he is entirely wise and absolutely certain. A man standing on a soap-

---

*The following letter from the Socialist Party Collection at Duke University is printed
with Lippmann's spelling, punctuation, and paragraphing unchanged. Ironically, after
writing this letter, Lippmann left the Socialist Party to become a Progressive.

box has to be cocksure. But about the tactics of a revolutionary movement only a fool is convinced that his is the last word. For we might as
well make up our minds to the fact that the debate over tactics will last as
long as the movement. For every year the situation changes, new factors
arise, and a living party has to readjust itself to meet them. That is why
hostility to "new" theories is such a discouraging business. These criticisms of Socialism which are coming from the younger men may be "half-
baked" and blundering: they are at least attempts to face a condition of
affairs that did not exist when the veterans were learning what they know.

Let me reply first of all to your question: What is the basis of attack
on the Schenectady administration? Its basis is the knowledge I gained as
Executive Secretary to the Mayor and member of the administration cau-
cus. I was present at the making of the first budget and the laying down
of the year's policy. The main outlines of my objections to the kind of
politics represented by Schenectady were published in the Call of June 9,
1912, under the title of "Schenectady the Unripe." The points of that
article have, I believe, been thoroughly confirmed by later events. I do not
propose here to rehearse all that, for our business is not with the criticism
of what is being done but with the discussion of something more effective.
I have met no informed Socialist who did not confess, at least privately,
that the Schenectady administration presented immense problems. You
admit it, of course, and you add to that statement the wider one that the
problems are typical. You have seen Milwaukee at first hand; it is very significant that after studying Schenectady you should feel that the Socialists
there "encounter the same kind of difficulties that every Socialist administration has encountered and the same kind of difficulties that for many
years every Socialist administration will encounter."

That difficulty can be stated quite simply on one very important issue: The economic policy of the administration. It is this,—the budget in
Schenectady was made on the principle that taxes must not be increased,
because high taxes would alienate the property-holders whose votes decided the election. In other words, the Schenectady Socialists know that they
owe their election to voters who would not stand for an increase of taxation. They know that they could not be re-elected if taxes were higher
than under the Democrats. The first principle of their economic policy was
to keep the tax rate where it was, or to reduce it if possible. This truth
about Schenectady has never been denied. The administration has boasted
of it. Now I say that this is a clean-cut issue between Socialism and anti-
Socialism, for it is quite clearly the business of a Socialist administration to
cut into the returns of property, take as much of them as possible to be
spent for social purposes. Any reformer would agree in a minute that the
"constructive" work of the Schenectady Socialists was admirable, no graft,

efficiency, parks, schools, medical attention, etc. But the ordinary reformer wishes these reforms without cutting into the returns on property. That
is why "low taxes" is the watchword of all good government activity.

Now the Schenectady administration chose deliberately to follow
the policy of the reformer. It couldn't help itself. It had been elected by
people who believed in reform, and it represents its constituency admirably. But on the only economic issue which it faced, the administration is
not a Socialist Administration. It is a pure and simple product of reform,
using some of the phrases of Socialism, but acting on the identical policy
that would inspire an administration conducted by John Purroy Mitchel or
Norman Hapgood. When I call it a reform government I am speaking as accurately as I can. It isn't the fact that Schenectady interested itself in dental clinics and playgrounds. I am not with those who despise these things
as unworthy of a "revolutionist." I say simply that when the amount of
playgrounds and the whole work of reform is made to depend on keeping
taxes where the Democrats left them, then the point of view is literally non-
Socialist. On the crucial question of whether the administration would cut
deeper into the returns on privilege, Schenectady said no.

And because of that, political action in Schenectady must be ineffective. It refuses to take the first step on which everything else hangs: it refuses to attack privilege.

Now if we are to arrive at an understanding of how to rejuvenate political action, we must find out why on this clean issue of policy, the Schenectady administration faltered. Such an analysis will lead us, I think, to
the source of their difficulties. From that there should emerge a clearer
sense of how to strengthen Socialist politics. I do not agree with you that
every administration must encounter the same difficulties. I do agree that
every administration will encounter them if it doesn't correct the underlying errors of Schenectady.

The main analysis is quite simple. The administration was elected by
non-Socialists. It represents them.

You can translate that very simple statement into a number of practical questions which must be answered before political action can have
any sound basis. Let me try to suggest a few of them.

1. Is it good policy to nominate a candidate for mayor who will poll
a personal vote large enough to decide the election?

2. Should Socialist campaigns be fought on issues like police corruption or paving graft?

3. What bid should be made for the progressive vote, disgusted with
the old parties and ignorant of Socialism?

4. If an administration is elected by non-Socialist votes, does it owe
any allegiance to the wishes of its non-Socialist supporters? Can the local

claim the right to control the action of officials, when the local represents a small minority of the voters?

5. What is the attitude of Socialist mayors towards disorderly strikes and strike-breakers?

6. What is the Socialist policy in taxation: What should it do in regard to its non-Socialist middle class supporters?

7. What is the Socialist policy towards vice?

8. What is the policy on school-boards? Is it "non-partisan" as reformers desire?

I mention these questions almost at random. They are, I think, all aspects of the same question, the most fundamental one that American Socialists in politics have had to face: where is the allegiance of Socialists elected by non-Socialists? If we can keep that issue before us it may be possible to save this discussion from running out into futile bickering. I should like to suggest that before anyone enters the argument he should face this question, and come to a clear understanding of what he really believes. I venture to predict that all the disagreements have their source right here: you will find that those who incline to some form of syndicalism have in the back of their minds the notion that an overwhelming political majority for Socialism is too slow a method of progress; you will find many Socialists who think they are very "practical" because they insist that we must play the political game and take any votes we can get; some of the greatest difficulties of the party turn on this point, such as our attitude toward the negro, towards the small farmer, and the little shop-keeper. But all this would take us too far afield, and I have no desire to wander all over the face of the globe. We are discussing political action especially in cities.

I do not know, of course, how you would answer the eight questions or the one question of which they are parts. I should say:

1. That votes cast for a candidate alone represent no strength for the movement.

2. That elections won on issues like graft, anti-Tammany, etc., etc., are mandates from the voters to clean out graft, not to strike at respectable privilege.

3. That the disgusted progressive vote represents no strength because it does not intend to stay with us on any essential issue.

4. That Socialists ought not, even if they could, go beyond the actual will of the constituency; *that administrations elected by non-Socialists do owe allegiance to non-Socialist voters.*

5. That a disorderly strike is an absolutely baffling problem, *unless* the great majority of the community are convinced Socialists.

6. That it is the business of Socialists to throw an increasing burden

187

of taxation on unearned incomes, and to spend the money socially.

7. That the policy of fighting vice with the police is a reformers' policy, not a Socialist's.

8. That non-partisan school-board appointments are an absurdity for Socialists who have a new philosophy of society, *and yet* partisan appointments are a form of tyranny unless they are made with the consent of the great mass of the citizens.

It is fairly clear, I think, that the keystone of our principal difficulties is that large and decisive group of progressive voters which holds the balance of power in America today. These progressives are hard to describe. They are more numerous than the Bull Moose; their national leaders include Roosevelt, Wilson, Bryan, La Follette; they are single-taxers and prohibitionists, anti-trust people, anti-Tammany, efficiency enthusiasts like John Purroy Mitchel, unclassifiable men like Brand Whitlock, Lindsey or Steffens; they are Collier's Weekly and the Saturday Evening Post, they are the muck-raking magazines, the social workers, the conservationists, white slave crusaders and woman suffragists; they are the most widely-spread element in public life. They hold their party ties lightly; they are today in a liquid condition, and under certain circumstances they will flow towards us. They are not afraid of Socialism, not of the name anyway. They like Socialism a great deal better than they do the Socialists.

The temper of these progressives is to use any political machine that will serve them. They have captured the Democratic Party in national politics; men like La Follette, Borah, Hadley still hope to control the Republican machine; there is, of course, the Bull Moose; they are powerful organizations like some of the granges, the People's Power League in Oregon, the Voters' League in Chicago—all of them instruments of this widespread progressive feeling. But that isn't the end. In a city like Schenectady, both old parties are utterly hopeless, the Bull Moose is weak, and the Progressives are quite ready to turn temporarily to the Socialists if they feel they can trust them. The path is smoothed for them if the candidate of the Socialists is a man who moved from progressivism to Socialism a year or so before, a popular man whom everybody knows. He becomes the link of an alliance between Socialism and the reformers. But note what happens: the reformers are harder to hold on to than the Socialists. They are free people who have signed no pledge and they are not tied to a ticket. They come when they please and go when they please. The whole campaign turns on keeping them in line. Everything is done to attract them, and the real Socialists stand around like a serious husband who has married a flirt.

It is this mass of progressives who create the puzzles of our political tactics. That, I think, is very clear for America.

It is essential then to understand the relation of the Socialists to the progressives.

The general attitude of the party press is that all reformers are either fools, crooks, or hypocrites. You will find Socialists arguing, as one of them did recently, that Mitchel must be all sorts of a knave because Hearst supported him, and McAneny a scoundrel because Hearst said he was. The rough assumption of all our political thinking is that the world is divided into Socialists and rascals. The assumption is false. In our less ugly moods we assume that society is divided into Socialists and conservatives. That assumption is false. Our politics assume that we alone represent every step in progress from personal honesty to the Cooperative Commonwealth. That is not true. We are not the whole of honest, nor the whole of progress, nor the whole of radicalism. It is the meanest kind of arrogance when our press or our speakers make a great fuss about Milwaukee's milk stations or Schenectady's grocery shop as if to say that if you want these undeniably good things you will have to vote for us. In the region of what we call our "immediate demands" it is sheer nonsense to pretend that we alone are capable or willing to carry them into effect. There is probably not an item in all the immediate demands of the Erfurt program that progressivism is incapable of accepting. And as for the execution of these reforms, well, you know as I do that the competent administrators have not yet swarmed into the Socialist Party.

But our assumption that we alone are to be trusted has got us into a very difficult position. We try to do the things that reformers can do at least as well as we, and we try to represent at the same time a profoundly revolutionary movement. Supermen might do it. We can't. The moment we go into competition with the reformers on their own ground, we are too busy for much else. It is quite an absorbing job to run even a dental clinic. The police force will keep any man busy. And the administration that is breaking its head off the daily problems of the police in a city is not going out of its way to encourage strikes or anything else that is likely to make new difficulties. And then, there is always before its eyes the great fact that supporters would leave in a minute if anything was done that they didn't like. There arises then the feeling that re-election is supremely important to prove to the world "that the Socialists have made good." And so in a thousand human complications the net is spun, and the Socialists are in the grip of the progressives. Then we wonder that political action is denounced.

If Socialists are to make anything of political action they have got to keep themselves clearly distinguished from the progressives. By clearly distinguished I do not mean a state of violent hatred towards Roosevelt and all his works. I do not mean a hallelujah chorus if Milwaukee installs the cost unit system and a cheap sneer if Philadelphia does it. To distinguish

189

clearly means for us to concentrate on that which is ours alone, to leave to the progressives what is theirs.

How is that to be done? I have been asked fifty times whether we can really reject votes that come to us. "Are you going into a campaign shouting 'Don't vote for us'?" It is perhaps hardly necessary to say to you that such argument is merely quibble. When a Socialist says that he wishes only Socialist votes, he doesn't mean that on election day he proposes to prevent anyone from voting his ticket. It is really quite easy to make it extremely improbable that the great mass of progressives will swing to us.

All it means is a really honest campaign. That is not pleasant, for we all like to see "results," and a big jump in the vote puts heart into the party. And yet I am convinced that political action will simply prove itself another of the age-long deceptions, unless it is conducted on the central principle that no fictitious size is any real strength. Those Socialists who talk as if we were going to measure our success by the standards of other parties have failed to grasp imaginatively what we are here for. We have nothing to gain by empty victories; every time we gain something which we do not really deserve, a new despair is born. If we cannot learn to play politics with a long vision and an ability to distinguish between Socialist power and the external clap-trap of victory, then we haven't learned the first steps in revolution, and our magnificent pictures of the future are the idle dreams of incompetent men.

The officials we elect are as powerful as the group they represent, no more so. The label Socialist will not make Socialists out of officials elected by progressives. If you keep that in mind, it becomes perfectly clear that the success of political action is determined before the officials are elected. The whole question which you ask me centers, then, in the campaign. You will understand, of course, that a Socialist campaign is not confined to six weeks of feverish electioneering before the vote is counted.

It includes the quality of propaganda, the kind of nominations, the nature of the platform, and the issues that are raised. You can readily see that everywhere here there is a choice, — a choice between the effort to build up a real Socialist constituency and the sham effort to pile up a vote. It is easiest perhaps to illustrate this with the platform.

The most interesting part of the platform in many ways is the section of "Immediate Demands." It represents the opening wedge of Socialist activity, a statement of where we would begin. Now so far as I can discover, the notion seems to be that our immediate demands should include desirable reforms capable of immediate realization. It's a list of good things worth having now. It's a sort of storehouse from which reformers are supposed to steal.

Whether they do or not is an academic question. The fact is that they do come around to endorsing most of our immediate demands. What do we do then? You know what we do: First, we shout "Thief"; then we shout "hypocrite,— if you really want these reforms you must let *us* carry them out . . . we had them first." This has been our position ever since the Progressive Party caught us napping.

Now the least we could have expected of the party was that it should set to work at once to map out a set of immediate demands far more radical than anything the Progressives had accepted. If reformers could go that far, it was clearly our business to move ahead. We did not need to attack the old reforms we had endorsed. They were just as valuable when the Progressives had accepted them. But it was our business to work out reforms that went beyond them.

On what principle? Fortunately an example exists, which I should like to call to your serious attention. Last spring in New York City a small group of us who had realized this predicament set about writing a municipal platform which should recognize the great political fact of the present time — that the progressives have become a conscious group in the community. We felt that the old platform was made before the progressives had appeared, and it was built on the assumption that the Socialists and the conservatives were the only two divisions of the voters. We knew this assumption was false. We knew that the Progressives represented a large body of earnest reform, and we recognized that this fact had changed the outlook of political action. We saw that it was folly for the Socialists to duplicate the work of the Progressives, and to attack them stupidly was worthy of the dog in the manger.

So we made an innovation in the structure of the platform. We divided the immediate demands into "Reforms endorsed by Socialists" and "Socialist Policies." This division has been very much attacked because no hair-line distinction is possible. That is true. But for the rough work of politics it is, I believe, a useful distinction. Under "Reforms Endorsed" we were able to place all those projects which are obviously desirable. You know that there are a hundred things of great value about which there is no class division because they involve no attack on profit. We desire those reforms in common with a great mass of people who are not Socialists at all. But there is nothing peculiar to us about them.

Now while we approve of them cordially, we cannot as a party afford to give much time to them. We have to concentrate on what is original in our message. But this does not mean that we are to talk the Cooperative Commonwealth, and despise immediate action. What we have to do is to devise a practical program for the next few years that would really affect the balance of power, that would really cut into profit, that would really put Socialists ahead in their essential work. Such a program is difficult to

191

formulate. But it has to be done. And it is on such a program of immediate demands that our campaigns must center.

One illustration may make this clear. Take the municipal ownership and operation of subways. That in itself is an immediate reform which will find no great opposition among the Progressives. We believe in it, and we should welcome its achievement. But we do not stop there. We say municipal ownership is worth having, but it is an installment of Socialism only when it is conducted on Socialist principles. The moment municipal trading becomes an immediate issue it is our business to draw the distinction between the reformer's policy and ours. The distinction is roughly this: that reformers propose to use the profits to reduce taxes; that Socialists propose to spend the profits socially. The difference is enormous. Municipal ownership under Socialists would pay for things that the people need; under reformers it would lighten the burden on property-owners. That is such a big difference that a great many "revolutionary" comrades won't see it at all.

For note what it means. The profits on a socialistically conducted subway would be a direct transfer from private dividends to the people; the profits on a reformist subway would be a transfer from stockholders to tax-payers. Landlords have everything to gain by a reformist enterprise, and the people very little; the Socialist method would be real socialization of capital. Now obviously, our campaigns must make this issue very clear: Municipal ownership is a reform we endorse; socialist municipal ownership is what we demand.

How profoundly this would change the quality of our campaigns you can see. There is no bait to the progressives in it. A whole pack of arguments are thrown overboard and the revolutionary issue is brought to the front. That is the way to keep the progressives from voting our ticket. Go to them with this statement: "We stand for municipal enterprise. We propose to operate public utilities for the public. We do not propose to take one cent of the profits to reduce the burdens on the tax-payers. We propose to spend it on raising wages, on reducing fares, improving service, and on reforms that would seem a luxury to you progressives. Out of the profits we propose to create new social opportunities, in schools, in city life, — opportunities which you will not endorse because they would cost too much."

What I have suggested here about municipal ownership can be extended, I think, to all the interests that politics touches. The Socialist policy on schools is yet to be worked out: there is contained in it a whole trunk full of revolutionary demands that are immediate and practical. There is a health program to be devised which will carry the party beyond anything the reformers are likely to accept. Taxation is a way of socializing wealth

192

that we have hardly explored.

If we really concentrate on immediate demands of this sort our progress will represent actual strength. There will be no mushroom victories, and the essential work of the movement will not be neglected. By an everlasting insistence on the specifically socialist position we shall save ourselves from the embraces of fickle friends.

Of course this means that we shall win less elections, and come into power more slowly. We shall have to stand by and let the Progressives look like the saviors of humanity. For those who find that too great a strain on their ambitions there is only one thing to do and that is to join the Progressives. If "doing something" means being in office or carrying through reforms, then the Socialist movement is the wrong place for them. We can part without bitterness. The progressives will be all the better for the addition of men who have had contact with Socialism, and Socialism will have lost nothing. For it cannot be repeated too often that the only strength of Socialism is its real strength.

The first objection that will occur to all this is that I am advocating mere talk. That is not true. I am advocating the assumption of political responsibility only when the constituency is ripe for it. The great danger, as in Schenectady, is to have the externals of power and none of its substance.

A second objection, certain to be raised, is that we must have political experience, and that we can't get that in our locals or in propaganda. That is true. No one who has watched the American movement can very well deny its deep need of experience. An evening at almost any local will convince an observer that whatever other virtues we may have, administrative efficiency is not one of them. I have watched a local of two hundred Socialists trying to audit fifty-cent bills by majority vote. The so-called practical wing of the party is composed largely of people who have a vivid sense of what a gigantic administrative problem Socialism will be, coupled with a vivid sense of what administrative dubs we are. And they feel that direct responsibility as in Schenectady is the only way there is of making the party prepare itself for practical affairs. There is, I believe, an enormous amount of truth in their position. We do need sorely to develop the capacity of dealing with actual problems. The debates which enliven the Call are often theoretical and verbal to an extreme: our criticisms of Congress or the mayor betray constantly the fact that the writer has never had to face the actual work of drawing up a bill or administering a department. It makes us arrogant, self-righteous, sectarian, and unjust. We blame officials for things absolutely beyond their control; we curse them often because we do not understand them. We announced on general principles that the subway contracts were a graft, but what the graft was we never took the trouble to state. If there is any party member who has made an analytical study of those contracts with the substitute proposal along Socialist lines, I have not heard of him. The first comment I read in the Call on John Purroy Mitchel's nomination announced that he was a pinhead. Now on the subject of municipal government Mitchel is undoubtedly not a pinhead. One could draw up a tremendous indictment against Mitchel, but on the question of his competence, administrative skill, and integrity no Socialist I know has the right to open his mouth. We become positive hypocrites, for if Mitchel were in Schenectady or Milwaukee, he would be doing just about what he has been doing and we should be hailing him as an example of the extraordinary capacity which the Socialist movement produces.

I do not wish then to underestimate the importance of the practical experience which so many comrades insist upon. But it does not follow that we must buy that experience by abandoning almost everything else that we believe. It is not necessary to crawl into office, and create political despair, just in order to remedy our incompetence. We can have experience without destroying the value of political action. Office is not the whole of politics.

We can if we have the energy, take an active part in every important controversy. The party could be represented at every hearing, could organize demonstrations: if the subway issue arises, the party ought to put forward its solution, and fight for it. It ought to make itself heard before every budget committee, every legislative inquiry on labor laws, conservation, schools. There should be trained representatives at every session of a government body, sent there not to write satirical articles, but to report to the party and keep it alert to new developments. There should be standing committees of experts on various phases of politics, and there should be machinery for presenting the issues to the party, and enabling it to take its stand. It would be an excellent beginning of the National Office appoint a committee to draw up suggestions as to how to carry on political action before the election of officials. Such a national inquiry could be supplemented with local committees that worked out the special details for particular communities.

Political action of this sort would be a blessing in all directions: it would give us all the habit of dealing constructively with immediate issues; it would be an unequalled form of propaganda; it would lay excellent foundations for any administration that we elected: it would ventilate the stuffy theoretical atmosphere of our discussion.

However, it is not the only way of gaining the experience we need. The unions themselves are miniature democracies, and active participation in their affairs by those who are eligible is not only absolutely essential

194

from the deeper aspects of Socialism: it is a real training for law-making and administration. But there is another field of activity that for business experience outweighs either politics or work in the unions. That is the cooperative. It is hard to realize sometimes how much we suffer in America from the lack of a strong cooperative movement. The time will come when we shall have to set about remedying that defect, for a working class with unions and no cooperatives is a one-legged man. The practice of cooperation is important in all sorts of ways: it is integral to any genuine revolution, it is the solution of many difficulties in capitalism, and from the point of view which we are discussing here, it is the only way I know of by which the working-class can have business experience combined with democracy. Cooperatives would supply us with capable administrators who had not been commercialized.

You see then that I do not advocate mere talk, and that I do not shirk the fact that practical experience is one of our greatest needs. I differ from the defenders of Schenectady in this, — that I think it is possible to get better training in a better way than by playing the political game of the old parties. The combination of extra-official politics, the unions and the cooperatives is a very ample field for training in administration.

Votes as an index of converts; campaigns without bait; political action year in year out without the immediate desire for office. That is, I think, the central policy that we must pursue.

But even that will be a delusion if we allow it to absorb our main interest. The work we are engaged in lies a great deal deeper than politics can ever go. Politics is very near the surface of life; it expresses rather clumsily forces that are much more important. For the currents that move the world do not start in legislatures; occasionally they reach the legislature. Revolutions are not made by statute, or Socialist congresses. All that politics can do is to clarify and put a sort of concluding stamp on revolutions that have worked themselves out in the life of the people. I need hardly say to you that we are concerned with the revolution, and interested in politics only because it can aid it.

Our great task to which politics is entirely subordinate is the organization of labor so that it understands its position, realizes its possibilities, and learns how to apply the power it possesses. Winning elections or fighting the subway issue are utterly trivial compared to the creation of this power among the working classes. Politics is only one small factor in this much more comprehensive work. Politics will be useful to labor only when labor has trained itself to self-government, has built its unions into centers of power, and saturated its daily life with a concrete and imaginative vision. That is the first work of the Socialist movement. If it is well done, our political action will reflect it. If it is neglected, no amount of fuss over the size of our vote will cover it up.

This then is the rough answer to your question: Political action in order to be effective must represent a power in the community behind it. That power is built out of economic forces made intelligent by conviction.

195

Votes must represent the size of that power: all other votes are a menace. Platforms must be written for the purpose of keeping the campaign to the essential issues. Propaganda and political action can be united by taking part in public affairs without the responsibility of office. Elections are the last goal of political action, and not the first. They should come only when the social forces are organized and ready.

This letter is very long, yet it is far too short for the subject. I have had to compress so much that many statements will appear unsupported by argument or evidence. I do not know how to avoid that. I hope you will read not to confute but to understand. I hope that in any discussion which may ensue no one will try to be smart and score debating points. They will only confuse what is already very confusing.

Fraternally yours,

Walter Lippmann

October 29, 1913

46 East 80th Street
New York City.

BIBLIOGRAPHIC ESSAY

The manuscript collection that was of greatest general use to the essays in this volume is the Socialist Party of America Papers at Duke University Library, Durham, North Carolina. Since these papers contain a large amount of material relating to Socialist locals, they are especially pertinent to the needs of any study dealing with municipal socialism. Other manuscript collections will be mentioned in the following discussion of the cities analyzed by the essays herein. A most useful guide to library and archival holdings is Bernard K. Johnpoll, "Manuscript Sources in American Radicalism," *Labor History* 14 (Winter 1973), 92–97. Another source valuable to all essays in this book is the U.S. Bureau of the Census, *Census of the United States,* for the decennial periods from 1890 through the present.

Of the four cities analyzed that elected Socialist administrations, Milwaukee has received the most previous attention by scholars. The following collections should be consulted for research materials on the history of Milwaukee socialism: the Daniel W. Hoan, Victor L. Berger, Emil Seidel, and Frederic F. Heath papers in the archives of the Milwaukee County Historical Society, as well as the papers of the Social Democratic party (Socialist party) of Milwaukee. The Society also has copies of county campaign manuals and proceedings of various conventions of the Wisconsin Social Democratic party. The Milwaukee Public Library houses relevant collections and the archives of the State Historical Society of Wisconsin contains related material, such as the papers of Morris Hillquit, Algie M. and May Wood Simons, and John M. Work. Party newspapers which are available include the daily, the *Milwaukee Leader,* 1911 to 1938, the weekly, the *Social-Democratic Herald,* 1900–1913, and the *Voice of the People,* a publication which appeared intermittently during local election campaigns.

Secondary works include: Sarah C. Ettenheim, ed., *How Milwaukee Voted, 1848–1968* (Milwaukee, 1970), Thomas W. Gavett, *The Development of the Labor Movement in Milwaukee* (Madison, 1965), Daniel Hoan, *City Government: The Record of the Milwaukee Experiment* (New York, 1936), Gerd Korman, *Industrialization, Immigration, and Americanization: The View From Milwaukee, 1886–1921* (Madison, 1967), Herbert F. Margulies, *The Decline of the Progressive Movement in Wisconsin, 1890–1920* (Madison, 1968), Sally M. Miller, *Victor Berger and the Promise of Constructive Socialism, 1910–1920* (Westport, Connecticut, 1973), Frederick I. Olson, "The Milwaukee Socialists, 1897–1941" (unpublished Ph.D. dissertation, Harvard University, 1952), and Olson's articles "The Socialist Party and the Unions in Milwaukee, 1900–1912," *Wisconsin Magazine of History* 44 (Winter, 1960–1961), 110–116, "Milwaukee's First Socialist Administration, 1910–1912: A Political Evaluation," *Mid-America* 43 (July 1961), 197–207, and "Victor Berger: Socialist Congressman," *Wisconsin Academy of Sciences, Arts and Letters* 58 (1970), 27–38, Robert C. Reinders, "Daniel W. Hoan and the Milwaukee Socialist Party During the First World War," *Wisconsin Magazine of History* 36 (August 1952), 48–56, Roger David Simon, "The Expansion of an Industrial City: Milwaukee, 1880–1910" (unpublished Ph.D. dissertation, University of Wisconsin, 1971), Bayrd Still, *Milwaukee: The History of a City* (Madison, 1948), David P. Thelen, *The New Citizenship: Origins of Progressivism in Wisconsin, 1885–1900* (Columbia, Mo., 1972), H. Yuan Tien, ed., *Milwaukee Metropolitan Area Fact Book, 1940, 1950, 1960* (Madison, 1962), Marvin Wachman, *History of the Social-Democratic Party of Milwaukee, 1897–1910* (Urbana, 1945), and Carl Wittke, *The German-Language Press in America* (Lexington, 1967).

In Schenectady, the office of the City Historian of Schenectady holds several manuscripts relating to socialism in that city. The *Proceedings of the Common Council of the City of Schenectady, New York* provides a formal account of city activities and the county enumerated its residents in the *Schenectady County Census Records, Enumeration of Inhabitants, 1915.* Mayor Lunn's and later the SP's paper, *The Citizen,* is valuable in analyzing Lunn's Administration; other useful newspapers are the *Schenectady Gazette, Schenectady Union-Star, Fulton County Democrat, Knickerbocker Press,* and the Socialist *New York Call.* Aside from Kenneth E. Hendrickson's earlier article on Schenectady in *New York History* 47 (January 1966), 22–40, one should see Robert Laurenty, "Socialism in Schenectady," *Hunter College Studies* 3 (1966), pp. 3–18.

The most useful manuscript collection for the study of Reading is the Darlington Hoopes Socialist Papers, which are available at Pennsylvania State University and on microfilm from Rhistoric Publications. The *Reading Labor Advocate* and the *Reading Eagle* provide valuable newspaper coverage while several interviews with old Socialists assisted in preparation of William Pratt's essay. James H. Maurer, *It Can Be Done* (New York, 1938) provides a first hand account. Henry G. Stetler, *The Socialist Movement in Reading, Pennsylvania, 1896--1936: A Study in Social Change* (Storrs, Connecticut, 1943), Kenneth E. Hendrickson, Jr., "The Socialists of Reading, Pennsylvania and World War I--A Question of Loyalty," *Pennsylvania History* 36 (October 1969), 430--50 and his "Triumph and Disaster: The Reading Socialists in Power and Decline, 1932--1939--Part II," *Pennsylvania History* 40 (October 1973), 381--411, William C. Pratt, "The Reading Socialist Experience: A Study in Working Class Politics" (unpublished Ph.D. dissertation, Emory University, 1969), and Raymond Ford, "Germans and Other Foreign Stock: Their Part in the Evolution of Reading, Pa." (unpublished Ph.D. dissertation, University of Pennsylvania, 1963) offer secondary analyses of the Reading situation. Upton Sinclair has written about *Jimmie Higgins* (Lexington, 1971 edition), the rank and filer, whose activities Professor Pratt explores in Reading.

No prior scholarly monograph or article has been written exclusively pertaining to the Bridgeport Socialist experience. Manuscript collections which were most valuable to study socialism in that city are: The McLevy and Schwarzkopf Collections at the University of Bridgeport; the Records of the W.P.A., Connecticut, 1935--1944, in the Connecticut State Library, Hartford; the Harry Hopkins Papers and the Official Files 300 in the Franklin D. Roosevelt Library, Hyde Park, N.Y., both of which contain detailed comments about localities throughout the United States, especially the latter which includes reports to James Farley about "Elections and Forecasts, Analyses and Results"; the collection at the Tamiment Institute Library, New York City; and the H-9500 file in Record Group 196 referring to public housing, National Archives, Suitland, Maryland. The scrapbook of former Bridgeport Socialist officeholder, Jack Bergen, assisted in the writing of the Bridgeport essay as did an oral history project conducted by the author; the oral history project is on file at the University of Bridgeport. The *New Leader* provided excellent coverage of the early years of the McLevy administration and the *Bridgeport Post* and *Telegram* offer daily reports of the city's municipal socialism. Two helpful official publications are the City of Bridgeport, *Manual* (the 1936 edition was used) and the *Municipal Register;* the latter provides voting returns for the year preceding the one in which the volume is published. Copies of the *Registers* and other useful material can be found in the Bishop Room of the Bridgeport Public Library. Aside from the U.S. Census, information about Bridgeport population and

Connecticut, in general, was found in Nathan L. Whetten and Henry W. Riecken, Jr., *The Foreign Born Population of Connecticut, 1940* (Storrs, Agricultural Extension Station, Bulletin 246, September 1943), Samuel Koenig and David Rodnick, *Ethnic Factors in Connecticut Life: A Survey of Social, Economic and Cultural Characteristics of the Connecticut Population* (New Haven, 1940), and Greater Bridgeport Regional Planning Agency, *Profile of Six Neighborhoods in the City of Bridgeport* (Trumbull, Connecticut, 1965). Information about the mayors of the nation's ninety-two largest cities was culled from the *World Almanac* for the appropriate years and the basic work concerning political realignment can be found in Jerome M. Clubb and Howard W. Allen, eds., *Electoral Change and Stability in American Political History* (New York, 1971), as well as in the other works cited in footnote 1 of the Bridgeport essay.

Several newspapers aided in the study of the abortive attempt to organize Oklahoma City. These include the Party's official paper, the *Oklahoma Pioneer,* and the Printer's Union sponsored *Oklahoma Labor Unit;* other papers pertaining to socialism in Oklahoma City include the *Social Democrat* (Oklahoma City), the *Daily Oklahoman,* and the *Oklahoma City Times.* A helpful official publication was the Oklahoma Department of Labor's 4th *Annual Report,* 1910–1911. Oscar Ameringer's *If You Don't Weaken* (New York, 1940), provides a first hand account of activities in the Sooner state. Secondary accounts can be found in Garin Burbank's two articles "Agrarian Radicals and Their Opponents: Political Conflict in Southern Oklahoma, 1910–1924," *Journal of American History* 58 (June 1971), 5–23 and "The Disruption and Decline of the Oklahoma Socialist Party," *American Studies* 7 (August 1973), 133–52; Keith L. Bryant, Jr.'s "Labor in Politics: The Oklahoma State Federation of Labor in the Age of Reform," *Labor History* 11 (Summer 1970), 259–76, and James R. Green, "Socialism and the Southwestern Class Struggle, 1898–1918: A Study of Radical Movements in Oklahoma, Texas, Louisiana and Arkansas" (unpublished Ph.D. dissertation, Yale University, 1972).

The only copy found, that for October, 1911, of the Passaic Socialist Monthly, *The Issue,* can be located in the Forstmann Public Library (Passaic) and is included in the Passaic Historical Collection of the library. Newspaper accounts of the change-of-government issue in Passaic are offered in the *Passaic Daily News* and *Passaic City (Daily) Herald.* The background of the city's socio-economic and political structure is investigated in Michael H. Ebner, "The Historian's Passaic, 1855–1912: A Research Model for New Jersey's Urban Past" in William C. Wright, ed., *New Jersey Since 1860, New Findings and Interpretations* (Trenton, 1972), pp. 10–34. Earlier interpretations include William J. Pape with William W. Scott, *The News' History of Passaic, From Earliest Settlement to the Present Day* (Passaic,

1899) and William W. Scott, *History of Passaic and Its Environs*, 3 vols. (New York and Chicago, 1927); the city's Jewish community is studied in *Jewish Roots, A History of the Jewish Community of Passaic and Environs* (Passaic, 1959). Ransome E. Noble, Jr., discusses *New Jersey Progressivism Before Wilson* (Princeton, N.J., 1946) and detail about progressive urban structural reforms can be found in: James Weinstein, *The Corporate Ideal in the Liberal State, 1900–1918* (Boston, 1968), Samuel P. Hays's widely reprinted, "The Politics of Reform in Municipal Government in the Progressive Era," *Pacific Northwest Quarterly*, 55 (October, 1964), 157–69, Melvin G. Holli, *Reform in Detroit: Hazen S. Pingree and Urban Politics* (New York, 1969), and Bruce M. Stave, ed., *Urban Bosses, Machines, and Progressive Reformers* (Lexington, Massachusetts, 1972).

The *Who's Who in Socialist America* (Girard, Kansas, 1914) served as the basis for the collective biography of the "salesmen-soldiers" of the "*Appeal* Army," and was found by James Green in the Yale University Library. Those wishing to obtain a first-hand account of Socialist debates and discussion should consult the *Proceedings of the National Congress* (sometimes Convention) *of the Socialist Party* (Chicago) for the year for which information is sought.

Useful books, of varying interpretation, that deal with socialism, workers, and radicalism are: Daniel Bell, *Marxian Socialism in the United States* (Princeton, 1967), William M. Dick, *Labor and Socialism in America, The Gompers Era* (Port Washington, New York, 1972), Melvyn Dubofsky, *When Workers Organize* (Amherst, 1968) and *We Shall Be All: A History of the IWW*, (Chicago, 1969), George Fischer, ed., *The Revival of American Socialism: Selected Papers of the Socialist Scholars Conference*, (New York, 1971), Ray Ginger, *Eugene V. Debs, A Biography* (New York, 1962), Bernard K. Johnpoll, *Pacifist's Progress: Norman Thomas and the Decline of American Socialism* (Chicago, 1970), Ira Kipnis, *The American Socialist Movement, 1897–1912* (New York, 1952), John Laslett, *Labor and the Left: A Study of Socialist and Radical Influences in the American Labor Movement, 1881–1924* (New York, 1970), John M. Laslett and Seymour Martin Lipset, *Failure of A Dream? Essays in the History of American Socialism* (Garden City, 1974), David Montgomery, *Beyond Equality: Labor and the Radical Republicans, 1862–1872* (New York, 1967), Howard Quint, *The Forging of American Socialism* (Indianapolis, 1964), Gerald Rosenblum, *Immigrant Workers, Their Impact on American Labor Radicalism* (New York, 1973), Murray B. Seidler, *Norman Thomas: Respectable Rebel*, 2nd ed. (Syracuse, 1967), David Shannon, *The Socialist Party of America* (Chicago, 1967), Frank A. Warren, *An Alternative Vision: The Socialist Party in the 1930's* (Bloomington, Indiana, 1974), James Weinstein, *The Decline of American Socialism, 1912–1925* (New York, 1967), and Betty Yorburg, *Utopia and Reality: A Collective Portrait of American Socialists* (New York, 1969).

Local case studies of municipal socialism not studied in this volume can be found in: Henry F. Bedford, *Socialism and the Worker in Massachusetts, 1886–1912* (Amherst, 1966) and his "The Socialist Movement in Haverhill," *Essex Institute Historical Collections* 99 (January 1963), 33–47, which appears as part of Bedford's book; Melvyn Dubofsky, "Success and Failure of Socialism in New York City, 1900–1918: A Case Study," *Labor History* 9 (Fall 1968), 361–75; Arthur Goren, "A Portrait of Ethnic Politics: The Socialists and the 1908 and 1910 Congressional Elections on the East Side," *Publication of the American Jewish Historical Society* 50 (March 1961), 202–38 reprinted in Joel H. Silbey and Samuel T. McSeveney, eds., *Voters, Parties and Elections* (Lexington, Mass., 1972), pp. 235–59; and a study of Buffalo by sociologist Elwin H. Powell, "Reform, Revolution, and Reaction: A Case of Organized Conflict," in Irving Horowitz, ed., *The New Sociology* (New York, 1964), pp. 331–56. A statewide case study is offered in Frederick A. Barkey, "The Socialist Party in West Virginia from 1898 to 1920: A Study in Working Class Radicalism" (unpublished Ph.D. dissertation, University of Pittsburgh, 1971).

Articles which study the Socialist relationship to immigrants, blacks, and women are: Charles Leinenweber, "The American Socialist Party and 'New' Immigrants," *Science and Society* 32 (Winter 1968), 1–25; Paul Buhle, "Debsian Socialism and the 'New Immigrant' Worker," in William L. O'Neill, ed., *Insights and Parallels: Problems and Issues of American Social History* (Minneapolis, 1973), pp. 249–77; R.L. Moore, "The Flawed Fraternity—American Socialists Response to the Negro, 1901–1912," *The Historian* 32 (November 1969), 1–16; Sally M. Miller, "The Socialist Party and the Negro, 1901–1920," *Journal of Negro History* 56 (July 1971), 220–29; and Mari Jo Buhle, "Women and the Socialist Party, 1901–1914," *Radical America* 4 (February 1970), 36–57. Herbert Gutman, "The Worker's Search for Power," in H. Wayne Morgan, ed., *The Gilded Age* (Syracuse, 1970), pp. 31–53 provides useful insight into how social structure affected working-class power, a point noted in this volume by James R. Green.

Varied interpretations of the success and failure of United States socialism are considered in: August C. Bolino, "American Socialism's Flood and Ebb: The Rise and Decline of the Socialist Party in America, 1901–1912," *The American Journal of Economics and Sociology* 22 (April 1963), 287–301; D.H. Leon, "Whatever Happened to an American Socialist Party? A Critical Survey of the Spectrum of Interpretations," *American Quarterly* 23 (May 1971), 236–58, which is a particularly useful essay; Sally M. Miller, "Socialist Party Decline and World War I, Bibliography and Interpretation," *Science and Society* 34 (Winter 1970), 398–411; Leonard B. Rosenberg, "The 'Failure' of the Socialist Party of America," *Review of Politics,* 31 (July 1969), 329–52; and Bryan Strong, "Historians and American Socialism, 1900–1920," *Science and Society* 34 (Winter 1970), 387–97. The second volume of Donald Drew Egbert and Stow Persons, eds., *Socialism and American Life* (Princeton, N.J., 1952), provided an extensive bibliography of materials relating to all aspects of American socialism, which is not as fresh today as it was two decades ago.

INDEX

204

CONTRIBUTORS

Garin Burbank is Assistant Professor of History at the University of Winnipeg in Canada. He holds three degrees from the University of California (Berkeley) and has published articles in the *Journal of American History,* the *Journal of American Studies,* and the *Chronicles of Oklahoma.*

Michael H. Ebner is Assistant Professor of History and Faculty Associate of the Wood Institute for Local & Regional Studies, Lake Forest College. He holds a Ph.D. from the University of Virginia; he has taught at Virginia, Lehman College, and The City College of New York. In 1973 he received an award for "Outstanding Teaching Contribution" from The History Society at C. C. N. Y. Ebner has written articles and reviews in numerous scholarly publications, including *Labor History,* the *Journal of Social History, Film & History, New Jersey History,* and *The History Teacher.* For many years he was active in Passaic politics. Ebner has also written on contemporary New Jersey public affairs in the *Newsletter of the Democratic Left,* a publication of the Democratic Socialist Organizing Committee. At Lake Forest College he offers courses in American social, political, and oral history.

James R. Green teaches social history at Brandeis University. His 1972 Yale University dissertation, "Socialism and the Southwestern Class Struggle, 1898–1918: A Study of Radical Movements in Oklahoma, Texas, Louisiana, and Arkansas," is now being prepared for publication. His essays have appeared in *Labor History, The Nation, Past & Present* and *Radical America,* a contemporary socialist journal of which he is an editor. He is now visiting lecturer in labor history at Warwick University's Centre for the Study of Social History in Britain.

Kenneth E. Hendrickson, Jr., is Professor and Chairman of the Department of History at Midwestern University in Wichita Falls, Texas, where he was named Hardin Distinguished Professor during the 1974-1975 academic year. He holds his Ph.D. from the University of Oklahoma and has published *Richard F. Pettigrew of South Dakota* (South Dakota State Historical Society, 1968) and articles in *Labor History, New York History, Pennsylvania History, North Dakota History,* and the *Pacific Historical Review.* He has received research grants from The New York State Office of Education, The American Philosophical Society, and The American Association for State and Local History.

Sally M. Miller presently teaches at the University of the Pacific in Stockton, California, where she is Associate Professor of History. Educated in the United States and Canada, she holds a Ph.D. from the University of Toronto, 1966. She has published articles on black history and American radicalism and is the author of *Victor Berger and the Promise of Constructive Socialism, 1910-1920* (Greenwood, 1973) and *The Radical Immigrant, 1820-1920* (Twayne, 1974). Her honors include Province of Ontario graduate fellowships, University of the Pacific Faculty Research Awards, a travel grant from the American Philosophical Society, and selection as "An Outstanding Educator of America."

William C. Pratt is Chairman of the Department of History at the University of Nebraska at Omaha. His doctoral dissertation "The Reading Socialist Experience: A Study in Working Class Politics" was written at Emory University and he received his degree in 1969. He has contributed to *The Nation,* the *Pacific Northwest Quarterly,* the *Journal of Southern History,* and Thomas G. Paterson's *Cold War Critics* (Quadrangle Books, Inc., 1971), and has delivered papers at national and regional meetings.

Bruce M. Stave is Professor of History at The University of Connecticut in Storrs. He specializes in U. S. urban history and holds degrees from Columbia University and the University of Pittsburgh, where he received his doctoral degree in 1966. He is the author of *The New Deal and the Last Hurrah* (University of Pittsburgh Press, 1970), editor of *Urban Bosses, Machines, and Progressive Reformers* (D. C. Heath and Co., 1972), co-editor with Leroy Ashby of *The Discontented Society* (Rand McNally, 1972), and has contributed articles and chapters to several journals and books. He is a member of the editorial board of the *Journal of Urban History,* was Fulbright Professor of American History in India, 1968-1969, and a National Endowment for the Humanities Fellow in 1974.

212